The Decline, Revival and Fall
of the British Empire

The Decline, Revival and Fall of the British Empire

The Ford Lectures and other essays

BY

JOHN GALLAGHER

Late Professor of Imperial and Naval History
University of Cambridge

Edited by Anil Seal

Cambridge University Press

CAMBRIDGE

LONDON   NEW YORK   NEW ROCHELLE
MELBOURNE   SYDNEY

Published by the Press Syndicate of the University of Cambridge
The Pitt Building, Trumpington Street, Cambridge CB2 1RP
32 East 57th Street, New York, NY 10022, USA
296 Beaconsfield Parade, Middle Park, Melbourne 3206, Australia

First published 1982

Printed in Great Britain
at the Alden Press, Osney Mead, Oxford

Library of Congress catalogue card number: 82-4291

British Library cataloguing in publication data
Gallagher, John
The decline, revival and fall of the British Empire.
1. Commonwealth of Nations – History
I. Title II. Gallagher, John
III. Seal, Anil
909′.0971241081   DA18

ISBN 0 521 24642 3

Contents

Acknowledgements

'Jack Gallagher in Trinity' by Graham Chinner is reprinted from the *Trinity Review*, Lent Term (1961), p. 26. © Graham Chinner 1961

'Jack Gallagher in Oxford' by Richard Cobb is reprinted from *The Cambridge Review*, 7 November 1980, pp. 21–4. © Richard Cobb 1980

'The Imperialism of Free Trade' by John Gallagher and Ronald Robinson is reprinted from the *Economic History Review*, 2nd ser. VI, 1 (1953), pp. 1–15. © R.E. Robinson and Estate of J. Gallagher 1953

'The Partition of Africa' by R.E. Robinson and J. Gallagher is reprinted from *The New Cambridge Modern History*, Volume XI, edited by F.H. Hinsley (Cambridge, 1962), pp. 593–640. © Cambridge University Press 1962

'The Decline, Revival and Fall of the British Empire' is the series of Ford Lectures delivered by John Gallagher in the University of Oxford in 1974. © Cambridge University Press 1982

'Congress in Decline: Bengal, 1930 to 1939' is reprinted from *Modern Asian Studies*, VII, 3 (1973), pp. 589–645. © Cambridge University Press 1973

The Editor wishes to acknowledge the help and encouragement of Ronald Robinson, Gordon Johnson, Tony Weir, Norman Stone, Maurice Cowling, Graham Chinner, Richard Cobb, and David Fieldhouse. He also would like to thank Deborah Swallow, Livia Breglia, and Tina Bone for their help in checking, subediting and typing the manuscript.

A.S.

Preface

John Andrew Gallagher, 1919–1980

THIS volume brings together some of the characteristic writings of John Andrew Gallagher, Vere Harmsworth Professor of Imperial and Naval History, Vice-Master of Trinity College, Cambridge, and Fellow of the British Academy, who died in Cambridge on 5 March 1980. Jack Gallagher was born on 1 April 1919, the only child of Joseph and Adeline Gallagher. From Birkenhead Institute, he came to Trinity in 1936 as a Scholar in History. At the outbreak of the war, he immediately enlisted in the Royal Tank Regiment and saw service in North Africa, Italy and Greece. He returned to Cambridge to complete his studies and was elected a Fellow at Trinity in 1948 for his research on the British penetration of West Africa. He taught History at Cambridge, becoming University Lecturer in Colonial Studies in 1950 and Dean of Trinity in 1960. In 1963 he was elected Beit Professor of the History of the British Commonwealth in Oxford and Fellow of Balliol College. In 1971 he returned to Cambridge to take up the Chair of Imperial and Naval History; in the following year he was elected Vice-Master of Trinity, a position he held until his death. In 1974 he delivered the Ford Lectures in Oxford on 'The Decline, Revival and Fall of the British Empire' and later that year he gave the Wiles Lectures at Belfast.

Gallagher's interest as an historian of imperialism lay first in Africa and later in India. To the modern understanding of the nature and operation of imperialism and colonial nationalism in both these regions, his contribution has been revolutionary. It would be difficult to exaggerate the formative effect that his facility for perceptive analysis and his capacity to present old matters in a new light have had upon students and colleagues alike for more than thirty-five years. But although the range of his influence was far-reaching, only those who worked closely with him or were taught by him have the full measure of the fertility of his intelligence and the special character of his impact. That impact was more by word of mouth than by publication, and his writings were distinguished more by their quality than by their quantity.

Gallagher liked to work in collaboration: on imperialism and Africa with Ronald Robinson (his successor in the Chair at Oxford) and later on India with the editor of this volume, his pupil and colleague at Trinity. Struck down by a long and cruel illness, Gallagher left much undone and many plans unfulfilled. Most of his research upon India in the twentieth century was not written up, even in the most preliminary way. But he did leave behind his notes for the Ford Lectures, and this volume brings their substance into print. Gallagher intended to work on the Ford Lectures and convert them from rough notes into polished prose. He died before he made progress with this project. This volume includes the editor's reconstruction of the lectures from Gallagher's notes.

In 1953 Ronald Robinson and John Gallagher challenged the conventional definitions of nineteenth-century imperialism with their manifesto on 'The Imperialism of Free Trade'.[1] Until then, empire had tended to be analysed as if rulers had no subjects and as if Europe's pursuit of profit and power was made in a world untrammelled by external forces. They enquired why, if there was no more to empire than the expansion of Britain, the Victorians liberated their more valuable colonies of settlement, while annexing other less valuable territories. Contraction did not fit existing theories of economic imperialism; the extension of rule seemed inexplicable if its causes were sought simply inside Europe. Discovering no compelling reason at the metropolitan centre for the drive into the tropics, they extended their enquiry beyond areas formally ruled to include the informal empire of influence, a notion which they were to make peculiarly their own. Local circumstance in overseas societies, whether the success of collaboration or the crisis of resistance, was the neglected factor which they called into play, since it governed much of the timing and character of imperial interventions and withdrawals.

During the next decade, Gallagher and Robinson came to define expansion as a set of bargains between European agents, sometimes with little backing from the metropolis, and their indigenous allies and opponents, who were primarily concerned to defend or to improve their position inside their own societies. Such a view made it impossible to continue to regard imperialism as an unified process. Step by step this led Gallagher and Robinson to discard monocausal and Euro-centric

[1] J. A. Gallagher and R. E. Robinson, 'The Imperialism of Free Trade', *Economic History Review*, 2nd ser. VI, 1 (1953), pp. 1–15, reprinted below, pp. 1–18.

hypotheses in favour of 'excentric' or peripheral assumptions.[2] *Africa and the Victorians*, which was published in 1961 and quickly accepted as a classic, set the theories to one side and analysed the calculations of the official mind in the decisions to advance or not to advance into Africa. Its main emphasis was upon Victorian perceptions of the partition of Africa at the time. If its argument centred upon Egypt, as some critics have complained, it was not the authors but the partitioners, drawn into yet another empire by the 'local' crisis, who are to blame. In 'The Partition of Africa'[3] the arguments about the role of local crises and proto-nationalisms were extended to the policies of other powers, especially of France.

By the time Gallagher went to Oxford in 1963, his partnership with Robinson had built a new framework for the study of imperial history; it had sparked off a continuing controversy and had helped to attract large numbers of scholars into the broad field of imperial history.[4] Taking on a new partner, Gallagher now turned towards British India to develop the logic of his view that imperialism was to be understood less by the study of policy and more by looking at the hard facts of colonial society which often buckled, refracted or broke it. In so far as the British empire had a true centre, it lay in India. Characteristically, Gallagher still preferred to work in collaboration. The powerful flow of published work from a 'school' of Indian history which he did so much to create is testimony to his capacity to inspire and direct.[5] That 'school' has helped to transform the historiography of modern India, from the commanding heights to the context at the base.

The emphasis shifted from the elegant exchanges between London and Viceregal Lodge to the brutal scrambles for resources among politicians at the more humdrum levels in India where the pickings lay. Old axioms about the omnipotence of imperial power were replaced by cannier notions that it was hobbled at every turn. Attention switched

[2] So described by Robinson in his 'Non-European Foundations of European Imperialism: Sketch for a Theory of Collaboration', *Studies in the Theory of Imperialism*, ed. E. J. R. Owen and R. B. Sutcliffe (1972), pp. 117–40.

[3] R. E. Robinson and J. A. Gallagher, 'The Partition of Africa', *New Cambridge Modern History*, vol. XI, ed. F. H. Hinsley (Cambridge, 1962), pp. 593–640, reprinted below, pp. 19–72.

[4] See, for example, Wm Roger Louis (ed.), *Imperialism. The Robinson and Gallagher Controversy* (New York, 1976).

[5] A new generation of historians of India, among them Gordon Johnson, Judith Brown, Christine Dobbin, David Washbrook, Christopher Baker, Christopher Bayly, Tom Tomlinson, David Page, Francis Robinson, Richard Gordon, Rajat Ray, Claude Markovits, Keith Jeffrey, Ian Coupland, Basudev Chatterji and Ayesha Jalal, were all students of that partnership.

from imperial fiats to Indian facts, from the generalizations of policy-makers and the ideologies of politicians to the concreteness of local studies. Thus the 'school' joined in demolishing casings which used to hold the subject together. As its provincial, and then its local, roots were laid bare, what once looked like a national movement of a people struggling rightfully and unitedly to be free appeared more like a ramshackle coalition, its power throughout its long career as hollow as that of the imperial authority it was supposedly challenging. Indian nationalism proved in large measure to be the rivalry between Indian and Indian, and its relationship with imperialism the clinging together of two unsteady men of straw. But if the assaults by Gallagher and his sepoys made it difficult to organize modern Indian history around the old notions of imperialism and nationalism, they were builders as well as demolition men. They put new life into old factors and helped to identify some of the forces which linked the politics of Indians in different arenas, whether the locality, the province or the nation. Their work made some of the conundrums of Indian history appear less intractable and generated another lively controversy. Gallagher's article, 'Congress in Decline: Bengal 1930 to 1939',[6] reprinted below, describes the complex interactions between the politics of the all-India centre and those of Calcutta and the districts of Bengal; it gives a tantalizing hint of the transformation that Gallagher, had he been able to bring this work to fruition, might have wrought in our understanding of India in the nineteen-twenties and thirties, the subject of his research during more than a dozen visits to the sub-continent.

By the early nineteen-seventies, Gallagher was bringing the analysis to bear upon the causes of the rise and decline of empires, in his Ford Lectures at Oxford and in the Wiles Lectures at Belfast. Moving easily from continent to continent, this master of synthesis encompassed most of the world which had changed markedly during his career as an historian. When he began his research, India was in the throes of being granted independence; in Africa the transition from empire to nation still seemed far away. 'The Imperialism of Free Trade' was written in a Britain dependent upon Marshall Aid; the chapters on Egypt in *Africa and the Victorians* were drafted during the Suez Crisis. In the sixties and early seventies, Britain dismantled most of her African empire. Not surprisingly, there had been large shifts in the thinking about imperial-

---

[6] This was published as part of a special issue of *Modern Asian Studies*, VII, 3 (1973), pp. 589–645, which Gallagher edited with Gordon Johnson and Anil Seal; it was reprinted as a volume entitled: *Locality, Province and Nation: Essays on Indian Politics 1870–1940* (Cambridge, 1973); see below, pp. 155–211.

ism as an historical process. Some of the old unities of the subject had been destroyed. Yet Gallagher argued that imperialism still deserved to be studied as an entity, if not an unity. However incompetent their management, all systems of influence or rule fitted into a construct of national interests. For a century and a half, India had underpinned the British world system in the eastern seas. Thus the study of an Indian locality, be it Allahabad or Madras, was part of a larger whole. To look only at the localities was to run the risk of missing the bird and bagging a few scraps of its plumage. The Imperial Grand Master, in Gallagher's eyes, had played simultaneous chess on innumerable boards, running into stalemates on many of them.[7] Since many of the factors inside empires were interdependent, it was an integrated game and had to be studied as such. Imperialism in the abstract, with a capital 'I', had never perhaps existed. Rather it was a question of examining the interactions between the expansive propensities of advanced states and the local circumstances in the regions into which they were expanding which influenced decisions about going in as well as their outcome. Since these regions contained peoples riddled and etiolated by internal rivalries, Europe was able to profit from their divisions. Hence the importance of the notion of collaboration which Gallagher deployed so skilfully. In some parts of the world, the imperial power was content to leave well alone; in others it had to come down harder upon the lives and times of its subjects. Such interventions were a key to what has rather romantically been called colonial nationalism.

Working by these charts, Gallagher encouraged the voyager to make landfalls upon unfamiliar shores: the inwardness of the relationship between imperial interventions and colonial divisiveness, a more realistic appreciation of the reasons why empires have broken down and the role in these affairs of colonial nationalism. In the Wiles Lectures, he touched upon the breakdown of the British empire in America in the later-eighteenth century. At the end of the Seven Years War, London, anxious to cut its metropolitan spending, tried to shift the burden of running America on to American backs. It took a more resolute hand in the administration of the Thirteen Colonies. This marked the end of the traditional policies of 'salutary neglect', and it upset a great many colonial applecarts. Americans of substance, once the collaborators of the British, now found their interests increasingly circumscribed.

[7] For an example of the interplay of crises in different parts of the empire, see J. Gallagher, 'Nationalisms and the Crisis of Empire, 1919–1922', in *Power, Profit and Politics: Essays on Imperialism, Nationalism and Change in Twentieth-Century India*, edited by C. Baker, G. Johnson and A. Seal, *Modern Asian Studies*, XV, 3 (July, 1981), pp. 355–68.

Although this did not quite amount to a second British invasion of America, Gallagher discovered consequences here similar to those he was to find in the second invasion of India in the eighteen-eighties or of tropical Africa in the nineteen-forties. Colonial subjects question imperial rule once it begins to do what it has always claimed in theory it had the power—perhaps even the duty—to do, but in practice has usually avoided doing. Paradoxically, one of the best ways of keeping an empire is by neglect; and one of the surest ways of losing it is by deepening imperial intervention. But every triumph of colonial nationalism manufactures its own mythology. Colonial revolutions need the appearance of unity; they do not possess its reality. Paul Revere carried the news of the Boston Tea Party to a divided America, where colony quarrelled with colony about boundaries and resources and faction fought faction inside each colony over local matters. In every continent and in every period colonial politics were honeycombed with dissension. This was one reason why in the seventeen-seventies the British were prepared to go over the brink into war; they still believed that they had powerful friends and allies inside America.

By 1974, when Gallagher came to review the course of nineteenth-century expansion, the view that the second quarter of the century was an age of anti-imperialism had largely been discredited. Historians now recognized it as a time when Europe had much to offer non-Europeans who were ready to work with it. Collaboration based upon a reciprocity of interests sometimes succeeded, and sometimes failed. All ages in modern times have been imperialist, the world today being no exception. It is just that some imperialisms have been luckier than others. Playing from strength imperialism could eschew formal dominion; playing from weakness it might be forced to move to systems of formal rule when faced with the alternatives of getting out altogether or getting in deeper. The methods varied, but the aims were strikingly the same. Forms of reliance upon informal influence were favoured during the first half of the century; later in the century there was a greater resort to annexation and rule. This resulted less from structural changes inside Europe and more from the difficulty of maintaining empires of mere influence. Conventional theories which attempted to explain the great age of imperialism in the later-nineteenth century were all trying to get to grips with a phenomenon whose very existence Gallagher came to doubt. The theorists of imperialism were victims of the vice of carving expansion into periods where everything was thought to be all of a piece; their viewpoints were unreal, their conclusions faulty. Despite the partitions and the racialist assumptions, splendidly mounted and framed in mediocre popular literature, there was little hard evidence of a determined imperialism at this time. Africa, dissected by a sinister geometry of straight lines and artificial frontiers, had added square miles by the million to the colonial spheres of the powers. Yet inside the unswerving frontiers of territories, obtained at next to no expense, attracting little immigration or capital and given next to no administration, the achievement was sparse and somewhat seedy. Before 1914, Europe had not seriously attempted the occupation of tropical Africa. In other parts of the world, partitions were discussed, but they were not carried out. Over China and the Ottoman empire, the striking fact is not rivalry between the powers but cooperation to limit their liability. Even the more serious disputes over Persia, Egypt and Morocco tended to be settled by the old device of *Kompensationspolitik*. Moreover, public opinion had no positive role in these matters. Governments followed forward policies, or backward policies, without much reference to it. The excitements over the fate of General Gordon or the French flying column in Indo-China were the emotions of the day, not steadily held points of view. Public attention concentrated upon ·domestic issues and its chief importance was to compel governments to act cheaply and speak simply in imperial matters. Public opinion was not significant in the making of empire. In the Ford Lectures Gallagher asked whether it was important in their unmaking.

This approach brought Gallagher's emphasis firmly back to the local circumstances overseas which either encouraged or obstructed the workings of European expansion. Colonial systems of rule, castigated as tyrannies by their critics or lauded as benevolent despotisms by their apologists, proved on closer examination to have been neither the one nor the other. They have always depended upon understandings between rulers and subjects. If colonial rule brought disaster to some of the ruled, it made opportunity knock for others. By winning government favour, and hence a firmer grip upon local patronage and power, some colonial subjects gained advantages over others. The stability of colonial rule owed not a little to the opportunities given by the rulers to the ruled for settling old scores without let or hindrance from above. But if divisions inside a colony helped the imperial power to build up systems of collaboration, deeper intervention unavoidably upset them. Gallagher saw India as a leading case. There the British had been content to leave many important aspects of governance to Indians, especially at the local level. In many parts of the Raj, the District Officer might appear to be the master of his little world, but it was the local bigwigs who really ran the district. At the base, British rule in India required the regular collection of revenue and the keeping of law and order. The convenient and economical system was to rely informally upon Indian notables to cover British bets. When Macaulay drafted his law codes for India, he had little idea how scant a bearing they would have on the short and simple annals of the poor and on the tyrannies of the local men who mattered. British overrule in India was a system of minimum intervention, an oriental version of 'salutary neglect'; one of the main interests of Gallagher's 'school' was to see how this system worked in India and why it failed.

One reason why it could not last lay in the continuing poverty of the Raj. It was always short of money; its taxes tended to be inelastic and India was inherently poor. In the later-nineteenth century, the poverty of government grew more alarming. There was no hope of hand-outs from London; Britain ruled India to take money out of it, not to put it in. The Government of India had to be self-supporting. So it had to develop the resources of its own taxpayers. This forced the government, however reluctantly, to move away from its old arrangements about power sharing and its old maxims about keeping taxes low and leaving things alone. Willy-nilly, it began to put pressure upon the old franchises and privileges of the local notables upon whom its rule ultimately depended. Intervention from above affected the systems of collaboration below: hence the device of representation in the various Council Acts and the growth of local self-government. In some cases, these developments stung the local bosses into organized political associations which could fight elections and defend their franchises against the meddling by government. In the new representative institutions men anxious to defend or to improve their conditions and brusquely treated by government could claim to be the spokesmen of larger interests. Associations set up mainly as local insurance policies went on by amalgamation and alliance to gather strength at provincial or even all-India levels. An electoral system based upon the representation of interests rather than numbers encouraged factions to proliferate; all manner of groups emerged and laid claim to government's recognition and support. As one group or faction formed what it was pleased to call a party, its rivals followed suit. Step by step the British had to play a series of political games with their Indian subjects. As they did so, they could reflect that if many were called, many could now be chosen. In India's version of Pandora's box there was no shortage of candidates for collaboration, but the old basis of rule was being eroded. The Raj had been secure so long as a balance could be struck between deploying India in the imperial interest and leaving much of India alone. Political security meant keeping India balkanized and not rupturing the autonomy of its discrete localities. But imperial interests demanded an interconnected and unified structure for a government which was increasingly active. Security might entail economic stagnation; but intervention stirred up a political hornets' nest. This was the fundamental dilemma which the British faced in India. If the problems that political growth created for the Indian empire did not appear formidable at the outset, in time they were to become so, not only in India but in other parts of the empire as well.

Inevitably, these are bland versions of the rich arguments that Gallagher elaborated about the imperial dilemma. In the Wiles and the Ford Lectures, he dwelt upon the oppositon to empire, at home as well as in the colonies. Even in the heyday of empire, anti-imperialism was something of an intellectual vogue among the radical and liberal squadron. But they were all attacking particular ways of running an empire rather than the empire itself. Lenin apart, the critics wanted to eat imperial cake while criticizing the imperial baker, especially in Britain. Before 1914 at least, this was not a serious constraint upon imperial policy. The working class, which had no reason to love the empire and thought that charity should begin at home, had no decisive impact upon expansion. Whatever its political potential, its vote was still working to the advantage of the two old political parties. As yet the Labour party had no views on colonies—until 1919 its programme did not even mention them. Whenever colonial issues impinged on British politics before the first war, it was because some politicians at home picked upon them, irrespective of their merits, as handy weapons in domestic factional fights. British imperialism was not seriously hobbled by domestic constraints before 1914. By then the British and the French empires did face new challenges from other powers across the world. But if their empires were overstretched, diplomacy could still plaster over the cracks. Neither domestic constraints nor international pressures seriously hampered the imperial powers before the First World War.

In the Ford Lectures, Gallagher grappled with some of the questions raised by the decline of the British empire. Had the decolonization of the last thirty years or so been the product of a long and slow decline? Should it be seen as a flame hissing along a fuse laid long ago? Should it rather be seen as a sudden and awful dissolution, the result of a powerful but random combination of events? If it was to be interpreted as possessing a long history, then the question was whether decolonization was a continuous process. Was it simply a matter of rolling along from bad to worse, from decline to fall, or did it happen in phases which moved from decline to revival and from revival to fall? This raised a deeper question. What really brought about the fall of the empire? Axiomatic to Gallagher's approach was the argument that deeper imperial intervention produced growing dilemmas for imperial rule. But was colonial nationalism the factor which finally made it impossible to stay on? Nationalist freedom-fighters (whose numbers seem dramatically to have risen since the fighting stopped) have claimed that Jack killed the Giant. Gallagher asked the nationalists for their identity cards and enquired whether other forces, the constraints of domestic politics and international difficulties, had been at work. Political growth overseas, domestic constraints in the metropolis and international pressures, these were the three factors which Gallagher considered in his survey of the decline, revival and fall of the British empire which is printed for the first time here.[8] It was a pioneering venture; it shows that the writings he himself published were but the visible tip of the iceberg of Gallagher's formidable influence, and suggests how our understanding of imperialism has suffered from his premature death.

Timing, Jack Gallagher was fond of remarking, is critical, whether in love affairs or in history; and of course he was lucky to be the right man at the right time for the task which faced him when he began his study of empires after his return from the war. As European empires declined and were dismantled, so their study called for their historian. Orthodox interpretations, by the apologists and critics of empire alike, had failed to fit the facts. They exaggerated the power of imperialism; they suffered from Euro-centric bias; they were sometimes wrong-headed, more often innocent. They did not explain what had happened, still less what was in the process of happening. The Marxist approach made a desert of understanding; and the freedom-fighters, who saw all their troubles as gifts from abroad, were bogged down in the sands of their own propaganda. Here was an opportunity for a remaking, in many ways a making, of the subject. It is fair to say that Gallagher and Robinson really created the subject known as the 'Expansion of Europe' in Cambridge, engineered an historiographical revolution (as Eric Stokes has described it), and put upon it the stamp of a distinctive 'Cambridge school'.

To these tasks, Jack Gallagher brought an unusual, and perhaps an unusually contradictory, combination of qualities: a ceaseless, darting intelligence, deployed over an enormous range of fact and fiction, a precise memory capable of performing remarkable feats of recall and

[8] See below, pp. 73–153.

cross-reference to support his mental gymnastics. His books, the only possessions he bothered about, contained works on history everywhere and in all eras—America, Russia, China, the Middle East, Europe, medieval and modern, the work of political theorists, memoirs of statesmen and soldiers, wars and more wars; but they also reflected his catholic taste for literature, in French and German as well as English, through which he vicariously lived a life which was both rich and strange. Contemptuous of those who could not raise their eyes from the specifics of their specialities, those who counted the number of angels on the head of a pin or carved prayers upon a cherry-stone, Gallagher yet had a respect for the monographic approach which made him a realistic and successful supervisor of research students. But he could put these monographs into a wider context—he had the imagination to transcend the minutiae of research.

It mattered that he himself had no *parti pris*. His origins were such that he was free from the moorings of tradition, the bonds of immediate loyalties. His father, a working-class Irishman, had returned from Canada to fight in the Great War, and thereafter remained as a railwayman in Liverpool where Jack grew up during the Depression. His mother, something of a Catholic puritan, would no doubt have liked Jack, her only child, to use his gifts in the priesthood, or at least to mark his entry into academic respectability by abandoning what she despairingly regarded as slovenly and Bohemian ways at odds with her expectations and his training. But Jack was irredeemably secular; and although there was always something very Catholic about his approach, he was not beyond a good old-fashioned anti-clericalism (and the Counter-Reformation supplied him with quantities of black humour).

It mattered that Jack Gallagher belonged, in effect, nowhere. He never married, and Trinity, where he came as an undergraduate and stayed on as a Fellow, was all-important to him, It gave him a sense of belonging which was irreplaceable, a no-man's land where the rich and the poor, the established and the *arriviste* shared the neutrality of its fellowship. He always regarded his Oxford days as a Babylonian exile, and was not always too polite to suppress his opinions. His friends in Cambridge were never quite sure why suddenly, and characteristically at the last moment, he applied for the Beit Chair in 'Siberia'; but his return to Cambridge was a campaign carefully planned and successfully executed.

From his rooms in College, and on his travels, Jack was content to observe, and sometimes even to enjoy, the world outside. He never conceived for himself an active role in its affairs. Still, his judgement was impeccable, and he prided himself on the gifts that he thought best for politicians—timing and management. He enjoyed 'the long slow game', building up alliances in College and Faculty, to make sure that his subject got backing and the right man was appointed. Yet sometimes it seemed that this was a cover for inaction, the cunctation of his hero, Quintus Fabius Maximus. His advice on Appointments Committees and in Fellowship Elections was such that he was always listened to with respect: his the foot on the brake, or, more rarely, the accelerator. For Jack believed that when action was necessary it should be swift and decisive with the 'mark of the lion's paw'. It was all a matter of priorities. Lectures, seminars, references for his students, reports on fellowship and doctoral dissertations, all were models of elegance and care; in matters which he took seriously (they did not include completing income-tax returns which he did not make for ten years, banking cheques for supervision and examining, or futile correspondence) he was utterly reliable.

He had a fantasy of himself as a Tammany Hall 'boss', a wheeler and dealer, sometimes a Police Chief, at others a machine-politician. But he was mainly an observer, always interested, always informed, weighing up the crimes and follies of mankind with a sardonic eye. Increasingly, it was the art of politics that interested him, not the great systems that historians had tried to impose on the subject. A sceptic, an enemy of humbug and cant, he took delight in seeing the stiff-necked, the high-minded, the consciously liberal, the philanthropic, the puritanical and the pussyfooted tripping themselves up and acting contrary to their professions. But if his view of political man owed something to the Namier approach, it had a richer and more human quality: everyone, the quick and the dead, who came under Gallagher's scrutiny, was subjected to comment in which the selfish, the ridiculous, the disreputable and the funny were given full play. But underneath a Shavian cynicism lay a sort of wistful Irish, perhaps Catholic kindness, an almost feminine intuition, an understanding and a concern which, because it did not expect much of human nature, felt called upon neither to despise nor to condemn, simply to enjoy, with melancholy and wit, the peculiarities it threw up.

It is not surprising that Gallagher was deeply intrigued by empires and their enemies. Where others had seen in them some great purpose at work, Jack perceived a less impressive reality. Happily adapting Bismarck's remark about the Polish noblemen to a more earthy 'fur coat and no knickers', he was amused but not deceived by the pomp and circumstance of empire, the governors in cocked hats, the troops in tropical garrisons, the colonial bishops gazing glassy-eyed out of sepia prints, just as he was fond of catching out the colonial nationalists who demanded 'freedom or death' and ended by politely declining both. His sense of irony and his love of paradox were such that he would revel in finding the hard under-belly of empire: Saints who abolished the slave trade to defend their dividends, progress that was more material than moral, Gandhians who were once non-cooperative and twice shy. Anything pretentious evoked his scorn. But he admired the sheer nerve, the sleight of hand, the political skills of management, whether of 'fabulous artificers' who 'galvanized' continents on paper, proconsuls who ran empires on shoe-strings or nationalist leaders who somehow painted a veneer of unity over gimcrack coalitions of feuding factions.

Gallagher was essentially a lonely man behind his prodigal openness; he always wore a mask and did not reveal much of himself to anyone. But he was, in his little world, the highest court of appeal. Not surprisingly, he got on wonderfully well with Rab Butler and admired men like Salisbury, or—more ruefully—Bismarck, who had the measure of mankind. His own vast reading, his experience of life vicarious and actual, and his humanity made him an invaluable adviser and critic. The more he went on, the more a flood of ideas, effortless allusions, a wicked humour, would come bubbling forth, inspiring his students and helping them to make the most of their talents. His teaching, on a wide variety of subjects, was always interesting, sometimes a monument of eccentricity (there was the famous occasion when he was discovered dancing the High-Life with a Nigerian lady instead of reading her work). Still, he never took care of his body, always trusting that his Irish frame would bear any strain he put upon it; he smoked heavily, drank whisky too often, avoided physical exertion and survived on a strange diet of cream buns, corned beef and miniature Mars Bars, which he kept (to the shock of more prudent souls) by his armchair. Ironically, the soldier who survived the assaults of the desert destroyed himself in the academic groves.

Jack Gallagher wanted his epitaph simply to read, 'Tank Soldier and Historian'. This is apt enough, though maybe not quite in the way he expected. For he cut an elegant path with great force through hugely complex subjects, bringing along a numerous, appreciative, supportive infantry, all of whom—and not merely those in his own field of imperial history—have cause to remember him with the deepest gratitude and affection.   Anil Seal

Trinity College, Cambridge
1 April 1982

JACK GALLAGHER IN TRINITY

FEW Deans, on first reading Grace in Hall, can have been greeted with such spontaneous applause as was Jack Gallagher. But if the undergraduate enthusiasm displayed on this occasion in any way arose from the expectation of a lax administration, it was sadly misplaced, as was soon apparent from the zeal with which Gallagher entered into the performance of his duties. Indeed, some idea of the effectiveness of his discipline may be gathered from his own statement that during the first six months of his régime, not one case of bear-baiting was reported from within the College, and there is every reason to believe that this happy state will continue.

In an age when disciplinary officers are commonly figures of great awe and majesty, Gallagher provides a most refreshing contrast. In appearance vaguely reminiscent of a merry monk, his tonsured head settles comfortably on ample shoulders, the whole stably supported on a trunk of generous, but not unbalanced proportions. During ecstasy of amusement, his eyes, set behind horn-rimmed spectacles, virtually disappear, while his mouth broadens between genial jowls, and erupts in throaty chuckles and gusty roars of laughter. In conversation, spasmodic and compulsive thrusts of an open hand emphasize his argument, while smoke from the eternal *Gauloise*, clenched between stubby fingers, envelops the scene. Certainly, it is as a conversationalist that the non-historian best knows Gallagher, for he is a *raconteur* of some accomplishment, embroidering the most mundane of tales with trimmings of Irish whimsy. An avid student of the paradox and of the preposterous, he has occasionally been known to compliment others who have shown promise in the exercise of this most sophisticated art, and it is a rare occasion indeed when he will repeat the epigrams of others without improvement. The whimsy of his humour is perhaps best displayed when he is able to draw upon his compendious memory, and upon his historian's ability to digest statistics and to regurgitate them at improbable times and in impossible guises, as in his oft-quoted remark that the completion of a lavatory on his staircase had consumed precisely one-fifth of the time required to erect St Paul's Cathedral. While the element of bluff is undoubtedly pre-eminent in such pronouncements, there is no evidence to suggest that Gallagher has ever been deterred from making a prediction by the possibility that it might prove correct, or from stating a fiction because it could be fact.

With his well-rounded figure and head so suited for coronation by the Vitellian Laurel Wreath, Gallagher can hardly be said to epitomize the athlete, yet perforce of circumstance he has led a far more adventurous life than many of his colleagues. Born in Birkenhead of Irish parents (in Erse, he affirms, O'Gallagher is a foreign invader) he entered Trinity as a scholar in 1937 to read history under Dr Kitson Clark, taking Part I in 1939. Enlisting in the army, he drove a tank through the desert campaign, and yearly on the vigil (or at any other opportunity) he will strip his sleeve and celebrate in suitable manner his deliverance at Alamein. He landed at Salerno, and after leaving Italy in an inflammatory condition he assisted in the preservation of the balance of power in Greece. Demobilization was followed by return to Trinity to take Part II in

1946 and a Fellowship in 1948; in 1950 he joined the teaching staff in history in the College and the University.

Even in these relatively peaceful times, however, Gallagher's research into Colonial History has led him to many of the world's trouble spots—India, the Congo, Algeria, and America. Nearer home, amidst the bursting book-shelves and relict furnishings of his rambling set in Nevile's Court, he dispenses knowledge and justice with sympathy and insight. His University and College duties, combined with frequent visits to satisfy his well-known taste in cathedrals [*scil.* bars], and his entanglement in the proofs of his forthcoming book on the development of the colonial concept in the nineteenth century, undoubtedly make Gallagher a busy man. And so it is hardly surprising that when the last lamp in the Great Court is long extinguished, and when in the pre-dawn hush the river-mist rises through Nevile's colonnade, four windows, brilliantly lit, proclaim that scholarship never sleeps, and neither does the Dean.

Graham Chinner
1961

JACK GALLAGHER IN OXFORD

'WAIT till Jack comes', they would say, 'he's quite a character', 'he will liven things up'. This was in the autumn of 1962, when I was first in Balliol. But Jack did not come; like the Cheshire Cat in reverse movement—and, later, I used to think that with his round face, his round glasses and his unblinking eyes, he looked rather like the Cheshire Cat (others were to describe him as the Living Buddha); and he was indeed from Cheshire—he was always about to be there, but never quite there. No-one, the Master of Balliol included, had any idea where in fact he *was*. Nor had he ever written to anyone to accept his Professorial Fellowship. It was an early training in what later one would come to regard as one of Jack's principal characteristics: his elusiveness. This was later illustrated, once he had moved into his rooms in the tower, above the library, by the lines of supplicants—Indian ladies in saris, the Lord Mayor of Addis Ababa, an assortment of Africans and Thais, and a clutter of undergraduates, waiting patiently, and with suitable oriental resignation, on the spiral staircase, all the way down from his closed door to the level of the Library. Was he in? Was he in Oxford? Would his door open? One could only wait. Jack too Moved in a Mysterious Way. He was fortunate, too, in respect of Balliol that the College was connected by an underground passage, little known to outsiders, to neighbouring Trinity, so that Jack, from his observatory in the Senior Common Room, on seeing the then current chairman of the Examiners, could make a rapid escape into Trinity Garden, and thence walk nonchalantly through Trinity Lodge into the Broad, until scouts had reported to him that the danger had passed and that the way was clear for him to return. Sometimes, if he were reading a magazine, he would ask me to stand look-out and report to him the stealthy approach of the long-suffering Chairman, who, soon used to Jack's wiles, sometimes took to approaching the Common Room obliquely, *en rasant les murs*, in the hope of escaping detection. Of course, Jack was long overdue with the papers that he was supposed to be setting or be marking. It was hardly surprising that, in the course of his eight years in Oxford, he developed a strong affection for Trinity Garden, a long rectangle of safety, up and down which we would walk, denouncing Enthusiasm, or planning our futures. It was the same with mail, when Jack turned up, all at once, and hardly ever at the beginning of the term, the Head Porter would hand him his mail: an enormous pile of beige envelopes. 'Put them in the bin, Bert', he would say. Sometimes it was as abrupt as that. At other times, he would say: 'Just look through quickly to see if there are any scented lilac envelopes, then put the lot in the bin.' Once he asked my wife to see if there were any lilac scented envelopes, but, of course, there never were. The Balliol porters have retained a sort of amazed and awed respect for Jack's manner of dealing with accumulated administrative correspondence.

Then, all at once, it was reported, on good authority, that Jack had been *seen*, not in Balliol, but in Queen Elizabeth House, a sort of seamen's home for transients. This was where I first saw him: a bedroom with twin beds, three tin trunks spilling out printed blue books marked Top Secret, Ten Copies Only, Restricted, for the Attention of the Viceroy, and with such titles as 'Report on Terrorist Activities in West Bengal', 'Report on Civil Disobedience in Bihar', 'Enquiry into the Attempted Murder of the Governor of Sind', mixed up with socks, shoes and shirts. It looked as if the room had been assailed by very rough seas, Jack round-eyed, was sitting on one of the beds. I introduced myself. It appeared that, from whatever mysterious quarter he had just come, reports had reached him concerning *me*, for he gave me a most charming, warm smile, and in his quiet, and pleasant voice, asked if I would like a drink. There was a bottle of *Black Knight*, Delhi whisky, on the top of the chest-of-drawers. The room really did look like a cabin.

After a spell in the seamen's home, Jack was finally installed in Balliol, first at the top of the Library tower, later in a penthouse flat at the top of the new building. I think he favoured heights as likely to discourage the more importunate of his visitors. They also offered him a clear view of approaching supplicants, giving him time to pull up the drawbridge if the enemy were sighted. He liked heights too because they gave him ready access to the College roof, used at regular intervals for his splendid and sometimes alarming parties. It was always something of a surprise to me that, in the course of these, none of his guests ever fell off the roof, crashing to the ground, though one, having put a burning cigarette in the face of one of Jack's pupils—he was also one of mine—was, on Jack's quiet orders, expelled *celerrime* down the spiral staircase. Jack was a marvellous host; but he would not tolerate bad manners. On the other hand, he had derived considerable pleasure at the antics of some of his guests: I can recall one of his former Trinity pupils whose bearded head suddenly fell sideways into his plate of nuts from which position it stared at us with glaucous eyes. Jack made some remark about his guest thinking he was John the Baptist. Later the same guest wandered off dazedly up and down the spiral staircase leading to High Table. One of Jack's fantasies—and he was rich and ingenious in these—was that we should organize a Widmerpool Dinner to which would be invited a careful selection of the biggest boors and the rudest dons that could be provided by the Common Rooms of both ancient Universities. This remained a project. But a number of Jack's guests, most from Trinity, behaved, to Jack's observant delight—one could tell this by the steady stare from behind the round spectacles and the attentiveness of his immobile, Buddha-like face—in a manner either dramatic or wholly incoherent. I can remember one who spent the rest of the night in a vain search for his car, scouring the whole of central Oxford for the missing vehicle, asserting, piteously, that it was yellow. When it was found, at midday the next day, parked by some laboratories, it turned out to be grey.

Nothing gave Jack greater pleasure than for a solemn occasion to go wrong and for pomposity to trip up in its own robes. One of the stories most often repeated from his extensive Cambridge lore—and our sister University, in Jack's accounts, always appeared much more accident-prone than the apparently staider institution further west—concerned the Inaugural Lecture of a newly elected Regius Professor of Moral Theology. The Professor, led in to the Senate House, preceded by the beadles, reached the dais, pronounced the single word 'I' and then fell down dead drunk. Jack returned to this account again and again with loving detail. Then there was another recurring theme on the subject of a Cambridge Professor whose marriage turned on and off *par éclipses*, the legitimate wife alternating with a recurrent mistress—a beautiful Slav; when the Professor was in one of his periodical returns back to his wife, the couple could be seen, parading in an open barouche—sometimes it was a victoria, sometimes a landau, sometimes a white Rolls—up and down King's Parade. It was in character that Jack adored W. C. Fields and took enormous satisfaction in old-fashioned musical-hall acts involving glasses and trays of drink flying through the air and as regularly being retrieved by a nimble waiter clad in a long white apron. There was something childlike in his pure enjoyment of the sight and sound of breakage, an enjoyment that I fully shared. The breakage was sometimes imaginary. On one occasion, I had brought in as a guest a young historian with a nose of Cyrano-like proportion; the nose was in scaffolding, following some major construction work on it. Jack passed me a note: 'Would you tell your guest that his nose has fallen into my soup?' In fact the nose was still on, beneath its elaborate super-structure.

Jack also showed a devastating readiness in his allocation of nicknames to those of whom he did not wholly approve, who were too solemn, too convinced, or took themselves too seriously. A colleague for a brief time in Oxford—his departure from Oxford was no doubt accelerated by Jack's presence there—a specialist in Indian history, was constantly referred to as the Grand Eunuch. A young research fellow whose surname reiterated his Christian one, was always addressed as Humbert Humbert, and indeed introduced as such to other guests. Balliol contained at one time both Genghiz Khan and Robespierre. Jack's persecutor, the Chairman of the Examiners, was named, for some reason, the Minstrel Boy. There was also a Barnsley Boy. An English Fellow from Merton—a splendid figure always clad in loud checks, and with a voice like a fog-horn—was described alternatively as Micawber or W. C. Fields. There were mysterious figures from Cambridge referred to as Hot Lips, Wet Leg, Boyo, Daddy, Rhino, Electric Whiskers. Jack himself was generally evoked as the Living Buddha; and, though he was not especially big, as Big Jack. He was a large man who somehow helped to fill any room in which he was sitting. In a group, such as at a College Meeting, he would be the first person one would pick out, his broad, solid and still presence as reassuring as that of some eighteenth-century Bishop of Peterborough, a Learned Theologian and of Moderate Piety, an Enemy of Enthusiasm. There was something very eighteenth century about Jack, he was certainly an Enemy of Enthusiasm, and he was the most English Irishman I have ever met. His presence was reassuring, because it radiated calm, carefully concealed kindliness, and immense good sense. It was hard to imagine that Big Jack, in what he liked to describe as his 'formative years', had once managed to insert himself through the turret of a tank. It was only fair that, in his descriptions of myself, for the benefit of others, he would refer to the Scavenger, to Gandhi, and to Lazarus. Others have said that, when seen together at table during Consilium dinner, we made as extravagant a pair as Laurel and Hardy. We certainly made a pair, especially at those convivial occasions, engaged as we were in a sort of a double act of impudence and irreverence, extravagance and fantasy. We always took care to sit well away from the main table, and among the more raffish and pleasure-loving members of the College. Our presence at the end of the peripheral table was marked by a fine array of bottles. When I first met Robbie Robinson—sliding down the banisters of Staircase XXII, with a bowler hat over his eyes—Jack introduced him as a bookie friend of his, warning me at the same time to keep a firm hold on my wallet. (Later, indeed for years, Jack made a point of announcing to all and sundry that I had stolen his large black overcoat, though I would have been completely lost in it. By a twist of irony that would have greatly appealed to Jack, after his death I was offered his large black overcoat, not in jest, but in all seriousness, by one of his dearest and most devoted friends.) Jack, to complete his role, needed a partner who would also be a foil. One of the younger Fellows of Balliol described the double impact of Jack and myself on the more puritanical elements of Balliol as the sudden arrival on the sober scene of 'those two wicked old men', unrepentantly and shamelessly calling for More Drink, More Wine. If Robbie was—and is—in the habit of dividing the world between 'the sort of chap I would not mind flying with' and 'not the sort of chap I would go flying with', Jack liked to tell a story in which Robbie and he decided to fly from Cambridge to Colchester in order to eat oysters. Flying over a town, Robbie had said: 'look, that is Colchester'. But, once they had landed, it turned out to be Peterborough. Robbie at the time was a Flying Proctor. In a much more important sense Gallagher & Robinson constituted a partnership of lasting value to historical scholarship. Though fundamentally a lonely man, and perhaps even a melancholy one (the allusion both to the scented lilac envelopes that never came and to Alexandra, the beautiful Greek girl, encountered on an island during Jack's three weeks' idyll of Missing Believe Killed, a recurrent figure in Jack's reminiscences late in the evening, no doubt indicated something that had been lost a very long time back) Jack loved the company of his own choice. I recall, with delight, a supper party at the 'Vine', in London, on Jack's birthday, which as he liked to point out, was on April 1st. Jack was not fortunate in the devotion of his close friends; he *deserved* them. And he needed them to bring him out. It was as if he had managed to surround himself with a small group of loyal retainers, extending from the Lodge to the inner fastnesses of Trinity, so that, when Jack moved, went on a journey, or on holiday, it involved a small *état-major*. Jack was not merely an Imperial historian, there was something Imperial about Jack. I often thought how suitable was the parting gift of the Fellows of Trinity on Jack's elevation to his Oxford chair: a group photograph of the Master of Trinity, George V and some marvellously stoned officers, at the manoeuvres held in Cambridge in 1910 or 1911. In Balliol, Jack withdrew into a tower, an object of some mystery: in Trinity, one felt that the whole College was built around him. Here indeed was the splendid palace of the Living Buddha.

Jack had breakfast fantasies, supper fantasies, and post-midnight fantasies. At breakfast, we would be invited to take a seat in the Great Train as in sedate slowness it steamed past Alpine fields thick with bright spring flowers, girls with straw-coloured hair in plaits, and very blue eyes, and dressed in grindels or brindels, approaching the train and smilingly holding up to its windows baskets of multicoloured fruit and gourds of rough peasant wine. The blue and gold carriages would pass on slowly, amidst a shower of rose petals, a beautiful Rumanian spy, her long lashes reaching halfway down her cheeks, posted at each window, would survey the happy, yodelling Alpine scene. Outside, sleet would be falling over the Garden Quad, while, opposite, Tommy Balogh plunged into the pink pages of the *Financial Times*. Breakfast was decidedly the time that took Jack on long Balkanic wanderings; it was then too that he evoked the Inaugural Lecture of the newly appointed Professor of Macedonian History at the University of Niš, a lecture entitled 'The Macedonian Problem'. First sentence: 'The Macedonian Problem is one of great complexity.' BANG. The Professor, his recently and lavishly endowed chair and his audience are blown sky-high, like Stambulisky in Sofia cathedral. A breakfast variant on the 'I' lecture of the Regius Professor of Moral Theology. It would still be sleeting; and the electric toaster had gone wrong again giving forth clouds of thick, acrid smoke. Young resident research fellows and visitors staying in guest rooms would bury themselves in their papers. One of the evening fantasies would be the battle of Jutland—Jack liked to read Arthur Marder, tucked up in bed in the tower, on stormy winter nights, while the west wind howled outside—twelve hundred men sent to the bottom in one blast, as the magazine blows up—laid out on the floor of the Senior Common Room, the Grand Fleet steaming at 30 knots, the high smoke stacks emitting a long trail of thick black smoke low over the dark oily waters, the German Fleet represented by Hartmut Pogge von Strandmann, wearing for the occasion a spiked helmet. The post-midnight fantasy would often be sparked off by a vengeful record of Serge Ginsbourg's on the subject of *la petite putain* whose little bottom almost burst from its tight envelope and in which the singer, to *un air de java*, evoked with affection *le petit père Ronsard*. But it could also take the form of excursions back into past memories of the Trinity Footlights. Jack was as partial to political music-hall as to the pointed and joyous cruelty of the *chansonniers*.

Jack had a healthy dislike for puritans, the politically convicted, radicals, revolutionaries, fanatics, ranters, and ravers. He distrusted legislation, believed that nothing could ever be solved by laying down rules to meet hypothetical situations, and hated theorists and generalizers. In Balliol, his was always the voice of calm pragmatism; and by his cool patience and gentle persuasion he often managed to prevent the College from taking some inconsidered step into sheer foolishness. He was a natural conservative in the best sense, and his presence often preserved the College from some act of singular folly such as might be inspired by the old, dangerous and rather arrogant notion that 'Balliol must lead the way', no matter where the way might lead: such, for instance, as the suggestion, put to a College meeting, that the unfortunate Rudi Dutschke should be admitted as a graduate student (in politics?). On this occasion, the College was saved from much potential trouble, not by Jack, but by Dutschke himself, who declared a preference for Cambridge. Jack was too much of a Trinity man ever to have made a true Balliol one; but he brought to the College the temperate wind of East Anglian common sense. However, while he undoubtedly enjoyed his years in Oxford, it would not be quite true to say that he enjoyed *all* his years in Balliol. Indeed, shortly before being elected to the Cambridge chair, he had been engaged, with backing in important circles, in engineering his physical transfer to Christ Church. The Cambridge election saved Oxford from what could have been a major and interesting constitutional row, and one that Jack would have enjoyed.

Undoubtedly what he enjoyed most in Oxford was the warm friendship both of Anne Whiteman, very much a kindred spirit, and of Hugh Trevor-Roper, whom he greatly admired for his concern for graduate researchers and for his good sense, as well as the possibility of building up a powerful group both of undergraduates and research pupils. He used to say that his Oxford pupils were the best that he had ever had; and, from the start, although a professorial Fellow, he readily undertook a great deal of undergraduate teaching for the College, starting the new Special Subject: the Making of the Ententes, which, because he taught it, soon became enormously popular. At Jack's Nuffield seminar, what was most impressive was not so much the papers read, excellent though many were, as the urbanity with which Jack presided over these meetings, and the throw-away comments with which he would conclude them: small pieces of pure gold and great elegance, for the possession of which the jostling crowds would eagerly scrabble. A chance suggestion of Jack's sent one of his pupils, Patrick Tuck (who later gave me a small Buddha as a reminder of our mutual friend), off on an investigation of French policies in Siam in the late-nineteenth century. A remark by Jack at a Balliol guest night induced one of my pupils, Peter Carey, to go off and study the possibly remote effects of the French Revolution on Java, resulting in Peter becoming a leading specialist of Indonesian history. It was Jack, too, who induced Chris Bayly, a Balliol man, whom he always described as the best pupil he had ever had in either University, to work on the organization of the Congress Party at a provincial level, in this case, that of Allahabad. Jack distributed wealth like a monarch on a royal progress, with languid ease and elegance. Ideas flowed from him apparently without effort, and at any hour of the day or of the night. This was not just because he was endowed with a very acute historical imagination and a natural facility of expression (his Ford Lectures were literary gems as well as being extremely witty), but also because he had travelled widely in India and Africa, as well as in Europe (much of it *aux frais de la princesse* while in the Armoured Corps), but also because he was very well read, especially in French.

I was greatly surprised—and flattered—to discover that he had read my own works in French, and that, through such writers as Jean Galtier-Bossière, he had acquired a pungent knowledge of Paris slang. The schoolboy who had been preached to by rough Irish fathers on the subject of 'that notorious atheist Jean [as in Jean Harlow] Jakes Rewso', in Birkenhead, had travelled a very long way since his days in that city's Institute. His understanding of the particularities of French colonialism was based as much on observation and sympathy as on reading. He liked to evoke his time on the *north* bank of the Congo Estuary, sitting on a café terrace, drinking his Ricard, and staring across at *Léo* (Léopoldville), while his French companions went on about *ces salauds de Belges*. One Balliol man he recommended to work on Faidherbe, another, on the tribal history of Senegal. The principal monument that Jack has left as a historian can best be traced in the ideas that he communicated to some hundreds of pupils, in both Universities. His felicity of expression was more often verbal than written; and it is typical of his courage and dedication that he insisted on lecturing when in great physical pain, in the last stages of his accumulated illnesses. Much of his conversational charm was injected into his lectures.

Jack's basic loyalty was to Trinity. Of Trinity he always spoke, in Oxford, with pride, describing how, in the days of G. M. Trevelyan, the Master would sit as in feudal splendour, while the emissaries from other Colleges would come and pick up the crumbs dropped from the Master's table, once the list of the College's choices had been read out. He loved to evoke this imperial scene. As a lonely man, without family—his father, a railwayman, died in his 80s in Jack's second year in Balliol—he was more attached than most both to institutions and to friends. It was fitting that he should have returned to Trinity, for this was his home. There, during his long series of illnesses, he was protected by the devotion of friends who included porters solicitous in the watchful protection of his privacy. In Trinity, his hospitality could acquire a suitably grand scale, even to the extent of offering to visitors the Judge's suite and the bed marked with a golden 'V' and a golden 'A' on red (when I slept in it, I was careful to sleep on the 'A' side). And in Trinity, in his rooms on the ground-floor of Great Court, he died in March this year. The whole College followed his coffin as it was borne to the Lodge. It was the saddest sight I have ever seen. And yet, such was the strength, the warmth of his personality, I can see and hear Big Jack is if he were in his room in the tower, or standing, holding the beer mug engraved with his name, in Balliol Buttery, or talking to the barman of the J.C.R. bar in Trinity, or sitting under the terrifying portrait of a cruelly Asiatic Henry VIII. Big Jack will live on in scores of grateful memories of those lucky enough to have known him and to have experienced his warmth, his humour, his elegance, his generosity and his elaborately concealed kindness. For he was a shy man who did good, as if he were pocketing the sugar or the silver spoons, by stealth, when he thought no-one was looking.

Richard Cobb
November 1980

The Imperialism of Free Trade

JOHN GALLAGHER AND RONALD ROBINSON

I

IT ought to be a commonplace that Great Britain during the nineteenth century expanded overseas by means of 'informal empire'[1] as much as by acquiring dominion in the strict constitutional sense. For purposes of economic analysis it would clearly be unreal to define imperial history exclusively as the history of those colonies coloured red on the map. Nevertheless, almost all imperial history has been written on the assumption that the empire of formal dominion is historically comprehensible in itself and can be cut out of its context in British expansion and world politics. The conventional interpretation of the nineteenth-century empire continues to rest upon study of the formal empire alone, which is rather like judging the size and character of icebergs solely from the parts above the water-line.

The imperial historian, in fact, is very much at the mercy of his own particular concept of empire. By that, he decides what facts are of 'imperial' significance; his data are limited in the same way as his concept, and his final interpretation itself depends largely upon the scope of his hypothesis. Different hypotheses have led to conflicting conclusions. Since imperial historians are writing about different empires and since they are generalizing from eccentric or isolated aspects of them, it is hardly surprising that these historians sometimes contradict each other.

The orthodox view of nineteenth-century imperial history remains that laid down from the standpoint of the racial and legalistic concept which inspired the Imperial Federation movement. Historians such as Seeley and Egerton looked on events in the formal empire as the only test of imperial activity; and they regarded the empire of kinship and constitutional dependence as an organism with its own laws of growth. In this way the nineteenth century was divided into periods of

[1] The term has been given authority by Dr C. R. Fay. See *Cambridge History of the British Empire* (Cambridge, 1940), II, 399.

imperialism and anti-imperialism, according to the extension or contraction of the formal empire and the degree of belief in the value of British rule overseas.

Ironically enough, the alternative interpretation of 'imperialism', which began as part of the radical polemic against the Federationists, has in effect only confirmed their analysis. Those who have seen imperialism as the high stage of capitalism and the inevitable result of foreign investment agree that it applied historically only to the period after 1880. As a result they have been led into a similar preoccupation with formal manifestations of imperialism because the late-Victorian age was one of spectacular extension of British rule. Consequently, Hobson and Lenin, Professor Moon and Mr Woolf[2] have confirmed from the opposite point of view their opponents' contention that late-Victorian imperialism was a qualitative change in the nature of British expansion and a sharp deviation from the innocent and static liberalism of the middle of the century. This alleged change, welcomed by one school, condemned by the other, was accepted by both.

For all their disagreement these two doctrines pointed to one interpretation; that mid-Victorian 'indifference' and late-Victorian 'enthusiasm' for empire were directly related to the rise and decline in free-trade beliefs. Thus Lenin wrote: 'When free competition in Great Britain was at its height, i.e. between 1840 and 1860, the leading British bourgeois politicians were . . . of the opinion that the liberation of the colonies and their complete separation from Great Britain was inevitable and desirable.'[3] Professor Schuyler extends this to the decade from 1861 to 1870: '. . . for it was during those years that tendencies toward the disruption of the empire reached their climax. The doctrines of the Manchester school were at the height of their influence.'[4]

In the last quarter of the century, Professor Langer finds that 'there was an obvious danger that the British [export] market would be steadily restricted. Hence the emergence and sudden flowering of the movement for expansion. . . . Manchester doctrine had been belied by the facts. It was an outworn theory to be thrown into the discard.'[5] Their argument may be summarized in this way: the mid-Victorian formal empire did not expand, indeed it seemed to be disintegrating, therefore the period was anti-imperialist; the later-Victorian formal

[2] J. A. Hobson, *Imperialism* (1902); V. I. Lenin, *Imperialism, the Highest Stage of Capitalism* (Selected Works, (n.d.), V; P. T. Moon, *Imperialism and World Politics* (New York, 1926); L. Woolf, *Empire and Commerce in Africa* (n.d.).

[3] Lenin, *Imperialism*, V, 71.

[4] R. L. Schuyler, *The Fall of the Old Colonial System* (New York, 1945), p. 45.

[5] W. L. Langer, *The Diplomacy of Imperialism, 1890–1902* (New York, 1935), I, 75–76.

empire expanded rapidly, therefore this was an era of imperialism; the change was caused by the obsolescence of free trade.

The trouble with this argument is that it leaves out too many of the facts which it claims to explain. Consider the results of a decade of 'indifference' to empire. Betweeen 1841 and 1851 Great Britain occupied or annexed New Zealand, the Gold Coast, Labuan, Natal, the Punjab, Sind and Hong Kong. In the next twenty years British control was asserted over Berar, Oudh, Lower Burma and Kowloon, over Lagos and the neighbourhood of Sierra Leone, over Basutoland, Griqualand and the Transvaal; and new colonies were established in Queensland and British Columbia. Unless this expansion can be explained by 'fits of absence of mind', we are faced with the paradox that it occurred despite the determination of the imperial authorities to avoid extending their rule.

This contradiction arises even if we confine our attention to the formal empire, as the orthodox viewpoint would force us to do. But if we look beyond into the regions of informal empire, then the difficulties become overwhelming. The normal account of South African policy in the middle of the century is that Britain abandoned any idea of controlling the interior. But in fact what looked like withdrawal from the Orange River Sovereignty and the Transvaal was based not on any *a priori* theories about the inconveniences of colonies but upon hard facts of strategy and commerce in a wider field. Great Britain was in South Africa primarily to safeguard the routes to the East, by preventing foreign powers from acquiring bases on the flank of those routes. In one way or another this imperial interest demanded some kind of hold upon Africa south of the Limpopo River, and although between 1852 and 1877 the Boer Republics were not controlled formally for this purpose by Britain, they were effectually dominated by informal paramountcy and by their dependence on British ports. If we refuse to narrow our view to that of formal empire, we can see how steadily and successfully the main imperial interest was pursued by maintaining supremacy over the whole region, and that it was pursued as steadily throughout the so-called anti-imperialist era as in the late-Victorian period. But it was done by shutting in the Boer Republics from the Indian Ocean: by the annexation of Natal in 1843, by keeping the Boers out of Delagoa Bay in 1860 and 1868, out of St Lucia Bay in 1861 and 1866, and by British intervention to block the union of the two Republics under Pretorius in 1860.[6] Strangely enough it was the first Gladstone Government which

[6] C. J. Uys, *In the Era of Shepstone* (Lovedale, Cape Province, 1933); and C. W. de Kiewiet, *British Colonial Policy and the South African Republics* (1929), *passim*.

Schuyler regards as the climax of anti-imperialism, which annexed Basutoland in 1868 and Griqualand West in 1871 in order to ensure 'the safety of our South African Possessions'.[7] By informal means if possible, or by formal annexations when necessary, British paramountcy was steadily upheld.

Are these the actions of ministers anxious to preside over the liquidation of the British empire? Do they look like 'indifference' to an empire rendered superfluous by free trade? On the contrary, here is a continuity of policy which the conventional interpretation misses because it takes account only of formal methods of control. It also misses the continuous grasp of the West African coast and of the South Pacific which British sea-power was able to maintain. Refusals to annex are no proof of reluctance to control. As Lord Aberdeen put it in 1845: '. . . it is unnecessary to add that Her Majesty's Government will not view with indifference the assumption by another Power of a Protectorate which they, with due regard for the true interests of those [Pacific] islands, have refused.'[8]

Nor can the obvious continuity of imperial constitutional policy throughout the mid- and late-Victorian years be explained on the orthodox hypothesis. If the granting of responsible government to colonies was due to the mid-Victorian 'indifference' to empire and even a desire to be rid of it, then why was this policy continued in the late-Victorian period when Britain was interested above all in preserving imperial unity? The common assumption that British governments in the free-trade era considered empire superfluous arises from over-estimating the significance of changes in legalistic forms. In fact, throughout the Victorian period responsible government was withheld from colonies if it involved sacrificing or endangering British paramountcy or interests. Wherever there was fear of a foreign challenge to British supremacy in the continent or sub-continent concerned, wherever the colony could not provide financially for its own internal security, the imperial authorities retained full responsibility, or, if they had already devolved it, intervened directly to secure their interests once more. In other words, responsible government, far from being a separatist device, was simply a change from direct to indirect methods of maintaining British interests. By slackening the formal political bond at the appropriate time, it was possible to rely on economic dependence

[7] De Kiewiet, *British Colonial Policy*, p. 224.
[8] Quoted in J. M. Ward, *British Policy in the South Pacific, 1786–1893* (Sydney, 1948), p. 138.

and mutual good-feeling to keep the colonies bound to Britain while still using them as agents for further British expansion.

The inconsistency between fact and the orthodox interpretation arises in yet another way. For all the extensive anthologies of opinion supposedly hostile to colonies, how many colonies were actually abandoned? For instance, the West Africa Committee of 1865 made a strong and much quoted case for giving up all but one of the West African settlements, but even as they sat these settlements were being extended. The Indian empire, however, is the most glaring gap in the traditional explanation. Its history in the 'period of indifference' is filled with wars and annexations.

Moreover, in this supposedly *laissez-faire* period India, far from being evacuated, was subjected to intensive development as an economic colony along the best mercantilist lines. In India it was possible, throughout most of the period of the British Raj, to use the governing power to extort in the form of taxes and monopolies such valuable primary products as opium and salt. Furthermore, the characteristics of so-called imperialist expansion at the end of the nineteenth century developed in India long before the date (1880) when Lenin believed the age of economic imperialism opened. Direct governmental promotion of products required by British industry, government manipulation of tariffs to help British exports, railway construction at high and guaranteed rates of interest to open the continental interior—all of these techniques of direct political control were employed in ways which seem alien to the so-called age of *laissez-faire*. Moreover, they had little to do, particularly in railway finance, with the folk-lore of rugged individualism. 'All the money came from the English capitalist' as a British official wrote, 'and, so long as he was guaranteed five per cent on the revenues of India, it was immaterial to him whether the funds which he lent were thrown into the Hooghly or converted into bricks and mortar.'[9]

To sum up: the conventional view of Victorian imperialist history leaves us with a series of awkward questions. In the age of 'anti-imperialism' why were all colonies retained? Why were so many more obtained? Why were so many new spheres of influence set up? Or again, in the age of 'imperialism', as we shall see later, why was there such reluctance to annex further territory? Why did decentralization, begun under the impetus of anti-imperialism, continue? In the age of *laissez-faire* why was the Indian economy developed by the state?

These paradoxes are too radical to explain as merely exceptions which prove the rule or by concluding that imperial policy was largely

[9] Quoted in L. H. Jenks, *The Migration of British Capital to 1875* (1938), pp. 221–22.

irrational and inconsistent, the product of a series of accidents and chances. The contradictions, it may be suspected, arise not from the historical reality but from the historians' approach to it. A hypothesis which fits more of the facts might be that of a fundamental continuity in British expansion throughout the nineteenth century.

II

The hypothesis which is needed must include informal as well as formal expansion, and must allow for the continuity of the process. The most striking fact about British history in the nineteenth century, as Seeley pointed out, is that it is the history of an expanding society. The exports of capital and manufactures, the migration of citizens, the dissemination of the English language, ideas and constitutional forms, were all of them radiations of the social energies of the British peoples. Between 1812 and 1914 over twenty million persons emigrated from the British Isles, and nearly 70 per cent of them went outside the empire.[10] Between 1815 and 1880, it is estimated, £1,187,000,000 in credit had accumulated abroad, but no more than one-sixth was placed in the formal empire. Even by 1913, something less than half of the £3,975,000,000 of foreign investment lay inside the empire.[11] Similarly, in no year of the century did the empire buy much more than one-third of Britain's exports. The basic fact is that British industrialization caused an ever-extending and intensifying development of overseas regions. Whether they were formally British or not, was a secondary consideration.

Imperialism, perhaps, may be defined as a sufficient political function of this process of integrating new regions into the expanding economy; its character is largely decided by the various and changing relationships between the political and economic elements of expansion in any particular region and time. Two qualifications must be made. First, imperialism may be only indirectly connected with economic integration in that it sometimes extends beyond areas of economic development, but acts for their strategic protection. Secondly, although imperialism is a function of economic expansion, it is not a necessary function. Whether imperialist phenomena show themselves or not, is determined not only by the factors of economic expansion, but equally by the political and social organization of the regions brought into the

[10] Sir W. K. Hancock, *Survey of British Commonwealth Affairs* (1940), II, pt I, 28.
[11] A. H. Imlah, 'British Balance of Payments and Export of Capital, 1816–1913', *Econ. Histo. Rev.* 2nd ser. V (1952), pp. 237, 239; Hancock, *Survey of British Commonwealth Affairs*, II, pt I, 27.

orbit of the expansive society, and also by the world situation in general.

It is only when the polities of these new regions fail to provide satisfactory conditions for commercial or strategic integration and when their relative weakness allows, that power is used imperialistically to adjust those conditions. Economic expansion, it is true, will tend to flow into the regions of maximum opportunity, but maximum opportunity depends as much upon political considerations of security as upon questions of profit. Consequently, in any particular region, if economic opportunity seems large but political security small, then full absorption into the extending economy tends to be frustrated until power is exerted upon the state in question. Conversely, in proportion as satisfactory political frameworks are brought into being in this way, the frequency of imperialist intervention lessens and imperialist control is correspondingly relaxed. It may be suggested that this willingness to limit the use of paramount power to establishing security for trade is the distinctive feature of the British imperialism of free trade in the nineteenth century, in contrast to the mercantilist use of power to obtain commercial supremacy and monopoly through political possession.

On this hypothesis the phasing of British expansion or imperialism is not likely to be chronological. Not all regions will reach the same level of economic integration at any one time; neither will all regions need the same type of political control at any one time. As the British industrial revolution grew, so new markets and sources of supply were linked to it at different times, and the degree of imperialist action accompanying that process varied accordingly. Thus mercantilist techniques of formal empire were being employed to develop India in the mid-Victorian age at the same time as informal techniques of free trade were being used in Latin America for the same purpose. It is for this reason that attempts to make phases of imperialism correspond directly to phases in the economic growth of the metropolitan economy are likely to prove in vain. The fundamental continuity of British expansion is only obscured by arguing that changes in the terms of trade or in the character of British exports necessitated a sharp change in the process.

From this vantage point the many-sided expansion of British industrial society can be viewed as a whole of which both the formal and informal empires are only parts. Both of them then appear as variable political functions of the extending pattern of overseas trade, investment, migration and culture. If this is accepted, it follows that formal and informal empire are essentially interconnected and to some extent interchangeable. Then not only is the old, legalistic, narrow idea of empire unsatisfactory, but so is the old idea of informal empire as a separate, non-political category of expansion. A concept of informal empire which fails to bring out the underlying unity between it and the formal empire is sterile. Only within the total framework of expansion is nineteenth-century empire intelligible. So we are faced with the task of re-fashioning the interpretations resulting from defective concepts of organic constitutional empire on the one hand and Hobsonian 'imperialism' on the other.

The economic importance—even the pre-eminence—of informal empire in this period has been stressed often enough. What was overlooked was the inter-relation of its economic and political arms; how political action aided the growth of commercial supremacy, and how this supremacy in turn strengthened political influence. In other words, it is the politics as well as the economics of the informal empire which we have to include in the account. Historically, the relationship between these two factors has been both subtle and complex. It has been by no means a simple case of the use of gunboats to demolish a recalcitrant state in the cause of British trade. The type of political lien between the expanding economy and its formal or informal dependencies, as might be expected, has been flexible. In practice it has tended to vary with the economic value of the territory, the strength of its political structure, the readiness of its rulers to collaborate with British commercial or strategic purposes, the ability of the native society to undergo economic change without external control, the extent to which domestic and foreign political situations permitted British intervention, and, finally, how far European rivals allowed British policy a free hand.

Accordingly, the political lien has ranged from a vague, informal paramountcy to outright political possession; and, consequently, some of these dependent territories have been formal colonies whereas others have not. The difference between formal and informal empire has not been one of fundamental nature but of degree. The ease with which a region has slipped from one status to the other helps to confirm this. Within the last two hundred years, for example, India has passed from informal to formal association with the United Kingdom and, since the Second World War, back to an informal connection. Similarly, British West Africa has passed through the first two stages and seems to-day likely to follow India into the third.

III

Let us now attempt, tentatively, to use the concept of the totality of British expansion described above to restate the main themes of the history of modern British expansion. We have seen that interpretations of this process fall into contradictions when based upon formal political criteria alone. If expansion both formal and informal is examined as a single process, will these contradictions disappear?

The growth of British industry made new demands upon British policy. It necessitated linking undeveloped areas with British foreign trade and, in so doing, moved the political arm to force an entry into markets closed by the power of foreign monopolies.

British policy, as Professor Harlow has shown,[12] was active in this way before the American colonies had been lost, but its greatest opportunities came during the Napoleonic Wars. The seizure of the French and Spanish West Indies, the filibustering expedition to Buenos Aires in 1806, the taking of Java in 1811, were all efforts to break into new regions and to tap new resources by means of political action. But the policy went further than simple house-breaking, for once the door was opened and British imports with their political implications were pouring in, they might stop the door from being shut again. Raffles, for example, temporarily broke the Dutch monopoly of the spice trade in Java and opened the island to free trade. Later, he began the informal British paramountcy over the Malacca trade routes and the Malay peninsula by founding Singapore. In South America, at the same time, British policy was aiming at indirect political hegemony over new regions for the purposes of trade. The British navy carried the Portuguese royal family to Brazil after the breach with Napoleon, and the British representative there extorted from his grateful clients the trade treaty of 1810 which left British exports paying a lower tariff than the goods of the mother country. The thoughtful stipulation was added 'that the Present Treaty shall be unlimited in point of duration, and that the obligations and conditions expressed or implied in it shall be perpetual and immutable'.[13]

From 1810 onwards this policy had even better chances in Latin America, and they were taken. British governments sought to exploit the colonial revolutions to shatter the Spanish trade monopoly, and to gain informal supremacy and the good will which would all favour British commercial penetration. As Canning put it in 1824, when he had clinched the policy of recognition: 'Spanish America is free and if we do

[12] V. T. Harlow, *The Founding of the Second British Empire, 1763–1793* (1952), pp. 62–145.

[13] Quoted in A. K. Manchester, *British Pre-eminence in Brazil* (Chapel Hill, 1933), p. 90.

not mismanage our affairs sadly she is *English*.'[14] Canning's underlying object was to clear the way for a prodigious British expansion by creating a new and informal empire, not only to redress the Old World balance of power but to restore British influence in the New. He wrote triumphantly: 'The thing is done . . . the Yankees will shout in triumph: but it is they who lose most by our decision . . . the United States have gotten the start of us in vain; and we link once more America to Europe.'[15] It would be hard to imagine a more spectacular example of a policy of commercial hegemony in the interests of high politics, or of the use of informal political supremacy in the interests of commercial enterprise. Characteristically, the British recognition of Buenos Aires, Mexico and Colombia took the form of signing commercial treaties with them.

In both the formal and informal dependencies in the mid-Victorian age there was much effort to open the continental interiors and to extend the British influence inland from the ports and to develop the hinterlands. The general strategy of this development was to convert these areas into complementary satellite economies, which would provide raw materials and food for Great Britain, and also provide widening markets for its manufactures. This was the period, the orthodox interpretation would have us believe, in which the political arm of expansion was dormant or even withered. In fact, that alleged inactivity is seen to be a delusion if we take into account the development in the informal aspect. Once entry had been forced into Latin America, China and the Balkans, the task was to encourage stable governments as good investment risks, just as in weaker or unsatisfactory states it was considered necessary to coerce them into more cooperative attitudes.

In Latin America, however, there were several false starts. The impact of British expansion in Argentina helped to wreck the constitution and throw the people into civil war, since British trade caused the sea-board to prosper while the back lands were exploited and lagged behind. The investment crash of 1827 and the successful revolt of the pampas people against Buenos Aires[16] blocked further British expansion, and the rise to power of General Rosas ruined the institutional framework which Canning's strategy had so brilliantly set up. The new régime was uncooperative and its designs on Montevideo caused chaos

[14] Quoted in W. W. Kaufmann, *British Policy and the Independence of Latin America, 1804–1828* (New Haven, 1951), p. 178.

[15] Quoted in J. F. Rippy, *Historical Evolution of Hispanic America* (Oxford, 1946), p. 374.

[16] M. Burgin, *Economic Aspects of Argentine Federalism* (Cambridge, Mass., 1946), pp. 55, 76–111.

around the Rio de la Plata, which led to that great commercial artery being closed to enterprise. All this provoked a series of direct British interventions during the 1840s in efforts to get trade moving again on the river, but in fact it was the attractive force of British trade itself, more than the informal imperialist action of British governments, which in this case restored the situation by removing Rosas from power.

British policy in Brazil ran into peculiar troubles through its tactless attempt to browbeat the Government of Rio de Janeiro into abolishing slavery. British political effectiveness was weakened, in spite of economic predominance, by the interference of humanitarian pressure groups in England. Yet the economic control over Brazil was strengthened after 1856 by the building of the railways; these—begun, financed and operated by British companies—were encouraged by generous concessions from the Government of Brazil.

With the development of railways and steamships, the economies of the leading Latin American states were at last geared successfully to the world economy. Once their exports had begun to climb and foreign investment had been attracted, a rapid rate of economic growth was feasible. Even in the 1880s Argentina could double her exports and increase sevenfold her foreign indebtedness while the world price of meat and wheat was falling.[17] By 1913, in Latin America as a whole, informal imperialism had become so important for the British economy that £999,000,000, over a quarter of the total investment abroad, was invested in that region.[18]

But this investment, as was natural, was concentrated in such countries as Argentina and Brazil whose governments (even after the Argentine default of 1891) had collaborated in the general task of British expansion. For this reason there was no need for brusque or peremptory interventions on behalf of British interests. For once their economies had become sufficiently dependent on foreign trade the classes whose prosperity was drawn from that trade normally worked themselves in local politics to preserve the local political conditions needed for it. British intervention, in any case, became more difficult once the United States could make other powers take the Monroe Doctrine seriously. The slackening in active intervention in the affairs of the most reliable members of the commercial empire was matched by the abandonment

[17] J. H. Williams, *Argentine International Trade under Inconvertible Paper Money, 1880–1900* (Cambridge, Mass., 1920), pp. 43, 103, 183. Cf. W. W. Rostow, *The Process of Economic Growth* (Oxford, 1953), p. 104.

[18] J. F. Rippy, 'British Investments in Latin America, end of 1913', *Inter-American Economic Affairs* (1951), V, 91.

of direct political control over those regions of formal empire which were successful enough to receive self-government. But in Latin America, British governments still intervened, when necessary, to protect British interests in the more backward states; there was intervention on behalf of the bondholders in Guatemala and Colombia in the eighteen-seventies, as in Mexico and Honduras between 1910 and 1914.

The types of informal empire and the situations it attempted to exploit were as various as the success which it achieved. Although commercial and capital penetration tended to lead to political cooperation and hegemony, there are striking exceptions. In the United States, for example, British business turned the cotton South into a colonial economy, and the British investor hoped to do the same with the Mid-West. But the political strength of the country stood in his way. It was impossible to stop American industrialization, and the industrialized sections successfully campaigned for tariffs, despite the opposition of those sections which depended on the British trade connection. In the same way, American political strength thwarted British attempts to establish Texas, Mexico and Central America as informal dependencies.

Conversely, British expansion sometimes failed, if it gained political supremacy without effecting a successful commercial penetration. There were spectacular exertions of British policy in China, but they did little to produce new customers. Britain's political hold upon China failed to break down Chinese economic self-sufficiency. The Opium War of 1840, the renewal of war in 1857, widened the inlets for British trade but they did not get Chinese exports moving. Their main effect was an unfortunate one from the British point of view, for such foreign pressures put Chinese society under great strains as the Taiping Rebellion unmistakably showed.[19] It is important to note that this weakness was regarded in London as an embarrassment, and not as a lever for extracting further concessions. In fact, the British worked to prop up the tottering Peking régime, for as Lord Clarendon put it in 1870, 'British interests in China are strictly commercial, or at all events only so far political as they may be for the protection of commerce'.[20] The value of this self-denial became clear in the following decades when the Peking Government, threatened with a scramble for China, leaned more and more on the diplomatic support of this honest British broker.

The simple recital of these cases of economic expansion, aided and

[19] J. Chesnaux, 'La Révolution Taiping d'après quelques travaux récents', *Revue Historique*, CCIX (1953), 39–40.

[20] Quoted in N. A. Pelcovits, *Old China Hands and the Foreign Office* (New York, 1948), p. 85.

abetted by political action in one form or other, is enough to expose the inadequacy of the conventional theory that free trade could dispense with empire. We have seen that it did not do so. Economic expansion in the mid-Victorian age was matched by a corresponding political expansion which has been overlooked because it could not be seen by that study of maps which, it has been said, drives sane men mad. It is absurd to deduce from the harmony between London and the colonies of white settlement in the mid-Victorian age any British reluctance to intervene in the fields of British interests. The warships at Canton are as much a part of the period as responsible government for Canada; the battlefields of the Punjab are as real as the abolition of suttee.

Far from being an era of 'indifference', the mid-Victorian years were the decisive stage in the history of British expansion overseas, in that the combination of commercial penetration and political influence allowed the United Kingdom to command those economies which could be made to fit best into her own. A variety of techniques adapted to diverse conditions and beginning at different dates were employed to effect this domination. A paramountcy was set up in Malaya centred on Singapore; a suzerainty over much of West Africa reached out from the port of Lagos and was backed up by the African squadron. On the east coast of Africa British influence at Zanzibar, dominant thanks to the exertions of Consul Kirk, placed the heritage of Arab command on the mainland at British disposal.

But perhaps the most common political technique of British expansion was the treaty of free trade and friendship made with or imposed upon a weaker state. The treaties with Persia of 1836 and 1857, the Turkish treaties of 1838 and 1861, the Japanese treaty of 1858, the favours extracted from Zanzibar, Siam and Morocco, the hundreds of anti-slavery treaties signed with crosses by African chiefs—all these treaties enabled the British Government to carry forward trade with these regions.

Even a valuable trade with one region might give place to a similar trade with another which could be more easily coerced politically. The Russian grain trade, for example, was extremely useful to Great Britain. But the Russians' refusal to hear of free trade, and the British inability to force them into it, caused efforts to develop the grain of the Ottoman empire instead, since British pressure at Constantinople had been able to hustle the Turk into a liberal trade policy.[21] The dependence of the

[21] V. J. Puryear, *International Economics and Diplomacy in the Near East* (1935), pp. 216–17, 222–3.

commercial thrust upon the political arm resulted in a general tendency for British trade to follow the invisible flag of informal empire.

Since the mid-Victorian age now appears as a time of large-scale expansion, it is necessary to revise our estimate of the so-called 'imperialist' era as well. Those who accept the concept of 'economic imperialism' would have us believe that the annexations at the end of the century represented a sharp break in policy, due to the decline of free trade, the need to protect foreign investment, and the conversion of statesmen to the need for unlimited land-grabbing. All these explanations are questionable. In the first place, the tariff policy of Great Britain did not change. Again, British foreign investment was no new thing and most of it was still flowing into regions outside the formal empire. Finally the statesmen's conversion to the policy of extensive annexation was partial, to say the most of it. Until 1887, and only occasionally after that date, party leaders showed little more enthusiasm for extending British rule than the mid-Victorians. Salisbury was infuriated by the 'superficial philanthropy' and 'roguery' of the 'fanatics' who advocated expansion.[22] When pressed to aid the missions in Nyasaland in 1888, he retorted: 'It is not our duty to do it. We should be risking tremendous sacrifices for a very doubtful gain.'[23] After 1888, Salisbury, Rosebery and Chamberlain accepted the scramble for Africa as a painful but unavoidable necessity which arose from a threat of foreign expansion and the irrepressible tendency of trade to overflow the bounds of empire, dragging the government into new and irksome commitments. But it was not until 1898 that they were sufficiently confident to undertake the reconquest of so vital a region as the Sudan.

Faced with the prospect of foreign acquisitions of tropical territory hitherto opened to British merchants, the men in London resorted to one expedient after another to evade the need of formal expansion and still uphold British paramountcy in those regions. British policy in the late, as in the mid-Victorian, period preferred informal means of extending imperial supremacy rather than direct rule. Throughout the two alleged periods the extension of British rule was a last resort—and it is this preference which has given rise to the many 'anti-expansionist' remarks made by Victorian ministers. What these much quoted expressions obscure, is that in practice mid-Victorian as well as late-Victorian policy-makers did not refuse to extend the protection of formal rule over British interests when informal methods had failed to give security. The fact that informal techniques were more often sufficient for this purpose

[22] Quoted in Cromer, *Modern Egypt* (1908), I, 388.
[23] Hansard, 3rd Series, CCCXXVIII, col. 550, 6 July 1888.

in the circumstances of the mid-century than in the later period when the foreign challenge to British supremacy intensified, should not be allowed to disguise the basic continuity of policy. Throughout, British governments worked to establish and maintain British paramountcy by whatever means best suited the circumstances of their diverse regions of interest. The aims of the mid-Victorians were no more 'anti-imperialist' than their successors', though they were more often able to achieve them informally; and the late-Victorians were no more 'imperialist' than their predecessors, even though they were driven to annex more often. British policy followed the principle of extending control informally if possible and formally if necessary. To label the one method 'anti-imperialist' and the other 'imperialist', is to ignore the fact that whatever the method British interests were steadily safeguarded and extended. The usual summing up of the policy of the free trade empire as 'trade not rule' should read 'trade with informal control if possible; trade with rule when necessary'. This statement of the continuity of policy disposes of the over-simplified explanation of involuntary expansion inherent in the orthodox interpretation based on the discontinuity between the two periods.

Thus Salisbury as well as Gladstone, Knutsford as well as Derby and Ripon, in the so-called age of 'imperialism', exhausted all informal expedients to secure regions of British trade in Africa before admitting that further annexations were unavoidable. One device was to obtain guarantees of free trade and access as a reward for recognizing foreign territorial claims, a device which had the advantage of saddling foreign governments with the liability of rule whilst allowing Britons the commercial advantage. This was done in the Anglo-Portuguese Treaty of 1884, the Congo Arrangement of 1885, and the Anglo-German Agreement over East Africa in 1886. Another device for evading the extension of rule was the exclusive sphere of influence or protectorate recognized by foreign powers. Although originally these imposed no liability for pacifying or administering such regions, with changes in international law they did so after 1885. The granting of charters to private companies between 1881 and 1889, authorizing them to administer and finance new regions under imperial licence, marked the transition from informal to formal methods of backing British commercial expansion. Despite these attempts at 'imperialism on the cheap', the foreign challenge to British paramountcy in tropical Africa and the comparative absence there of large-scale, strong, indigenous political organizations which had served informal expansion so well elsewhere, eventually dictated the switch to formal rule.

One principle then emerges plainly: it is only when and where informal political means failed to provide the framework of security for British enterprise (whether commercial, or philanthropic or simply strategic) that the question of establishing formal empire arose. In satellite regions peopled by European stock, in Latin America or Canada, for instance, strong governmental structures grew up; in totally non-European areas, on the other hand, expansion unleashed such disruptive forces upon the indigenous structures that they tended to wear out and even collapse with use. This tendency in many cases accounts for the extension of informal British responsibility and eventually for the change from indirect to direct control.

It was in Africa that this process of transition manifested itself most strikingly during the period after 1880. Foreign loans and predatory bankers by the 1870s had wrecked Egyptian finances and were tearing holes in the Egyptian political fabric. The Anglo-French dual financial control, designed to safeguard the foreign bondholders and to restore Egypt as a good risk, provoked anti-European feeling. With the revolt of Arabi Pasha in 1881, the Khedive's Government could serve no longer to secure either the all-important Canal or the foreign investors' pound of flesh.

The motives for the British occupation of 1882 were confused and varied: the desire, evident long before Disraeli's purchase of shares, to dominate the Canal; the interests of the bondholders; and the over-anxiety to forestall any foreign power, especially France, from taking advantage of the prevailing anarchy in Egypt to interpose its power across the British road to India. Nearly all Gladstone's Cabinet admitted the necessity of British intervention, although for different reasons, and, in order to hold together his distracted ministry, the Prime Minister agreed.

The British expedition was intended to restore a stable Egyptian government under the ostensible rule of the Khedive and inside the orbit of informal British influence. When this was achieved, the army, it was intended, should be withdrawn. But the expedition had so crushed the structure of Egyptian rule that no power short of direct British force could make it a viable and trustworthy instrument of informal hegemony and development. Thus the Liberal Government following its plan, which had been hastily evolved out of little more than ministerial disagreements, drifted into the prolonged occupation of Egypt it was intent on avoiding. In fact, the occupying power became directly responsible for the defence, the debts and the development of the country. The perverse effect of British policy was gloomily summed up by Gladstone: 'We have done our Egyptian business and we are an Egyptian government.'[24] Egypt, then, is a striking example of an informal strategy misfiring due to the undermining of the satellite state by investment and by pseudo-nationalist reaction against foreign influence.

The Egyptian question, in so far as it was closely bound with the routes to India and the defence of the Indian empire itself, was given the highest priority by British policy in the 'eighties and 'nineties. In order to defend the spinal cord of British trade and empire, tropical African and Pacific claims were repeatedly sacrificed as pawns in the higher game. In 1884, for example, the Foreign Office decided that British vulnerability in Egypt made it unwise to compete with foreign powers in the opening scramble for West Africa; and it was therefore proposed '. . . to confine ourselves to securing the utmost possible freedom of trade on that [west] coast, yielding to others the territorial responsibilities . . . and seeking compensation on the east coast . . . where the political future of the country is of real importance to Indian and imperial interests.'[25] British policy was not one of indiscriminate land-grabbing. And, indeed, the British penetration into Uganda and their securing of the rest of the Nile Valley was a highly selective programme, in so far as it surrendered some British West African claims to France and transferred part of East Africa to Germany.

IV

Thus the mid-Victorian period now appears as an era of large-scale expansion, and the late-Victorian age does not seem to introduce any significant novelty into that process of expansion. The annexations of vast undeveloped territories, which have been taken as proof that this period alone was the great age of expansion, now pale in significance, at least if our analysis is anywhere near the truth. That the area of direct imperial rule was extended is true, but is it the most important or characteristic development of expansion during this period? The simple historical fact that Africa was the last field of European penetration is not to say that it was the most important; this would be a truism were it not that the main case of the Hobson school is founded on African examples. On the other hand, it is our main contention that the process of expansion had reached its most valuable targets long before the

[24] Quoted in S. Gwynn and G. M. Tuckwell, *Life of Sir Charles Wentworth Dilke* (1917), II, 46.
[25] F.O. Confidential Print (East Africa), 5037.

exploitation of so peripheral and marginal a field as tropical Africa. Consequently arguments, founded on the technique adopted in scrambling for Africa, would seem to be of secondary importance.

Therefore, the historian who is seeking to find the deepest meaning of the expansion at the end of the nineteenth century should look not at the mere pegging out of claims in African jungles and bush, but at the successful exploitation of the empire, both formal and informal, which was then coming to fruition in India, in Latin America, in Canada and elsewhere. The main work of imperialism in the so-called expansionist era was in the more intensive development of areas already linked with the world economy, rather than in the extensive annexations of the remaining marginal regions of Africa. The best finds and prizes had already been made; in tropical Africa the imperialists were merely scraping the bottom of the barrel.

The Partition of Africa

JOHN GALLAGHER AND RONALD ROBINSON

I

SINCE the nineteenth century began, the Europeans had been strengthening their hold over those parts of the world selected during the era of mercantilism. Australasia, India, South-east Asia, above all the Americas—they were either temperate regions peopled with white immigrants or tropical countries already under white rule. Step by step the mode of white expansion had altered: liberalism and industrial growth shifted the emphasis away from colonies of formal empire to regions of informal influence. But whatever the form it had taken, the groundwork of European imperialism had been truly laid long before the cartographical exercises in partition at the end of the century. Africa was the last continent to win the interest of the strategists of expansion; it seemed to them that here they were scraping the bottom of the barrel.

Dividing Africa was easy enough for the Europeans. They did it at that moment in history when their lead over the other continents was at its longest. Economic growth and technical innovation gave them invincible assurance and force. Their culture and political organization gave them a carrying power to match their iron ships and high-velocity guns. That Europe had the capacity to subjugate Africa was self-evident; but had her rulers any firm wish to do so?

Twenty years were enough to see the continent carved into symmetries devised by the geometers of diplomacy. By the end of the century only Morocco and Ethiopia were still independent, and their turn was coming. But the statesmen who drew the new frontier lines did not do so because they wanted to rule and develop these countries. Bismarck and Ferry, Gladstone and Salisbury, had no solid belief in African empire; indeed they sneered at the movement as something of a farce. A gamble in jungles and bush might interest a poor king such as Leopold II of the Belgians, or a politician on the make such as Crispi, but the chief partitioners of the 1880s glimpsed no grand imperial idea behind what they were doing. They felt no need of African colonies and in this they

reflected the indifference of all but the lunatic fringe of European
business and politics. Here their historians must follow them. For all the
hindsight of social scientists, there was no comprehensive cause or
purpose behind it. In all the long annals of imperialism, the partition of
Africa is a remarkable freak. Few events that have thrown an entire
continent into revolution have been brought about so casually.

Why then did statesmen bother to divide the continent? It used to be
supposed that European society must have put out stronger urges to
empire in Africa at this time; and all sorts of causes have been suggested
to support the supposition. One and all, however, they suffer from a
tiresome defect: of powerful new incentives there is remarkably little
sign. Only after the partition was long over and done with did capital
seek outlets, did industry seek markets in tropical Africa. As late as the
end of the century the European economy went on by-passing these poor
prospects in favour of the proven fields of America and Asia. Neither is it
realistic to explain the movement by some change in the temper of the
European mind. The pride and pomps of African empire did not suit the
popular taste until late in the 1890s when the partition was all but
completed. Only after Africa lay divided and allotted did European
opinion embrace the mythology of empire. Defined as a movement of
white men to transform African society, as they had transformed the
societies of India or Java, imperialism was not the cause of partition. It
was one of the side effects.

This is not to say that there is no rational explanation. It is only to
suggest that no single, general cause underlay a movement to which so
many things contributed at random. All of them must be included, for it
was their concatenations that brought on the partition. And these
cannot be revealed unless the view is wrenched away from the
standpoint that has obscured it hitherto. Scanning Europe for the
causes, the theorists of imperialism have been looking for the answers in
the wrong places. The crucial changes that set all working took place in
Africa itself. It was the fall of an old power in its north, the rise of a new in
its south, that dragged Africa into modern history.

From these internal crises, erupting at opposite ends of the continent,
there unfolded two unconnected processes of partition. That in southern
Africa flowed from the rise of the Transvaal on its gold reefs, from a
struggle between colonial and republican expansion that reached from
Bechuanaland to Lake Nyasa. It eventually drove South Africa into the
Jameson Raid and the Boer War. The second crisis was the breakdown
of the Khedivate in the Egyptian revolution of 1879–82. Their
misdealings with this new proto-nationalism brought the British

stumbling on to the Nile and trapped them there. This was crucial. It led to bad blood between them and the French in a quarrel that was to spread over all tropical Africa before being settled at Fashoda in 1898.

Hence Europe became entangled in tropical Africa by two internal crises. Imbroglios with Egyptian proto-nationalists and thence with Islamic revivals across the whole of the Sudan drew the powers into an expansion of their own in East and West Africa. Thousands of miles to the south, English efforts to compress Afrikaner nationalists into an obsolete imperial design set off a second sequence of expansion in southern Africa. The last quarter of the century has often been called the 'Age of imperialism'. Yet much of this imperialism was no more than an involuntary reaction of Europe to the various proto-nationalisms of Islam that were already rising in Africa against the encroaching thraldom of the white men.

II

Muslim rebellion drew Ferry into the unplanned occupation of Tunis which was the prelude to the partition; Muslim revolution in Cairo drew Gladstone into his Egyptian bondage and set off the partition proper. The peoples of this part of North Africa had much to protest about. By 1880 consuls, money-lenders, engineers and philanthropists from over the water had organized both these countries into chaos. Since Egypt commanded a route to British India, since Tunis counted in French Mediterranean policy both the Khedive and the bey had been playthings of Anglo-French expansion for three-quarters of a century. Although neither power could be indifferent to the fate of these areas, neither wished to turn them into colonies. Anxious to keep the Ottoman empire intact, the British chose to watch over Suez from Constantinople. Enjoying the fruits of unofficial hegemony in Tunis and Cairo, the French felt no desire for another Algeria. But European investment and trade had increased since the 1830s and it was from investment that the crash came in the 1870s, that golden age of Islamic insolvency when the Commander of the Faithful at Constantinople was himself hammered into bankruptcy. In Cairo and Tunis the financial advice of Europe hardened into something like dictation. Debt commissioners took charge of the revenues so blithely mortgaged by their rulers; payment of the coupon became the first charge on their governments; in the eyes of their peoples the two potentates had become mere debt collectors for the infidels. Inevitably they went from financial catastrophe to political disaster. Their armies, as the least rigid and most westernized group in these states, threatened a *putsch*; or the tribes of the marches talked of revolt. The more they squeezed money from landlord and peasant, the nearer came revolt against their rapacity. By 1881 Egypt and Tunisia were sliding into the ruin which overtook almost all the non-European polities in the nineteenth century that essayed a programme of European-style development. Islam provided neither the law nor the ethos nor the institutions for such work, and the rulers discovered that they could not modernize without loosing their authority or their independence.

In spite of the bankruptcy, the French were far from anxious to occupy Tunisia. But with Italian encouragement after 1877 the grand peculator, Mustapha ben Ismail, replaced Khérédine, the tool of France, as first minister and set about rooting up the concessions which gave Paris the option over the economic and political future of the country. Here was a new situation. Making good these options would require more than gunboats and peddlers of contracts.

Many in Algeria, but few in France, called for a punitive expedition. There were admirals and generals who looked forward to adding Tunis to their domain in Algeria, there was rubbing of hands among speculators at the prospect of the *coup de Bourse* which would come if their government ended by guaranteeing the debts of a defeated bey. But most French politicians saw more risk than gain. 'An expedition to Tunis in an election year?', the premier, Ferry, exclaimed to his Foreign Minister. 'My dear Saint-Hilaire, you cannot think of it!' But Gambetta, the President of the Chamber, was for intervention, and this was decisive. Assured of his aid, the government at last unleashed the army. On 22 April 1881 the military promenade into Tunisia began.

How large were the French intentions? They were remarkably small for the so-called age of imperialism. Gambetta, defining the expedition's aims, wrote: 'We ought to extort a large reparation from the bey . . . take a large belt of territory as a precaution for the future, sign a treaty with effective guarantees, and then retire . . . after having made a show of force sufficient to assure for ever a preponderant position there, in keeping with our power, our interests and our investments in the Mediterranean.' With Ferry also, the aim was to reassert external sway rather than to acquire a new colony and these limited aims were mirrored in the Treaty of Bardo, extorted from the bey on 12 May 1881. It merely announced a French protectorate. By itself this meant only long-range control of his external relations; and even so mild a commitment as this was ratified in the Chamber with a hundred and twenty abstentions. The French occupation of Tunisia was not a matter of forward policy-making in Paris. It came in response to the deepening crisis inside Tunisia itself. The Treaty of Bardo was merely an arrangement with a discredited Muslim ruler whose surrender to France could not bind his subjects.

Within his kingdom, as in Algeria, preachers of the *Sanusi* religious order were whipping up rage against the Christian invaders; a rebellion in Oran was followed by another in the south around the holy city of Kairouan. Holy war was proclaimed, a Khalifa was recognized, the tribes farthest from Tunis flocked to join the movement. Here in essence was the same situation as that which had produced the savage wars of Abd-el-Kader in Algeria during the 1840s and was to produce the Muslim theocracy of the Mahdi in the Egyptian Sudan—lightning explosions of fanaticism against the overlordship of the foreigner and the unbeliever.

Crushing the rising offered no difficulties to the generals, but it presented thorny problems to the politicians. One thing was now clear. The basis of the old system of informal control had gone for good, swept aside by political and religious revolt from below. By the summer of 1881 France had to make the same hard choice in Tunisia as Abd-el-Kader had presented her with in Algeria. She had either to get on or get out. Either the paper protectorate had to be made good, or it had to be torn up. Making it good would entail yet more criticism from the Chamber. In October the rebellion was broken. But the general dislike of African adventures in the Chamber meant that its endorsement would be oblique and ambiguous. Gambetta induced the new Chamber to resolve on the 'complete fulfilment' of the Treaty of Bardo. Behind this dexterously vague draftsmanship, the reality was quite different. The invaders of Tunisia were now compelled to conquer and rule a people whom they could no longer dominate from outside.

So devious an occupation was far from marking the start of a new imperialism. It was not the result of a profound impulse in French society to enlarge the empire in Africa. It was electorally risky. It brought obloquy upon its sponsors. It struck no spark of that Gallic love of *gloire* so often brought in by historians when the problems surrounding French expansion become too puzzling. The protectorate was no more than a continuation of the old move into Algeria, a conclusion of the old informal expansion into Tunisia.

The partition of the African tropics which began two years later was not the result of the Tunisian mishap, or of Leopold's schemes and Bismarck's wiles, or of the squabbles of white merchants and explorers on the spot. What drove it on was the Suez crisis and the repercussions of that crisis.

A recognizably modern nationalist revolution was sweeping the Nile Delta by 1882; its leaders are much more familiar figures today than the pro-consuls who put them down. The Egyptians were reacting against increasing interference over the past six years by Britain and France. Anxious to renovate the crumbling state on which their amicable dual paramountcy and their security in India and the Mediterranean in large part depended, they had acted with a high hand. At their behest, the Khedivate had been clothed in the decencies of constitutional monarchy, the army cut, and the landlords obliged to pay their dues; the Khedive Ismail had been sent packing, Tewfik raised in his place and two-thirds of the revenue sequestrated to satisfy the bondholders. Small wonder that the Notables were using the constitution to break their foreign fetters. The mulcted peasantry was at the point of revolt. Muslim gorges were rising against Christians; the army had mutinied to recall dismissed comrades, and the pashas were defending their fiscal privileges in the guise of patriots ridding the country of the foreigner. By January 1882 all were uniting against the Anglo-French Financial Controllers and the Khedive who did their will. The French consul reported that Tewfik had lost all prestige; the British that Arabi and his colonels had practically taken over the country.

What was afoot in Egypt was far more serious than the collapse of the bey had been. Here also was 'an anti-European movement . . . destined to turn into fanaticism';[1] but this time it had the professional army at its head. Gladstone, then Prime Minister, anticipated 'with the utmost apprehension a conflict between the "Control" and any sentiment truly national, with a persuasion that one way or the other we should come to grief.' 'Egypt for the Egyptians [was] the best, the only good solution to the Egyptian question.' This was true. But as the 'union between [Britain and France] on that . . . question was the principal symbol' of their overall *entente*, both gave priority in the crisis to keeping in step. Each might grumble at going it together, neither desired to go it alone. The unpopularity of the Tunisian adventure was enough to deter Freycinet's ministry from another promenade in North Africa. Gladstone's Liberals, who had just retired from the Transvaal and Afghanistan and washed their hands of Tunis and Morocco, still had their scruples about meddling abroad. Yet something had to be done. Clearly the ideal solution, the only one as Gladstone had said, was to come to

[1] French consul in Cairo to Freycinet, 21 February 1882, Archives du Ministère des Affaires Etrangères [henceforth, AE], Egypte 72.

terms with Arabi. This was tried. Paris offered him a paid holiday to
study European armies; London tried to reconcile him to the Khedive.
But Egyptian feelings were too heated for Arabi to agree to the one
condition that seemed indispensable: abiding by the Financial Control.
So long as he refused this, the British feared a foreign thrust at the
jugular vein of Suez, and the French feared Turkish intervention which
would bring the aid of Islam nearer to their dissident subjects in Tunis
and Algeria. On 6 January 1882 the joint note announced the
conclusion of Gambetta, unwillingly subscribed to by Gladstone. The
Khedive must be supported and the Control upheld. What was not
announced was the equally emphatic conviction of the two governments
that landing an army in Egypt for this purpose would defeat its own
object. Freycinet could not move because the Chamber was opposed,
and so an invasion would hand Egypt to the British on a plate.
Gladstone's Cabinet too was in a dilemma. Intervening single-handed
would mean a breach with France. A joint intervention would give
France a half-share in the route to the East. Granville at the Foreign
Office listed the objections: 'Opposition of Egyptians; of Turkey;
jealousy of Europe; responsibility of governing a country of Orientals
without adequate means and under adverse circumstances; presump-
tion that France would object as much to our sole occupation as we
should object to theirs.' The official case against going into Egypt was
overwhelming. As Disraeli had said, 'Constantinople [was still] the key
to India, not Cairo and the Canal'. At few times in the century had
Anglo-French rivalry in the Mediterranean been so composed. Added
to that, the late-Victorian pessimism about the possibilities of making
English gentlemen of 'Orientals' made another strong argument against
conquering new Indias. All the plans therefore were for staying out and
solving the problem from outside.

But effective as the arts of 'moral influence' had been hitherto in
bending pashas and mandarins to European whims, they were to prove
worse than useless against Arabists, Mahdists and Boxers whose mass
defiance signalled the political awakenings of Islam and the Orient.
Instead of sobering the colonels and saving the Control, the pressures of
gunboat diplomacy and the European Concert only added to the
charismatic appeal of Arabi, *el Misr*, the 'Egyptian'. The Anglo-French
naval demonstration of June provoked a massacre of Europeans at
Alexandria. This destroyed Arabi's credit with the English Liberals, and
although the French squadron sailed away, Beauchamp Seymour was
allowed to bombard the Alexandrian forts to show that Britain at least
was in earnest. This old-fashioned device proved the critical blunder,

the point of no return. Arabi proclaimed a *jihad* against the British, rioting spread to the interior. According to the dogmas of strategy, if Suez was in jeopardy, it must be protected at any cost. According to Anglo-Indian orthodoxy, the *jihad* challenged imperial prestige throughout the Muslim East. Hence for Gladstone's ministers, 'the question [was] no longer what form of intervention is . . . most unobjectionable, but in what form it can be most promptly applied'. No chance of French or international cooperation was left. But in applying their conventional routine of threat and bluff to cow the Egyptians, the British had raised the stakes so high that now they had to win by any means. On 16 August Sir Garnet Wolseley and the redcoats landed on the Canal for another small colonial war. They routed the Egyptian army at Tel el Kebir, imprisoned Arabi and reinstated Tewfik. Gladstone's Government pledged its word that as soon as the Canal was safe and Tewfik strong, it would bring the troops home and leave the Egyptians 'to manage their own affairs'.

There is no doubt that this is what the Liberals meant to do. Like the French in Tunisia, they simply intended to restore the old security through influence without extending their rule. The expedition was to be a Palmerstonian stroke of the kind that had brought the Turk to reason in 1839–41, had chastened the Chinese in two Opium wars, the Ethiopians in 1869 and the Ashanti in 1874. Many months passed before they realized that, having rushed in, they could not rush out again; that they had achieved the occupation which above all they had wanted to avoid. By 1884 they had to confess privately that 'the theory on which we originally undertook [to go in] . . . however plausible, has completely broken down'. The models for intervention proved as outdated as the Crystal Palace. From start to finish the British had miscalculated. They had gone to restore the *status quo ante Arabi*, and discovered that it no longer existed. They had come to restore a khedive and found him a cypher without the authority of British bayonets. And so they had gone in and they could not get out.

What first opened their eyes was another crisis in Africa. After Mehemet Ali had conquered the eastern Sudan for Egypt, the Khedive Ismail had laid heavy tribute upon its people. At the same time, he had put down the slave trade, thus depriving them of their chief means of staving off the tax-collector or his bastinado. He had employed white governors to impose Christian ethics on his Muslim subjects. Detesting the imperialism of Cairo, the Sudanese struck back at the Egyptians once they had been disarmed by revolution and invasion. As so often in Muslim Africa, the liberation movement took the form of a puritan revolution against the religious latitudinarianism of the foreign ruling class. In 1881 the Mahdi, Mohammed Ahmad, began his preaching and the revivalist Dervish orders forged the politically discontented sheikhs and deposed sultans, slave traders and tribes, into an army and a state. At first the implications of the *Mahdia* were hidden from the British in Egypt behind a curtain of sands, until news came in November 1883 that the Mahdists had cut the Egyptian troops in the Sudan to pieces. Without soldiers or money, Tewfik could not hold Khartoum. There was no resistance left between the Mahdi and Wadi Halfa. Just as the British were handing back Tewfik a much qualified independence and withdrawing their troops from Cairo, the Mahdi's advance compelled them to stand in defence of the frontiers of Lower Egypt. At last the sinister truth dawned in London. As ministers complained: 'we have now been forced into the position of being the protectors of Egypt'. As with Arabi, so with the Mahdi, there was no chance of striking a bargain of the old mid-Victorian sort. Against fierce Egyptian opposition Gladstone ordered Tewfik to abandon the Sudan and stop the drain on his exchequer, while Gordon was sent to his death at Khartoum attempting the impossible. In enforcing the abandonment, Baring practically had to take control of the khedivial government and, the tighter he gripped it, the deeper the British became involved in its financial difficulties. By this time the unpopularity of the Egyptian fiasco matched that of the Tunisian affair in France. It was increasingly clear that Gladstone's Ministry had made fools of themselves. They had hoped to set up an independent Egyptian Government; but hampered by the *Mahdia*, the loss of the Sudan, the bankruptcy and the Control's unpopularity with the proto-nationalists, they found no Egyptian collaborators to whom they could transfer power with safety. Nor could they retire so long as the infuriated French refused to admit the exclusive paramountcy in Cairo which they claimed as their due reward. For if they left, the French would upset their influence, or the Egyptian nationalists or Sudanese invaders might upset the financial settlement, and all the dangers of the Suez crisis would arise again.

In the event, the *Mahdia* had trapped the British in Egypt in much the same way as the southern rising had caught the French in Tunisia. No sooner did a European power set its foot upon the neck of the Ottoman rulers of the coastal cities than the nomads of the inland steppes and deserts seized their chance of throwing off the pashas' yoke. Hence the Europeans found the régimes which they had come to discipline or restore falling about their ears and they had to stay and pick up the pieces. Gladstone wearily summed up the result of dealing as if they were politically uninhabited with an Egypt in revolution and a Sudan in religious revival: 'we have done our Egyptian business; we are an Egyptian government.'

The longer the British garrisons remained, the stronger grew the arguments for staying. By 1889 the 'veiled protectorate' had become a necessity for imperial security in the world. As Salisbury said, 'the appetite had grown with the eating'. Sir Evelyn Baring and the Anglo-Indian officials who governed in the name of the Khedive, brought from Calcutta to the Nile their professional distrust of nationalists. It became inconceivable that the Egyptians could be trusted to govern themselves. Arabist sentiment still smouldered. In taking over the country, the English had stopped its politics in a state of betwixt and between. Its obsolete Turkish rulers had fallen, but its rising liberal leaders had been put down. So Baring had to rule until native authority revived, but native authority could hardly revive while Baring ruled. If evacuation was impossible for internal reasons, it soon became impracticable on external grounds. Eventually the occupation drove France into the arms of Russia; and this combined menace in the Mediterranean, together with the further crumbling of Turkish power, enhanced Egypt's importance to Britain. After 1889, therefore, the resolution was to stay and keep the lid on the simmering revolution, rather than withdraw and invite another power to straddle the road to India. Henceforth England's statesmen were to be bewitched with the far-fetched fancies of the Nile-valley strategy. To be sure of the canal and lower Egypt, they were to push their territorial claims up the Nile to Fashoda and from the Indian Ocean to Uganda and the Bahr-al-Ghazal.

On an Olympian view, the taking of Egypt might seem to have been the logical outcome of two great movements of European expansion since the end of the eighteenth century. One was the long build-up of British trade and power in the East; the other was the extension of Anglo-French influence which had so thoroughly disrupted Ottoman rule in Egypt and the Levant that the routes to the East were no longer safe. Certainly this long-term logic set limits to the problem. But what determined the occupation of Egypt in concrete terms was not so much the secular processes of European expansion as the Arabist and Mahdist revolutions against its encroaching mastery. When they baffled the customary informal techniques of France and Britain, it was too late to find any other solution but conquest and rule.

The shots of Seymour at Alexandria and Wolseley at Tel el Kebir were to echo round the world. It transpired in the end that their *ricochets* had blown Africa into the modern age. The onslaught on Arabi opened the long Anglo-French conflict over Egypt which more than anything brought on the division of East and West Africa. Up to the 1890s it was merely a partition on paper. The politicians in the European capitals at least intended it to go no farther than that. Hitherto they had ignored the clamour of their merchants, missionaries and explorers for advances in tropical Africa. They had done so with good reason. Communications were difficult; the tribes of the hinterlands seemed lost in chaos; there were grave doubts whether the African could be persuaded to work, or whether he could work at anything worth producing; prospects of trade or revenue seemed gloomy indeed. If governments had sometimes bestirred themselves to help private traders and sent frigates along the coasts to atone for the sins of slave trade, such acts were not intended as commitments. Since large or stable authorities were few and far between, even the simplest methods of informal expansion worked badly in tropical Africa. Clearly, then, this was no place for colonies. For decades before 1882, therefore, a gentlemen's agreement between the powers saw to it that the petty quarrels of their merchants and officials on the coasts did not become pretexts for empire.

But when Gladstone stumbled into Egypt that era ended. To the French, the veiled protectorate was the worst humiliation since Sedan. Their canal and the country which they had nursed since Napoleon's landing had been snatched away under their very noses. This broke the Liberal *entente* and kept Britain and France at odds for twenty years. Once in Egypt, moreover, Britain became highly vulnerable to continental diplomacy. To set Egyptian finances in order, she needed German support against French vetoes in the Debt Commission, if her ministers were to avoid asking their critical Parliament to subsidize the Khedive. By altering European alignments thus, the Egyptian occupa-tion for the rest of the century gave the powers both incentive and opportunity to break the traditional understandings about tropical Africa. While Baring played the puppet-master in Cairo, the French sought to force him out by loosing their pro-consuls against exposed British interests in unclaimed Africa; while the Germans did likewise to extort more British aid in their European affairs. Once the powers began to back their nationals' private enterprises for diplomatic purposes, commerce south of the Sahara ceased to be a matter of restricted influence over coasts; it became a business of unlimited territorial claims over vast hinterlands. In this roundabout fashion, Arabi's revolution and Gladstone's blunder exaggerated the importance of intrinsically tiny disputes in tropical Africa and brought the diplomatists to the auction rooms.

III

On the western coasts before October 1882 there were few signs that the *modus vivendi* was to end so abruptly. Wars between producers and middlemen chiefs along the unpacified lines of supply were strangling the British and French trading stations on the Bight of Benin. For twenty years past, the Colonial Office had been thinking of giving up the Gambia, the Gold Coast, Lagos and Sierra Leone. The French Government had left the Ivory Coast and in 1880 it was thinking of moving out of Dahomey and Gabon 'because of the trivial scale of French interests there'.[2] With the turmoil in the hinterlands, the unofficial *pax* rigged up by the palm-oil traders was ceasing to work; but London and Paris refused to replace it with the extravagant order of colonial rule.

The only regions where Europeans had broken through the middlemen chiefs who closed all ways inland, had been along the three great rivers. On the Senegal by 1865 General Faidherbe had carried French influence up-river to Kayes. Sixteen years later their men in the field had visions of going on to bring the formidable Muslim states of the western Sudan under their sway and of building a trans-Saharan railway between Senegal and Algeria. This scheme went back into a pigeon-hole. In 1881, however, an Upper Senegal Command was formed and Colonel Borgnis-Desbordes was instructed to throw a chain of posts from Bafoulabe to Bamako on the Upper Niger. But as soon as the soldiers ran into trouble, the politicians of Paris cut their credits and talked of scrapping the command. The statesmen in London and Paris refused to quarrel about this expansion of Senegal which pointed no threat to the chief centre of British trade three thousand kilometres away on the Lower Niger.

Nor were there the makings of a West African 'scramble' here, where Liverpool merchants throve without the aid of colonial government. By 1881 George Goldie had amalgamated the most enterprising of the Niger firms into the National Africa Company, the better to monopolize the up-river traffic and drive out French competitors. This was Anglo-French rivalry of a sort, but only at the level of private traders

[2] Minister of Marine to Foreign Minister, 6 January 1874, AE, Mémoires et Documents, Afrique (henceforth, AEMD), 58. Foreign Minister to Minister of Marine, 31 January 1880, AEMD Afrique, 77.

cutting each others' throats in the ordinary way of business. So long as the Anglo-French *entente* lasted, their governments had no wish to become involved, as Goldie discovered when he was refused a royal charter for his company. They were as uninterested in the merchants and explorers jostling in the no-man's-land along the Congo river. Disraeli's ministers had rejected the Cameron treaties which offered them a political option on the inner basin. Leopold II of the Belgians was to be more reckless. Under cover of the International African Association which he floated in 1876, this inveterate projector was plotting a private Congo empire under the innocent device of a free state. In 1879 Stanley went out to establish its claims. To preserve a hinterland for its poverty-stricken posts on the Gabon, the French government asked Brazza to pick up counter-treaties that would 'reserve our rights without engaging the future'. All this was but the small change of local rivalry that had gone on for decades. Brazza's was a private venture of passing interest to his government. Leopold's Congo scheme had as little chance of being realized as a dozen others he had hatched for concessions in China, the Philippines, Borneo and the Transvaal. The Belgian Government would have nothing to do with it. Nor, as the King admitted, would investors subscribe a centime until the powers recognized his rights in the Congo. But what was the chance that they would then be so generous as to endow his house with a great estate which he was too puny to seize for himself? As long as France and Britain could agree, his hopes of becoming an African emperor were exceedingly thin.

But immediately the British ejected the French from the Dual Control in October 1882, these minor intrigues in West Africa were drawn into their quarrel over Egypt. In Paris there was less talk of jettisoning outposts and more speculation about extending claims to strengthen the diplomatic hand against the English. Treich Laplène was allowed to expand French influence on the Ivory Coast. More important, the French consul on the Lower Niger started a flurry of treaty-making, menacing the chief British trade on the coast. Early in 1883 Granville tried to renew the old self-denial arrangements by offering the French exclusive influence on the Upper Niger if they would respect the *status quo* on the lower river. But the time for such happy understandings had gone. As the ambassador reported, the breaking of the Egyptian gentlemen's agreement had so outraged the French that a West African standstill was now out of the question. So by November the Foreign Office could see nothing for it but to send out consul Hewett to bring the Niger districts under treaties of protection and 'prevent the possibility of our trade there being interfered with'. His sailing was delayed for six months. Neither the Treasury nor the Liverpool traders could be persuaded to pay his fare!

At the same time, the Anglo-French estrangement overturned the hands-off arrangements on the Congo. Paris scorned Granville's efforts to renew them. In November 1882 the Chamber ratified Brazza's treaty of claim to the right bank of the river instead. A month later, Granville countered by accepting Portugal's ancient claims to the Congo in return for guarantees of free trade. To the French this treaty seemed West African insult added to Egyptian injury; 'a security taken by Britain to prevent France . . . from setting foot in the Congo Delta'; a violation of an undertaking that went back to 1786. In riposte, Ferry mounted a diplomatic onslaught against the Anglo-Portuguese agreement. Once she had obtained a pre-emptive right over Leopold's holdings, France pressed the counter-claims of the Congo Free State as if they were already her own. At the end of March 1884 the most powerful statesman in Europe took a hand. His own metaphor for it was much more revealing: he would take up his 'Egyptian baton'.

With Egypt dividing them, France and Britain both courted German favour; Granville needed Bismarck's help to extricate his government from their financial troubles in Cairo; while Ferry solicited it in resisting the Anglo-Portuguese Treaty and English ambitions in Egypt—'a consideration which dominated all others' in Paris. The Chancellor could sell his support to the highest bidder; or if need be, he could encourage the weaker contender against the stronger, and so keep the Egyptian issue from being settled. In any case there would be something for Germany; Heligoland might be recovered from England; a number of colonial trifles could certainly be picked up; better still, an isolated France might be diverted from allying with Russia or rejoining Britain into a healing *rapprochement* with the conquerors of Alsace-Lorraine. In March Bismarck began to try out these ideas. He hinted at German help for France if she pressed her rights in Egypt. But Ferry, suspecting that Bismarck did 'not want to do anything to annoy England, but . . . [would] be delighted to see her opposed by others, especially by [France]', negotiated an Egyptian agreement with Britain. In June the English were promising to evacuate the country in 1888, if the French would agree to neutralize it on Belgian lines thereafter.

With the Egyptian baton falling from his grasp, it was time for Bismarck to stiffen the French with offers of German support, if they would raise their terms to Granville. Time also to remove Ferry's suspicions by proving that Germany had serious reasons of her own to act with France against Britain. There were none in Egypt, as the Chancellor had often declared. So for verisimilitude, he blew the petty Anglo-German trade disputes around the African coasts into a noisy anti-British demonstration. In May he pressed the German Government's protection over Lüderitz's concession at Angra Pequena, on the barren south-west coast of Africa. A month later, he denounced the Anglo-Portuguese Treaty and demanded an international conference to decide the Congo's future. At the beginning of July he proclaimed Togoland and the Cameroons to be German protectorates. There was no popular cry for African colonies inside the Reich; and as Bismarck always insisted, he himself was 'against colonies . . . which install officials and erect garrisons'. But paper claims to protectorates cost nothing, and they were good bait to draw France away from Britain into an *entente* with Germany. Surprisingly, this devious diplomacy succeeded. At the London Conference of July, Bismarck, together with the French Chamber and bondholders, contrived to wreck the Anglo-French agreement over Egypt. To drive the wedge home, he proposed a Franco-German *entente* on West African questions. In August the French accepted. 'After the bad treatment inflicted on us by England', wrote de Courcel, 'this *rapprochement* is essential to us under penalty of utter and most dangerous isolation.' To show good faith, the Germans joined France in backing Leopold's Congo Free State. By October 1884 the two powers had agreed to settle the fate of the Niger as well as the Congo at an international conference in Berlin; and the British, who had conceded all Bismarck's African claims and dropped the Portuguese treaty lest 'a breach with Germany . . . make our chances of honourable extrication from the Egyptian difficulty even less than they are', were compelled to attend.

To strengthen their governments' hands in the coming negotiations, consuls and merchants were now treaty-making wherever they hoped to trade on the west coast. Astonished ministers in London observed that 'the attention of European Powers is directed to an unprecedented extent to . . . the formation of Settlements on the African coast'. Forestalled by Nachtigal in the Cameroons, Hewett rushed around the Niger Delta bringing the chiefs under British protection to block the Germans and French there. On the Lower Niger, Goldie bought out the *Compagnie du Sénégal* and the *Société française de l'Afrique Equatoriale*, and sent Joseph Thomson to outrun a German expedition for treaties with the northern Nigerian emirates of Sokoto and Gandu. Meanwhile, the French, who had no great hopes of the Lower Niger, were advancing down the upper river from Bamako, occupied by Galliéni in 1883, and were extending their treaties along the Ivory and Slave Coasts. Governments had let the local expansionists off their leashes, now that the Egyptian occupation had merged territorial claims in Africa with power-politics in Europe. How high the symbolic importance of these trivial African clashes had risen was shown when the French and English went meekly to their little Canossa at Berlin. The two leading naval and colonial powers in the world were bidding for West African commerce under the hammer of a third-rate naval person who hitherto had had no colonies at all.

In strange contrast to the zealots on the coasts, the statesmen who met in Berlin at the end of 1884 found each other reasonably accommodating. The conference in fact was something of an anti-climax. Before it had ever met, it had served its main purposes. The Egyptian baton had thwacked Gladstone back into line. The Franco-German *entente* had been formed; and it had kept Granville from declaring a protectorate in Egypt and from taking exclusive charge of its finances. Toward the end of the meeting, indeed, Ferry and Granville were agreeing in the London Convention to pump an international loan into the Khedivate and to continue international control of its revenues. Though they were left pining for the British to leave Cairo, the French had at least prevented them from digging-in any deeper. Hence the West African disputes which had served as outer markers for these evolutions of grand diplomacy were easily dismissed in Berlin. And public opinion in Europe took scant notice of the manner of their going.

The diplomats dealt briskly enough with the outstanding trivia. Who should be saddled with the responsibility for free trade and navigation on the Niger; and on the Congo? How little the powers cared, they showed by recognizing the legal personality of the Congo Free State. It was Leopold's year for a miracle. The lions agreed to toss him the lion's share of the Congo basin, while contenting themselves with the scraps. Ferry took for France a much more modest sphere; the region around Brazzaville on the north bank was to be the Gabon's hinterland. For the rest, the Congo river was placed under an international régime and its conventional basin, covering most of Central Africa, became a free-trade area. Having conceded the Congo, Granville was able to keep international authority out of the Niger. Control of the lower river went to Britain, that of the upper river to France, arrangements which merely preserved the *status quo*. Though the Berlin Act laid it down that territorial claims on African coasts should depend on effective occupation, this magical phrase was left so vague that it meant almost nothing.

Far from laying down ground rules for the occupation of Africa, the statesmen at Berlin had no intention of playing that game. Despising colonial ventures in tropical Africa, they had extended their hands-off arrangements largely in order to avoid it. The last thing they wanted was to commit themselves to administering such comparatively unimportant places. Once these countries had been saved from foreign clutches by adjusting their international status, the diplomats planned to wash their hands of them. Except in the Cameroons and Togoland, where the traders refused such gifts, Bismarck gave over his paper protectorates to the Germans trafficking in them. The British hastened to do the same with the Lower Niger. In June 1886 Goldie at last got his monopoly chartered under the title of the Royal Niger Company; this was 'the cheapest . . . way of meeting' the obligations accepted at the Berlin Conference. Until 1891 the Foreign Office hoped to saddle the Liverpool firms with the governance of the Niger Delta, just as it had fobbed on to Goldie the costs of administering the lower river. But these merchants refused the privilege. There was nothing for it but to put the Niger Coast protectorate squarely under the rule of London. Throughout the British attitude to the Niger had been negative: 'so long as we keep other European nations out, we need not be in a hurry to go in.' Whatever this dictum rings of, it does not sound like imperialism.

The politicians of Paris were equally averse to colonizing their new spheres. True, Ferry was saying by 1885 that France must have colonies for all the usual reasons—investment, markets, prestige, the civilizing mission—but he had been swept out of office in March by the critics of his colonial adventures: the Freycinet who had followed him in office did not wish to follow him out again. Plainly, the French Congo was a new white elephant. The Gabon was an old one. The French Government treated both of them with scorn. In 1887 it stopped its annual subsidy to the Gabon[3] and loftily warned Brazza, the administrator of the Congo, that 'we cannot stay indefinitely in a period of costly exploration'.[4] Until the 1890s there were only fifteen French officials in the region. Its annual export was only worth £1,500.[5] Paris was no less sceptical about its possessions in the Gulf of Benin. All the Quai d'Orsay could find to say in their favour was that 'even if we admit that they are of small value . . . [they] are bargaining counters which . . . may be useful for

---

[3] Head of West African Mission to Décazes, 19 October 1885, 25 March 1886, Archives du Gouvernement-Général, Afrique Equatoriale Française (henceforth AEF), 2 B, 28.
[4] Freycinet to Brazza, 12 April 1886, AEMD, Afrique, 94.
[5] Memo. no. 70, 24 January 1890, AEF, Rapports sur la Situation Intérieure, October 1886–February 1890.

our interests elsewhere'. The heads of the Ministry of Marine 'show[ed] themselves very lukewarm, not merely to the development, but to the maintenance pure and simple of the French holdings in West Africa'. [6] On the Upper Niger too, they felt no enthusiasm for turning their sphere into a full-blown colony. At the Berlin Conference, neutralization of the river and free trade along its entire course had been the most they had wanted.[7] But when the British made the Niger Company the monopolists of free trade on the lower river, they may have fooled themselves, but they did not fool the French. The glaring paradox behind this goaded Freycinet into declaring a protectorate over the Upper Niger in 1887 to forestall an extension of so bizarre a theory of free trade.[8] Politically, he meant to go no farther than a vague network of alliances with the Muslim rulers of the area, and early in 1887 Galliéni signed treaties with Amadu Shehu and Samori, by far the most powerful of them. His agreements did not commit France, he explained, neither would they cost her anything. They were simply meant 'to enlarge the limits of our future commercial empire and to close these regions to foreign designs'. Trade was supposed to bind these Muslim states to France:[9] but there was not enough of it. 'It is only retail business,' Galliéni's successor reported, 'the means of transport are lacking for anything larger.'[10] All that Paris had envisaged on the Upper Niger was a small, cheap and conditional option on the region.

If the diplomats and commercial travellers after the Berlin Conference had been deciding these West African affairs on their merits, things would have gone no farther than that. But as usual they had reckoned with an Africa without the Africans. So their intentions were one thing; the outcome on the spot was another. Driven on by the Egyptian crisis, the West African 'scramble' could no longer be halted at will. The old stand-still arrangements could no longer stand. In the end, even paper protectorates were to perform that special alchemy which makes one people regard the remote lands of others as 'possessions' and itself as responsible for their well-being. But it was not working strongly yet; imperial sentiment in Europe was the least of the reasons for the scramble. They are rather to be found in West Africa itself. The diplomatic flurry had compelled governments to back their traders'

[6] Foreign Ministry memo., 15 April 1887, AEMD, Afrique, 83.

[7] Memo. by Services des Colonies, 17 July 1885, Archives de Ministère de la France d'Outre Mer (henceforth MFOM), Afrique, IV, 12 B.

[8] Under-Secretary of Colonies to Freycinet, 1 March 1886, MFOM, Sénégal, IV, 84.

[9] Memo. by Galliéni, 24 September 1887, MFOM, Sénégal, IV, 90; Galliéni to Under-Secretary of Colonies, 30 July 1887, *ibid.*

[10] Memo. by Archinard, 19 August 1889, MFOM, Sénégal, IV, 93 A.

THE PARTITION OF AFRICA

efforts to break through the middlemen chiefs and trade up-country. So a rivalry for commercial options was spreading as a result from the coast to the interior, with every port competing against its neighbours for a hinterland and its officials plunging deeper into the politics of the African bush. Even so, most of the powers held these local tendencies in check. Germany ceased to extend her claims once the diplomatic manoeuvres of 1884 and 1885 had been completed, content to take diplomatic advantage of the Anglo-French dissension to improve her position in Europe. No more ambitious were the British, on the west coast at least. Not only were they wary of going too far in their dealings with powerful Muslims in the backlands, they parsimoniously reined back all advances until local trade and colonial revenue had developed sufficiently to pay for them. What they had on the Niger, they held; but elsewhere the English usually let West Africa go.

It was to the French that it went. For the next fifteen years they made all the running in the western parts of the continent; but not altogether by choice. It would be puerile to argue that they were driven on by a search for glory—most Frenchmen had no idea of the whereabouts of Bafoulabe. Admittedly, the established influence of the military in their colonial affairs made the politicians prone to give their army in Africa its head. But what necessitated their headlong conquest of the middle Niger, the northern Ivory Coast and the western Sudan after 1887 was a series of involuntary imbroglios with the fighting Muslim theocracies of these regions. The hapless policy-makers of Paris had designed no more than a vague paramountcy over them. It was bad luck that, like the Egyptians, the Mahdists and southern Tunisians, the theocrats preferred the *jihad* to working with the French and so dragged them into vast imperial conquests instead. The paper partition had set the French army to grips with a reviving and recalcitrant Islam. In subjugating it, the paper empire had to be occupied.

In the history of Africa, the long expansion of Islam since the eighth century dwarfs the brief influence of Europe. From the western Sudan between the Senegal and Lake Tchad, between the coastal forests and the Sahara, the puritanic Almoravides had set forth to rule over Spain and the Maghreb. Here the golden empires of Mali and Ghana had risen and fallen; here Muslims and animists had struggled for centuries. Yet the difficulty of assimilating tribes into nations had foiled the making of enduring states. By the seventeenth century, Islam here was at best the cult of aristocracies lording it over a mass of pagan subjects. But from the later eighteenth century, the creed was on the march once more. United by the spread of Muslim brotherhoods with their calls for religious reform, the Tokolor and Fulani peoples rose in holy war upon their decadent Muslim rulers, riveting new empires upon the animists. At the end of the nineteenth century, when the British bumped into them in what is now northern Nigeria, their force was spent, and the Fulani emirs who had inherited the disunited provinces of the Sokoto empire were unable to resist British suzerainty. But the French had no such luck with the Tokolor and Manding empires to the west. By 1864 El Hadj Omar at the head of the *Tijani* order had brought the western Sudan from Futa to Timbuktu under his sway. When the French confronted this empire, Amadu Shehu, his successor, was imposing conformity to his version of Islam, and so overcoming the cleavage between rulers and ruled to forge a unified power. It was in the nature of such empires, founded in holy war, bound together by theocracy and the brotherhood of all believers, that their commanders could no longer command if they cooperated with a Christian power. Amadu and Samori were the prisoners of their own systems of leadership, unable to work their treaties with France without destroying their own authority. Both chose to fight rather than to abdicate. By 1889 Paris found out that Galliéni's loose protectorate meant a far-reaching military conquest.

All the traditions of the Ministry of Marine were against it. 'It is the negation of all our policy', the governor protested, ' . . . it means starting a holy war . . . poor Senegal.'[11] But covered by Étienne, the Algerian Under-Secretary for Colonies, the local army commanders seized their chance.[12] In 1890 Colonel Archinard broke the power of Amadu. Thenceforward protests from Paris could not stop the sand-table thinkers of the Upper Senegal Command from encompassing and crushing the embattled Muslim aristocracies one by one. In 'absolute violation of orders',[13] Archinard next invaded Samori's empire. For the next eight years that potentate and his mobile Sofa hordes kept the French army in hot pursuit from the Upper Niger to the Ivory Coast. Grappling with him and other disaffected Muslim leaders, the French were to end by occupying the entire western Sudan. Having gone so far against their will in the 1880s, logic brought them to rationalize these haphazard conquests in the 1890s. French Africa was to be all of a piece; Senegal and Algeria to be joined with the hinterlands of the Guinea, Ivory and Dahomian coasts; these in their turn to be linked with the French Congo at the shores of Lake Tchad.

---

[11] Vallon to Under-Secretary of Colonies, 22 March 1890, MFOM, Sénégal, IV, 95 C.

[12] Memo. by Archinard, 19 August, 1889, MFOM, Sénégal, IV, 93 A.

[13] Etienne to Governor of Senegal, 14 April 1891, MFOM, Sénégal, 91 B.

For the most part, the British looked on and acquiesced. As Salisbury put it ironically, 'Great Britain has adopted the policy of advance by commercial enterprise. She has not attempted to compete with the military operations of her neighbour.' Her priority in Africa lay in protecting the position in Egypt and, from 1889, in closing off the Nile valley for this purpose. In hope of damping down the Egyptian quarrel, Salisbury saw no harm in offering another round of West African compensations to France between 1889 and 1891. This vicarious generosity cost nothing either to give or to take, so Paris accepted it. The Gambian hinterland was signed away to French Senegal; that of Sierra Leone to French Guinea. But it was the Convention of August 1890 that gave the French their largest windfall; and once again the Egyptian priorities of the British shook the tree. To compensate Paris for the Heligoland–Zanzibar Treaty of 1890, in which the Germans gave him a free hand at Zanzibar and over the Nile, Salisbury cheerfully consigned to France the 'light soils' of the Sahara and the western Sudan between Algeria, Senegal and the Say–Barruwa line resting on Lake Tchad. This enormous paper concession of other people's countries the Quai d'Orsay accepted with the same irony with which it was given:

Without any appreciable effort, without any large sacrifice, without the expense of exploration . . . , without having made a single treaty . . . we have induced Britain to recognize . . . that Algeria and Senegal shall form a continuous belt of territory. . . . Political access to Lake Tchad *seems* important . . . . It may become the nodal point for trade routes. . . . But in striving to extend our activity towards central Africa, there is a more important consideration, bound up with more pressing and concrete interests. We want to get it recognized once and for all that no European nation can ever resist our influence in the Sahara and that we shall never be taken in the rear in Algeria.[14]

For the colonial zealots, there may have been enchantment in such a view. But for the technicians of national security these large but unconsidered trifles were worth picking up only so far as they improved French security in North Africa, and so in the Mediterranean. Like their counterparts in London, it was not so much a new empire as the future of their old interests in Europe and the East that they were seeking in Africa. For the French this meant security in Algeria's hinterland. But it also meant security in Egypt. So Salisbury's bargains could not end the scramble for Africa. France would take all she could get in the west. But she could not afford thereby to be appeased along the Nile.

[14] Foreign Ministry memo., 'Considérations sur le projet d'arrangement franco-anglais', 13 August 1890, AEMD, Afrique, 129.

IV

On the east coast, the Egyptian occupation had also shattered the old *modus vivendi*. Up to 1884 naval power had given Britain the leading influence from Port Natal to Cape Guardafui—an influence exerted through the puppet Sultan of Zanzibar, partly to keep other powers off the flank of the route to India, chiefly to put down the Arab slave trade. Unlike West Africa, the east coast had no large states on the mainland. Neither was there any large trade. Ivory was hauled by slaves, cloves were grown by slaves, caravans were stocked with slaves; commerce of this sort had fallen foul of European prejudices and it was being snuffed out. In doing this the powers kept on good terms with each other. In 1862 the British and French had made one of their gentlemen's agreements to respect the Sultan's independence. True, his régime was failing. Europe had used him to impose the anti-slavery ethics of Christendom upon his Muslim subjects, and this was over-stretching his authority as their religious head. Yet no government wanted a colony where there was so little to colonize. In 1878 the Foreign Office had refused to back the shipowner William Mackinnon in developing a concession of Zanzibar's mainland possessions. Four years later it turned a deaf ear to the sultan's pleas for what amounted to a British protectorate. London and Bombay considered that this would call for expenditure 'out of all proportion to the advantages to be gained'. Towards the end of 1884 Karl Peters could tout his blank treaty forms around Tanganyika acting as commercial traveller for the struggling *Kolonialverein*; yet Gladstone's Ministry would not hear of a Kilimanjaro protectorate.

But in February 1885 a new factor upset this equilibrium. Bismarck recognized the agreements of Peters—the man he had previously called a mountebank. As the Berlin West African Conference was disbanding, the Chancellor rigged up a paper protectorate for the German East Africa Company. Britain and France were reaching agreement on Egypt's finances. The time had come to pick another small African quarrel with Granville and to give another boost to the *entente* with France. Once again the Egyptian baton did its work. London accepted Bismarck's claims and bade the sultan of Zanzibar do the same. As Gladstone put it: 'it is really impossible to exaggerate the importance of *getting out of the way the bar to the Egyptian settlement* . . . [and] wind[ing] up at once these small colonial controversies.' Just the same, the India and Foreign Offices did not wish to be ousted from the entire coast, for the harbours at Mombasa and Zanzibar had some bearing on the security of

India. The upshot was another paper partition. In their East African agreement of October 1886, Salisbury and Bismarck divided the mainland, giving the northern sphere to Britain, the southern to Germany. But the governments meant to keep out of the lands they had earmarked. Here at last was Mackinnon's chance. London chartered his British East Africa Company, so as to put a sentry on its claim; to the south Berlin placed the German company in possession.

These paper insurances, casually fobbed off on traders, left the old political hands elegantly bored. Granville and Derby agreed that 'there [was] something absurd in the scramble for colonies'. They were 'little disposed to join in it'. Gladstone welcomed Germany's protectorates. Salisbury did not mind either, so long as they guaranteed free trade. German support in Cairo and Constantinople was cheap at the price. In Berlin and Paris the statesmen were taking their new possessions just as lightly. But here, as in West Africa, they were committing themselves to more than they bargained for. By 1889 the German company was at war with Bushiri and the Swahili slaving chiefs; and the Berlin Government had to rescue and replace its penniless caretaker so as to save face. Mackinnon's company was heading for ruin as well, so little did British investors value the attractions of East Africa. This was far more serious. By this time, the hinterland of the British sphere had become entangled with the security of the Nile valley and Salisbury's plans for the safety of India in Egypt.

Baring's failure to come to terms with Egyptian nationalists was partly responsible for this far-fetched design. The continuing occupation had directly shifted the Mediterranean balance. In 1887 Salisbury had sent Drummond Wolff to Constantinople to make what was probably his last serious offer to evacuate the Nile Delta. The troops would sail away within three years if the powers would agree that they could sail back again in case of need. The Porte accepted. But French and Russian diplomacy combined to wreck the agreement. Salisbury pondered the meaning of this debacle. British influence at Constantinople was not what it had been. Plainly the chances of patching up and packing up in Egypt had dwindled since 1885. Despite Bismarck's manoeuvres, France was now moving out of isolation and into the *Franco-Russe* toward the end of the 1880s. Worse still, Salisbury found that there were not enough ironclads to fight their way through the Mediterranean against such a combination. How then could the Turk be propped up against Russia? As the margin of security shrank at Constantinople, Salisbury saw the need of broadening it at Cairo. To be safe in Egypt he adopted the policy of keeping other powers out of the Nile basin. Fear lay behind this policy, the alarmist calculation that 'a civilised, European power . . . in the Nile valley . . . could so reduce the water supply as to ruin [Egypt]'. So from 1890 the British ran up their bids, claiming a sphere along the whole river and its approaches, from Mombasa and Wadi Halfa to Lake Victoria Nyanza. To gain as much as this, they were ready to tout compensations over most of the continent. As the British pivot began to swing from the Asiatic to the African shores of the eastern Mediterranean, the second phase of partition spread from Uganda and Ethiopia to the Zambezi river, from the Red Sea to the Upper Niger. By 1891 there was little more of Africa left to divide. The partition was all over, bar the ultimatums.

Without much cavil, Berlin agreed to stay out of the Nile basin. Haunted by her nightmare of coalitions, Germany was more trapped by European circumstances than any other of the partitioners. In March 1890 William II and Caprivi had decided to abandon the Reinsurance Treaty with Russia. They made no difficulty about scrapping many of their options in East Africa in return for a visible *rapprochement* with Britain in Europe. Gaining Heligoland and the extension of their sphere from Dar-es-Salaam westward to Lake Tanganyika and the northern end of Lake Nyasa, they agreed to a formal British protectorate over Zanzibar; they gave up their claims to Witu, which would otherwise have blocked British access to Lake Victoria from Mombasa; and they cut back their claims in the north, so conceding Uganda to the British and shutting themselves out of the Upper Nile valley. For Salisbury, things could not have been better. 'The effect of this [Heligoland–Zanzibar] arrangement', he congratulated himself, 'will be that . . . there will be no European competitor to British influence between the 1st degree of S[outh] latitude [running through the middle of Lake Victoria] and the borders of Egypt.' On paper, at least, his chief purpose had been achieved. This entailed scrapping Rhodes's romantic idea of a Cape-to-Cairo corridor between the Congo Free State and German East Africa. But Salisbury was no romantic. And in any case he had also cleared all German obstacles out of the way of the British South Africa Company's advance into what is now Rhodesia. After Berlin, he dealt with Lisbon. By the Anglo-Portuguese Treaty of 1891, Salisbury threw back the musty claims of Mozambique in Matabeleland to secure the company's claim there. This was partition with a vengeance. But Salisbury had not finished yet. Next it was the turn of the Italians.

No European nation had moved into Africa with less authority or less enthusiasm than they. In 1882 their government had bought the Bay of Assab from an Italian firm; three years later it had occupied the Red Sea port of Massawa with British encouragement. Better the Italians than the French or the Mahdists. This brought the new Romans into contact with the Ethiopians. Questioned about the possibilities of the new sphere two years later, di Robilant, the Foreign Minister, refused 'to attach much importance to a few robbers who happen to be raising dust around our feet in Africa'. But things were to be different. The old system of ministries living on the freedom-fighting of the *Risorgimento* gave way to a confusion that Francesco Crispi contrived to dominate from 1887 to 1896. Before he came to office he had opposed imperialism. After the old Redshirt had reached the head of the régime of which he had once been the critic, he had to find a new field for his extremism. He found it in African expansion. For successful radicals this was not unusual at the end of the century. The new brand of full-blooded imperialism was occasionally the resort of *arrivistes* moving from left to right; for in joining the old oligarchs, they gave up much of their former domestic stock-in-trade. Chamberlain forgot about his unauthorized pro-gramme; Gambetta's heirs turned their backs on the *nouvelles couches*: Crispi passed laws against the socialists. As the least disturbing issue for the transitional ministries to which they belonged, they were all permitted to express overseas the nonconformism they had to muffle at home.

The empty wharves of Massawa gave Crispi his chance for originality. Without a hinterland they would continue to crumble. To avenge the Italian defeat at Dogali at the hands of the Ethiopian Ras Alula, Crispi launched a punitive expedition whose gains were organized into the colony of Eritrea in 1890. More than that, he embarked upon a design for informal paramountcy over Ethiopia. It was full of conundrums, but when the Negus Yohannes was killed in battle with the Mahdists in 1889, the Italians imagined that their erstwhile protégé, Menilek, Ras of Shoa, would continue to be their man as Negus. He seemed to be a westernizer. He looked like a client. By the treaty of Ucciali, signed on 2 May, Rome claimed that he had accepted its protection; Menilek denied it—after taking delivery of the four million lire and thousands of rifles with which the Italians had endowed him. For the moment, Eritrea seemed to have a bright future of trade with Ethiopia. A year later the di Rudini ministry in pursuit of more trade pushed their colony's frontier westwards to Kassala, which lies on a tributary of the Nile, flush inside the Dervish country.

Fecklessly, the Italians were being drawn into the dangerous vortices of Dervish and Ethiopian politics, as the British had been drawn into those of Egypt, and the French into those of Tunis and the western

Sudan. They were rushing in to meddle with two African societies, ferociously united through a species of proto-nationalism against the unbelievers; but their catastrophe was yet to come. What concerned Salisbury and Baring in 1890 was that these Roman inroads into Ethiopia and the eastern Sudan had brought them closest to the sacred serpent of the Nile. Italian expansion into the realms of the King of Kings was not unwelcome in London. It had the merit of blocking any French advance on the Nile valley from the Red Sea ports of Djibouti and Obok. But the thrust on Kassala was a different story. Salisbury was not shutting the French and Germans out of the valley to let the Italians in. Early in 1891, therefore, he brought them to sign a treaty in which they agreed 'to keep their hands off the affluents of the Nile'; and rewarded them by recognizing their claim to preponderance over much of the Horn of Africa.

By edging towards the Triple Alliance and signing away huge stretches of unoccupied Africa, Salisbury had bought safety in Egypt from the Germans and Italians. But it was not to be bought from the French. All the donations of 'light soils' in West Africa would not soothe them into letting bygones be bygones in Egypt. Instead of consenting to leave the Nile alone, Paris, with increasing support from St Petersburg, demanded evacuation. More and more firmly, London refused. Egypt was still the deep rift between France and Britain. The way to the Nile still lay open from the west. Hence the partition of Africa went furiously on into the 1890s.

It is familiar enough, the diplomacy which contrived the astonishing partitions of the 1880s; but the motives behind them are stranger than fiction. As they drew their new map of Africa by treaty, the statesmen of the great powers intended nothing so simple or so serious as the making of colonies there. There were traders and missionaries who clamoured for imperial aid for their enterprises; but it was not they, it was the politicians who decided: and the politicians had no time for the notion that state action should develop the tropics in the interest of national prosperity. Trade, and the political influence that went with it, might expand in Africa; or again it might not. In either case the statesmen were happy to leave the matter to private energies. For tropical Africa at the end of the nineteenth century this meant that next to nothing would be done, for private business was as yet utterly unready to do it. Then were 'claims for posterity' the objects? There is a grain of truth in this old view, but it was more a rationalization after the event. As they sliced up more and more of the continent, the politicians found it easier to explain their actions in terms of new markets and civilizing missions than in terms of the more sophisticated and less high-minded concepts on which their minds were privately running.

Those who presided over the partition saw it with a cold and detached view. It was not Africa itself which they saw; it was its bearing on their great concerns in Europe, the Mediterranean and the East. Their preoccupations were tangential to the continent to a degree possible only in the official mind. They acted upon their traditional concepts of national interests and dangers. They advanced, not the frontiers of trade or empire, but the frontiers of fear.

From a European point of view, the partition treaties are monuments to the flights of imagination of which official minds are capable, when dealing with a blank map of two-thirds of a continent. The strategists anticipated every contingency; the diplomats bargained for every farthing of advantage; while the geographers showed them the where-abouts of the places they were haggling over. From an African standpoint, the main result of their efforts was to change the inter-national status of territory on paper. Turning *res nullius* into *res publica* made work for lawyers. It was to be a long time before it made work for Africans.

This perpetual fumbling for safety in the world at large drove the powers to claim spheres, to proclaim protectorates, to charter com-panies; but in almost all cases this was done with no purpose more positive than to keep out others whose presence could conceivably inconvenience a national interest, no matter how speculative or unlikely. So Bismarck had laid out a paper empire in 1884–85 mainly to make a Franco-German *entente* look plausible. Caprivi had added to it in 1890 to make an Anglo-German *rapprochement* feasible. So Gladstone had moved into Egypt to protect Suez; Salisbury had laid out the ground-plan of British East Africa to be safe in Egypt and Asia. In the main, British Africa was a gigantic footnote to the Indian empire; and much of the long struggle between France and the Muslims was an expensive pendant to her search for security in the Mediterranean. Perhaps the only serious empire-builders of the 1880s were Crispi and Leopold, and they merely snatched at the crumbs from the rich men's tables. For the rest, there was indeed a 'scramble in Africa'. But it was anything but a 'scramble for Africa'.

Yet if the procedures of the partition were diplomatic and European rivalries affected it, this is far from saying that it was caused chiefly by the workings of the European power balance. Had this been so, these new empires would have ended as they began—on paper. Anglo-French competition, which had given the Germans their chance in Africa, had sprung from the English fiascos with Egyptian revolutionaries and Mahdists; it was to quicken as these imbroglios merged into those of the French with the Muslims of the western Sudan and into those of the Italians with the Christian nationalists of Ethiopia. The European pretensions provoked new African resistances, and these compelled further European exertions. So the partition gained a new momentum. The quickening occupation of tropical Africa in the 1890s, as distinct from the paper partitions of the 1880s, was the double climax of two closely connected conflicts: on the one hand, the struggle between France and Britain for control of the Nile; on the other, the struggle between European, African, Christian and Muslim expansions for control of North and Central Africa. Having embarked so lightly on the African game, the rulers of Europe had now to take it seriously.

V

What was the nature of this continent into which Europe was spreading? If 'Africa' is merely a geographical expression, it is also a sociological shorthand for the bewildering variety of languages, religions and societies that occupy it. At one end of the scale in aptitude and achievement, the white men found peoples organized in minute segmentary groups, lacking any political authority at the centre, and finding their social cohesion in the unity of equals, not in the unity imposed by a hierarchy. These merged into a second type, the segmentary states where kingship had made little lasting impression upon the particularism of tribal kinships, where the forces of assimilation had been baffled. At the other end of this range came the sophisticated Muslim states and the military confederacies of the most dynamic Negro and Bantu nations. As the Europeans began to deal with Africa, they met trouble from societies of all these types. But their scuffles with the warriors of the segmentary systems have no great significance from the standpoint of the partition: for the rivalries of the kinships and tribes within them almost always provided collaborators, as well as rebels against alien control. But in the case of the organized African states things were very different. Their reception of the white man had a profound effect on the partition of the nineteenth century, just as it left a fiery legacy for the African nationalism of the twentieth.

They reacted in different ways. Some began by resisting, but went down before the first whiff of grapeshot, and have remained passive until only yesterday. Others accepted their new overlords only to rebel within a decade. Others again were flatly opposed to white influence in any shape or form, and were beaten down only after years of savage guerrillas. Yet there were other peoples who came easily to terms with the European, signing his treaty forms, reading his Bibles, trading with his storekeepers. How are these differences to be explained? What led Africans to bare the teeth or to smile a welcome, to come to school or to fight a war to the death? It depended perhaps upon the kind of unity they possessed and on the state of its repair.

From what little is known about it, African political history has shown an extremely high turn-over of régimes. Like the kingdoms of Europe in the Middle Ages, they were chronically short of reserve power at the centre against the overmighty subject and the turbulent priest. Much more than the medieval governments of Europe, they lacked the binding principles of political association which could assimilate conquered neighbours into loyal subjects. This seems to have been particularly true of animist Africa. An animist people, bound together by the web of kinship and by an ancestral religion, could hardly extrapolate these points of union to those it had conquered. In the states which they created, rulers and ruled tended to remain divided. In organization, the empires which they founded were but tribes writ large; and as kinship loyalties loosened down the generations, their provinces split off and their centres fell into disorders. So much of the history of African polities runs through very-short-term cycles of expansion and contraction, like the heavings of a diaphragm. Hunting for gold or salt or slaves, they might enlarge their territories, but this geographical expansion usually led in the end to political crack-up. How they reacted to the inroads of Europe, therefore, was partly determined by the point they had reached in their cycle of growth and decay. At a time of down-turn, their rulers would have strong reasons for striking a bargain with the new invaders. But challenged during a period of upswing, they might choose to fight it out to the end. Yet again, the more urbanized, commercial and bureaucratic the polity, the more its rulers would be tempted to come to terms before their towns were destroyed. On the other hand, the more its unity hung together on the luxuries of slave-raiding, plunder and migration, the less its aristocracy had to lose by struggling against the Europeans.

Here then were two of the many variables in settling the issue of cooperation or resistance. Not a few animist states whose economy was predatory and whose expansion was in progress fought for their independence. Both the Matabele and the Dahomians did so; but once they were beaten they stayed beaten. Perhaps the low generality of their creeds made them highly vulnerable to the culture of their conquerors.

The work started with powder and shot could be completed with the New Testament, and many who came to fight remained to pray. Within a decade of the running up of the Union Jack, the Baganda and Nyasa had taken avidly to the new learning and were staffing the government offices of East and Central Africa. In French Equatorial Africa the Bacongo became the agents of white administration, just as the Baluba were to do in the Katanga.

Such docility was possible among the Muslims, too, when it was a question of dealing with settled Islamic states which had flowered into bureaucracies and passed their peak. For their staid and venerable sultans and *almamys* there was as small an attraction in calling a *jihad* as there was for the Bey of Tunis. Yet apparently religion had much to do with the issue. In many other Muslim polities the harsh imperatives of the Koran were readily obeyed. The plain fact is that the longest and bloodiest fighting against the forces of Europe was carried out by Muslims. No European blandishments could charm them into becoming good neighbours. The task was one for fire-power, not philanthropy.

Robber empires, still expanding into black Africa, still mobile, still led by prophets of the faith—there were good reasons why they could not yield. They were incomparably better fitted to defy and resist than the animists. Islam's insistence on the equality of all believers under one law, together with its extensive brotherhoods and orders, provided firmer strands of unity which transcended the bonds of mere kinship and ancestral religions. Moreover, it postulated a principle of universal Godhead above any of the local deities and fetishes which divided black Africa. Supra-tribal Muslim institutions and discipline sometimes presented a coherent and continuous resistance. They also made surrender to Christian powers impossible without dissolving the forces of Muslim authority and empire. For many of these fierce foes had fashioned their power out of a sort of Muslim protestantism—attempts to purge Islam of scholiast accretions by moving back to the pristine purity of the Koran of the desert and rejecting the authority of the corrupted Caliphate at Constantinople. On the frontiers of the faith, it was new prophets who combined this stern, unbending fundamentalism with the thirst of tribes for independence and conquest. Muhammad al-Mahdi in the Sudan, Sayyid al-Mahdi among his Sanusi, Amadu Shehu and Samori of the Sofas, Rabih—all of these were prophets or caliphs of prophets and local theocrats. They were no less leaders of independence movements. Independence in African terms meant expansion and the dependence of others upon them, so they became conquerors of infidels for the true faith. After all, it is only armed prophets who have not been destroyed.

To survive, embattled theocrats of this sort had to be proof against the politics of influence practised by invading Christendom. The new dispensations which they preached had made obsolete all the cities and kingdoms of this world. They called upon all to return to God according to their revelation or be destroyed by him. If they compromised with the enemy after such preachings, they would be digging their own graves. Something of this adamantine attitude to unbelievers still rings in the Mahdi's message to the Christian Emperor, Yohannes of Ethiopia: 'Become a Muslim and peace will be unto you. . . . If on the other hand you choose disobedience and prefer blindness . . . [have] no doubt about your falling into our hands as we are promised the possession of all the earth. God fulfils His promises. . . . Let not the Devil hinder you.'[15] African Christianity, at least in Ethiopia, produced the same unyielding toughness. Shadowy and bizarre though the monophysite creeds of the Coptic church might be, they helped to rally national solidarity behind the Emperor when the Italians brought the time of troubles.

The deadliest enemies of European expansion into Africa were those states suffused by Islam or Christianity, both of them supra-tribal religious organizations capable of forging tribes into national unities. Believing that the white man was an infidel as well as an invader, these Copts and Muslims faced him, strong in the knowledge of a righteous cause. Meeting with so complete a self-confidence, the white men were pushed into choices they would have preferred—indeed, that they expected—to burke. There was no sensible negotiating to be done with theocrats, still less any converting. Their opposition raised local crises which could not be glossed over. Once the theocracies had been aroused by the challenge of Europe, it became a matter of everything or nothing. Dragged ever deeper into reactions which their own coming had provoked, the powers were forced in the 1890s to occupy the claims which they had papered on to the African map in the 1880s. The spectacular expansion that resulted has often been called imperialism. But at a deeper level it was a reflex to the stirrings of African proto-nationalism.

[15] Mahdi to Negus Yohannes, 1884–85, quoted in G. N. Sanderson, 'Contributions from African Sources to the . . . History of European Competition in the Upper Valley of the Nile', Leverhulme Conference Paper, University College of Rhodesia and Nyasaland, 1960.

VI

Whether they liked it or not, the white men were now committed to making sense out of the abstract dispositions of the 1880s. The harsh facts of Africa compelled it. For the French, lured on by British acquiescence and the dashing strategies of their colonial soldiers, there was no escape. In pursuit of Amadu the army had been drawn westward to Timbuktu. It was soon to go on to Gao, and the Upper Niger Command modulated into *Soudan Français*. In Paris the politicians had had enough. In 1891 and 1893 they called a halt to the soldiers, announcing that 'the period of conquest and territorial expansion must be considered as definitely over'.[16] Already the problem was how to make their new acquisitions pay; but the colonels, with one hand on their Maxims and the other on their next set of proofs, were bent on routing out Muslim resistance yet farther afield, in Futa Jalon and the Upper Volta. Paris turned up its nose at the new provinces. But the very fact of pacification gave them a fictitious value—since hard-won territory could hardly be given up. So step by step the army eventually involved Paris in the economics of development. When Trentinian took over the Sudan in 1895 the era of the sabre had ended. With the coming of government investment to push the railway up to the Niger, closer administration became possible and the battlefield was turned into a colony.

Gradually, the French grew more entangled in Dahomey and the Congo. In 1890 General Dodds, covered by Etienne in Paris,[17] slipped the leash and crushed the pagan slave-raiding confederacy of Dahomey, which had proved an impossible neighbour to the French on the coast. The way was open for a thrust inland. By 1894 French agents were reconnoitring Nikki; they were poised to invade the undefined western flanks of Goldie's monopoly on the lower Niger; what was more, they had seen a chance of uniting Dahomey with their fields of influence on the Senegal, Ivory Coast, Upper Volta and Upper Niger. Since 1889 the colonial zealots had been pressing the government to go one better still. Belatedly they would rationalize all the incongruous advances of the past decade by joining these territories to the starveling French Congo. The junction and symbol of this geographical romanticism was to be Lake Tchad.

After ten years in which their diplomats and soldiers had played ducks and drakes with West Africa, there emerged a group in Paris who

[16] Delcassé to Grodet, 4 December 1893, MFOM, Soudan, I, 6 A.

[17] Etienne to Governor of Senegal, 4 December 1891, MFOM, Sénégal, I, 91 B.

demanded that the French empire should be taken seriously for its own sake. In 1890 their private subscriptions sent Crampel from Brazzaville to establish French sway in the regions of Lake Tchad and so ensure 'the continuity of our possessions between Algeria, Senegal and the Congo'.[18] So little did this pipe-dream charm the Quai d'Orsay that in August they signed away the Tchad corridor to Britain. In protest Crampel's supporters toward the end of 1890 organized the *Comité de l'Afrique française*—the first serious pressure group in favour of a tropical African empire; but at no time did it attract any powerful business interests; and though it had the blessing of Etienne, its direct political influence was not spectacular. There was a certain grandiloquent appeal in the *Comité*'s idea of turning Tchad into the linch-pin of French Africa, but it was the risks, not the rhetoric, which moved the politicians. Coming down to the lake from the north meant striking across the Sahara, but this was clean contrary to the policy of the Government-General at Algiers. Since the slaughter of the Flatters expedition by the Touareg in 1880, Algiers had turned down project after project for Saharan penetration on the ground that it would be 'too dangerous'.[19] There were equally sharp objections against moving on Tchad from the west. If the thrust went along the Upper Niger, it would have to fight its way through Muslim opposition, which might have awkward repercussions in the newly organized French Sudan; as late as 1898 the Government-General in Saint-Louis was against such an advance.[20] The only practicable route seemed to be from the south. In 1891 the *Comité* sent Dybowski, and Brazza sent Foureau, on missions towards the lake from the Congo. Both were hurled back. Once more, French expansion had contrived to entangle itself with Muslim resistance. The wreckage of the Arab slaving state in the Bahr al-Ghazal had driven its survivors into the Wadai country. Here they were reorganized by Rabih into a strong, predatory state, which saw the Europeans as dangerous rivals. Another theocracy was in the making. Rabih 'found in religion more support and strength than a mere desire for loot would have given to a band of adventurers';[21] and after he had moved on to the Bagirmi country by the shores of Tchad, the support of the Sanusi, coupled with

---

[18] Crampel to Under-Secretary of Colonies, 12 March 1890, MFOM, Afrique, 5. Dossier Crampel, 1890–91.

[19] Governor-General, Algeria, to Colonies, 19 May 1896, MFOM, Afrique, 10. Dossier Foureau, 1896.

[20] Governor-General, French West Africa, to Colonies, 12 July 1898, MFOM, Afrique, 11. Dossier Mission Voulet au Lac Tchad.

[21] Clozel to Colonies, 26 August 1895, MFOM, Afrique, 9, Dossier Clozel.

the military skills he brought from Egypt, made him a formidable opponent.

For Brazza, the Commissioner-General of the Republic in the Congo, the *Comité*'s drive on Tchad was doubly welcome. It pushed out his frontiers, and it attracted the interest of Paris towards his neglected colony; it remained for him to associate the minority enthusiasm of the Lake Tchad school with a serious national interest that would appeal to the cynics of the Quai d'Orsay. In 1891 he was suggesting to Paris that the expeditions towards Tchad 'can . . . produce a situation for us which . . . will allow us to start negotiations with Britain about reciprocal concessions over the Egyptian question . . . '.[22] This was the germ of the French Fashoda strategy. In August 1891 Liotard was sent to the Ubanghi-Shari country, the western gateway to the Nile valley, with instructions to use the well-tried Brazza methods of influence on the small sultans there. If Paris were to take the plunge into reopening the Nile question, here was a possible method of doing so, and here were the means to hand.

VII

Paris was to take the plunge. Like all the crucial moves in the struggle for tropical Africa, this was decided by a turn in the chronic Egyptian crisis. Salisbury had taken some of the heat out of it by simply refusing to discuss it. The French had hoped for better times when the Liberals came back in 1892, but Rosebery, the new Foreign Secretary, told Paris point-blank that the Egyptian issue was closed. In January 1893 the Khedive timidly tried an anti-British *coup*. Cromer shouldered him back into subservience; but the crisis had its bright side for Paris. It showed that the revolutionary situation in Egypt was far from played out. It suggested that the nationalists inside the country might be usefully allied with pressure from outside to turn the British out of their citadel. The chances of external action were brightening as well. By 1893, with the *Franco-Russe* all but consummated, the strategic position in the eastern Mediterranean looked much more secure to the Ministry of Marine, once the Tsar's warships had visited Toulon. The politics of deference were over.

Paris therefore had good reason to take a higher line in the Egyptian affair. From the diplomats' viewpoint, the partition of Africa was a large-scale example of game-theory. One of the rules of the game was

[22] Brazza to Colonies, 18 April 1891, AEF (unclassified); same to same, 6 June 1891, AEF, 2 B.

that control of a river's course amounted to a forcing bid for territory. So it had been on the Niger. So it had been on the Congo. Why not install a French force on the Upper Nile? The Nile was Egypt, as everyone knew. Once the *infanterie de Marine* had straddled the river, the famous Egyptian question could be reopened with a vengeance. In May 1893, Carnot, President of the Republic, revived the Brazza scheme. A task-force could follow the old route towards Tchad, filter north-west through Liotard's empire of influence in Ubanghi-Shari, and then strike hard for the Nile. They would have to join it south of the Mahdists' country, since the Dervishes did not welcome visitors. But one theocracy was as good as another. Striking the river south of Khartoum would allow the French to work with Menilek, who was hunting for European rifles and sympathy. A handful of Frenchmen on the Nile would be picturesque; but joined by an Ethiopian army they would be portentous.

The contest for Egypt and the Mediterranean was speeding up again. As it did so, one remote African polity after another was enmeshed into its toils: the starveling colony of the Congo, the theocracies around Tchad, the petty Muslim oligarchies of Ubanghi-Shari, the wanderers in the marshes of the Bahr al-Ghazal, the Coptic state of Ethiopia, the stone-age men living around the sand-bank at Fashoda. As for the two European powers whose rivalry had provoked this uproar, they each strained every nerve to race the other to the dingy charms of the Upper Nile. There had been a time when light soils were booby prizes. Only the remarkable insights of late nineteenth-century imperialism could have seen them as pearls beyond price.

But the Fashoda scheme was risky. The Quai d'Orsay could not assume that the British would sit smoking their pipes in Cairo while the French were pitching camp by the banks of the Nile; and so the policy-makers in Paris held back the colonial *enragés*. To their minds, the scheme of planting the tricolour on the Nile was not a colonial scheme but a diplomatic weapon; they hoped to use it as a *bâton soudanais* to thwack the British into an Egyptian negotiation. Hence the Fashoda plan went in stops and starts, to be dragged out of the pigeon-holes whenever London grew refractory. Before Paris had summoned up the nerve to carry it out, London was taking precautions against it. On their side, the British were hard at work building up positions of strength in the valley of the Nile. It was in Uganda that they were building. Goaded by the Foreign Office, Mackinnon's company had sent Lugard inland to Buganda, to tighten Britain's hold on the headwaters of the river. The country was in uproar, through the struggles of rival factions, goaded on

by British Protestant, French Catholic and African Muslim missionaries. Early in 1892 Lugard managed to set the Protestants into
precarious authority: but vindicating the principles of the Reformation
had exhausted Mackinnon's finances, and he ordered Lugard to
withdraw from Uganda. This alarmed the government. Already,
military intelligence in Egypt was predicting that once the company
moved out of Uganda, the French forces in Ubanghi would move in; and
the Africanists in the Foreign Office conjured up French threats on all
sides. To them, and to Lord Rosebery, the best defence lay in going
forward. Formally occupying the country would shut out the French
from the sources of the Nile; linking it by rail with Mombasa would
make it a base for shutting them out of the upper valley as well. But the
Gladstonians in the Cabinet would not go so far as Rosebery. The best
he could do was to send Portal to Uganda to report on the pros and cons
of holding it.

Both London and Paris were to find that their insurance premiums
were too low, for now another partitioner, and one much suppler and
subtler than Carnot or Rosebery, declared an interest in the Nile. To a
remarkable extent, Leopold II of the Belgians combined the unction of a
monarch with the energy of a businessman. For all their modest
beginnings, it is Rockefeller, Carnegie and Sanford who offer the closest
parallels with this royal entrepreneur. Like them, he gambled on
futures; like them, he formed cartels out of chaos; like them again, he was
careless of the consequences. Leopold had been given the Congo since
his Independent State was the régime which divided the powers least. It
was his own money and not the taxpayers' which was used for
embellishing the new royal demesne. But since Leopold's African flutter
was not an act of state but a private venture, it had to show a cash
return—no easy matter this, in the Congo, where there seemed to be no
minerals and where the population showed no great zest in working for
the market. To keep his private empire going, Leopold badly needed
something to export. There was ivory; there was ebony; but these trades
were in the hands of the Arabs, especially those of the eastern regions
of the Congo. Leopold would have come to terms with them if he
could, but his treaties of trade and friendship had no attraction for
these oligarchs and oligopolists lording it over the Negro. So it came to
war, and this drove the Congo Free State deep into the Arab territories
which lay between it and the Nile. In 1891 its missions were setting up
posts in Ubanghi, in 1893 in the Bahr al-Ghazal, and in the same year
the forces of Van Kerckhoven struck as far as Lado on the Upper Nile
itself.

Such spirited advances were welcome neither in Paris nor in London. They were especially awkward for the French. Leopold's men were undoubtedly spilling north of the rough frontier proposed in 1887 between his sphere and theirs on the Congo; but when they tried to draw the frontier with some precision in 1892–94 the negotiations showed that none of the diplomats had the faintest idea of the lie of the land. What was more, these probings by the Free State showed how weak French authority was on the ground in the Ubanghi-Shari, scheduled as the launching-site for a move on Fashoda. Rosebery too had his troubles. He could order Portal to extend the British sphere from Buganda to the north; after the Liberals had succeeded at last in dropping their pilot, Gladstone, he could bring Uganda proper under a formal protectorate. But in the unreal game the powers were playing for the Upper Nile, the paper bargains of diplomacy still seemed the best insurances. In May 1894 Rosebery clinched two agreements. In the first place, the Italians became a holding company for British interests in Ethiopia. By recognizing a Roman hegemony over Ogaden and Harar, Rosebery could take it for granted that the Negus would not be of much use to French plans, so long as the Italians were sitting on his border. Secondly, the British tried to neutralize Leopold. By the Anglo-Congolese agreement he was assigned Equatoria and much of the Bahr al-Ghazal, so as 'to prevent the French who are about to send an expedition to [the Bahr al-Ghazal] from establishing themselves there, and to settle with the Belgians who are there already. . . . The presence of the French there would be a serious danger to Egypt.'

Elegant as this paper-work might be, it was all in vain. Rosebery's ill-judged attempt to settle the Egyptian issue on the Upper Nile only provoked the French to greater exertions. In Paris the Colonial Minister thought that the Anglo-Congolese Treaty 'seems to call for new measures on our part'.[23] One of these was to revive, with £70,000 worth of credits, the scheme of going to Fashoda by way of Ubanghi-Shari. But even now Hanotaux at the Quai d'Orsay managed to pour water into the Colonial ministry's wine. The expedition was to advance along the Ubanghi; but it was ordered 'to avoid breaking into the Nile valley'.[24] By August the second counter-measure was complete. The Anglo-Congolese treaty had been broken by the classic method of a joint Franco-German denunciation. Much to Hanotaux's relief, the Ubanghi

---

[23] Minister of Colonies to Monteil, 13 July 1894, MFOM, Afrique, III, 16–19 (dossier 19 B).

[24] *Idem*; revised draft, with emendations by Hanotaux.

striking-force could now be side-tracked out of harm's way, to try conclusions with Samori on the Ivory Coast.[25]

Rosebery was forced into direct negotiations with Paris. He was reported as saying 'Take all you want in Africa, provided that you keep off the valley of the Nile',[26] and like Salisbury before him it was in West Africa that he hoped to give his generosity full play. The hinterlands of the Gold Coast and the borderlands between the French and British spheres on the Lower Niger might all go in return for safety in Egypt. But since the French no less than the British thought much more highly of Egypt than they did of the west coast, there was no basis for a bargain. So the exchanges over the Nile and the Niger grew angrier, until in March 1895 Grey publicly warned the French that any advance into the Nile valley would be taken as an 'unfriendly act'. Sabres were beginning to rattle.

If the contention for Egypt and the Nile had been kept on the diplomatic level hitherto, it was now to burst into active conquest and occupation. As it neared its climax, the partition, which had begun almost frivolously, became hectic. It had been going on for so long that some of the new generation of politicians—the Delcassés and Chamberlains, had come to take it seriously, not only as a matter of old-fashioned power-politics but as a question of African colonies. The partition had brought them to a kind of geopolitical claustrophobia, a feeling that national expansion was running out of world space, and that the great powers of the twentieth century would be those who had filched every nook and cranny of territory left. Yet it was not ambitions or rivalries of this sort which drove France and Britain into carrying out their Nile strategies. It was the defeat of the Italians by the resurgent proto-nationalists of Ethiopia.

How this quasi-feudal, monophysite realm of the Lions of Judah survived the onslaughts of Islam and the Galla nomads through the centuries is a question. From the mid-eighteenth century, the emperors had been shadows, the king-makers all powerful. But after the accession of Teodros II in 1855 the Emperor and his feudatories slowly reunited to meet the growing menace of foreign invasion. Their disunity had prevented any effective resistance when Napier's columns marched to Magdala in 1867 to release the imprisoned British consul. When Crispi, hoping to buttress his divided ministry with colonial success, occupied Tigré and ordered the Italian army forward into the Ethiopian highlands in 1896, he relied on the same weakness. His General,

[25] Minister of Colonies to Monteil, 22 September 1894, *ibid.*
[26] French *chargé* in London to Hanotaux, 22 September 1894, AE Angleterre, 897.

Baratieri, knew better. Italian expansion, he observed, was provoking among the Ethiopians 'a kind of negative patriotism'.[27] The Negus Menilek was not only equipped with modern fire-power through the courtesies of white-man's diplomacy, he also had the great Rases of Tigré, Gojam, Harar and Wollo behind him. At Adowa on 1 March 1896 these Ethiopian proto-nationalists crushed the Italians. It meant the freedom of Ethiopia and the fall of Crispi. It also meant the first victory of African proto-nationalism. The Mahdists as well as the Ethiopians were moving against Italian Eritrea. The Italian outposts of Kassala on the Atbara tributary of the Nile looked like being cut off altogether.

Adowa so sharply transformed the politics of the Nile basin that twelve days later Salisbury ordered the Egyptian army under Kitchener to invade the eastern Sudan. This decision, so he informed Cromer, 'was inspired specially by a desire to help the Italians at Kassala; . . . to prevent the Dervishes from winning a conspicuous success which might have far-reaching results; and to plant the foot of Egypt rather further up the Nile'. It is true that the plight of the Italians seemed fortunate to the British. The Kaiser urged Salisbury to do something to help his unhappy partner in the Triple Alliance; and this meant German help in unlocking the Egyptian treasury to pay for the invasion. But if the Italian defeat gave the opportunity of attacking the Mahdists, the Ethiopian victory made it necessary to do so. Hitherto the English had done everything possible to keep out of the Egyptian Sudan. 'If the Dervishes have occupied the valley of the Nile', Salisbury had told Cromer in 1890, 'they do not pledge the future in any way . . . they can destroy nothing, for there is nothing to destroy.' Without engineering skills, they could not tamper with the Nile flow. 'Surely . . . this people were [sic] created for the purpose of keeping the bed warm for you till you can occupy it.' Even in 1897 Cromer was opposing the advance on Khartoum, as it would only lead to the acquisition of 'large tracts of useless territory which it would be difficult and costly to administer properly'. Plainly then they were not hastening to conquer another colony. They cautiously ordered the invasion, to forestall the French *coup* on the Upper Nile which Menilek's victory seemed to have made practicable.

This calculation was wrong but reasonable. English complacency about such a *coup* had rested hitherto on the hope that a French force from the west would be unable to fight its way through to the Nile; or if it

[27] S. Rubenson, 'Ethiopia in the Scramble', Leverhulme History Conference Paper, University College of Rhodesia and Nyasaland, 1960.

did, that it would get no help from Menilek under the Italian heel; or if it did get such help, that the Egyptian army could conquer the declining Dervish state before any dangerous Franco-Abyssinian combination could take place. Adowa transformed Salisbury's view of these possibilities. Rid of the Italians, the Ethiopians were much more formidable than had been supposed; and if, as Salisbury suspected mistakenly, they were prepared to act as allies of France, they would be formidable indeed.

The disappearance of the Italians seemed to have put new life into the Mahdists as well. It was known that Menilek was angling for an alliance with them. Not only did this make it less likely that Kitchener would be able to break through the Mahdists and forestall the French at Fashoda; it also raised the spectre that the French might launch a Mahdist-Ethiopian alliance against Egypt itself. Here the British stakes were too great to permit such risks. And Salisbury's government decided to take precautions in time. So opened the last great crisis in the partition of tropical Africa. Like its predecessors, it had been generated by the turn of events in Africa itself.

Predictably the invasion of the eastern Sudan provoked Paris to substantiate Salisbury's fears by invading it from the west.[28] Three months after Kitchener started for Dongola, Marchand left for Brazzaville, *en route* for Fashoda; and Lagarde went back to Addis Ababa to clinch the alliance with Menilek and arrange for the rendezvous with Marchand on the Nile. Whether the Egyptian army, dragging its railway from the north, could beat down the Khalifa and reach Fashoda ahead of the French seemed increasingly doubtful. So Salisbury was forced to try forestalling them from the south. He pressed on the building of the railway from Mombasa to supply the base in Uganda, and in June 1897 Macdonald was ordered to march from there along the Nile to Fashoda 'before the French get there from the west'. So the Anglo-French struggle for the Nile had set in motion four invasions of the Egyptian Sudan. French forces were now toiling towards it from east and west, British forces from north and south.

For long Salisbury was much more worried about the threat from Ethiopia than that from Marchand's expedition. Early in 1897 Rennell Rodd, the British envoy to Menilek, reported that he seemed very much under French influence; there seemed to be Frenchmen occupying high posts and assuming higher titles in the Ethiopian administration. In October the Emperor appeared to be cooperating in sending Bon-

[28] Memo. by Archinard, 20 January 1896, MFOM, Afrique, 14.

champs's Franco-Ethiopian expedition along the river Sobat to Fashoda. In fact, Menilek merely intended to play off the French against the
British who seemed a greater threat to his independence. Unknown to
them, he had already made an agreement with the Mahdists. As for the
joint expedition from Addis Ababa to the Nile, Bonchamps complained
that 'the Ethiopians did not help the mission; they did all they could to
stop it from heading towards the Nile'.[29]

If Salisbury had known all this, he need not have troubled to conquer
the rest of the Sudan. But, on the evidence to hand in London, things
looked gloomy indeed. Having reached Berber, Kitchener found the
Mahdists much stronger than expected, and remembering Hicks
Pasha's catastrophe in the desert, he asked for white troops. Ministers
were most reluctant to send the redcoats. But Macdonald's force which
was to have covered Fashoda from the south had not even set out,
because his troops had mutinied and the Baganda had rebelled. Like the
French strategy in the east, British strategy in the south had gone astray.
There was nothing for it but to press the conquest of the Sudan from the
north. In January 1898, perhaps as much from fear of a mythical
Dervish counter-attack as from fear of the French moving on Fashoda,
the British sent Kitchener his white reinforcements with orders to
capture Khartoum. So at last the English army's imbroglio with the
Dervishes dragged them into vast conquests of unwanted territory in the
eastern Sudan, much as the French army since 1889 had been drawn
into the western Sudan by their entanglements with the fighting Muslim
theocracies of Amadu and Samori. In the event the fanaticisms of
proto-nationalism had done far more to bring European imperialism
into Africa than all the statesmen and business interests in Europe.

All these threads came together in the summer of 1898. On 2
September Kitchener's machine-guns proved stronger than the Khalifa's Mahdists at Khartoum. An Anglo-Egyptian condominium was
soon riveted upon the Sudan. Six weeks earlier a sorely-tried Franco-
Ethiopian expedition had struggled up to the confluence of the Sobat
and the Nile near Fashoda, expecting to find Marchand. He was not
there. After a Russian colonel had planted the French flag on an island
in the Nile, they went away. Three weeks later Marchand himself
reached Fashoda. It was deserted. But not for long. On 19 September
Kitchener's regiments came up the river in their gunboats and sent him
packing.

At first sight it looks as though a British steam-roller had been sent to

[29] Memo. by Bonchamps, 'Reasons why Junction with Marchand was Impossible',
n.d., MFOM, Afrique, III, dossier 36 A.

crush a peanut at Fashoda. Salisbury had spent millions on building railways from Lower Egypt and Mombasa through desert and bush to Lake Victoria and the Upper Nile; he had launched a grand army into the sands and gone to the verge of war with France—and all to browbeat eight Frenchmen. Was the Nile *sudd* worth such exertions? No less an architect of expansion than Queen Victoria herself opposed a war 'for so miserable and small an object'. Yet this anti-climax at Fashoda brought the climax in Europe. For two months it was touch and go whether France and Britain would fight each other—not simply for Fashoda but for what that lonely place symbolized: to the British, safety in Egypt and in India; to the French, security in the Mediterranean. It was Paris that gave way. In the turmoil of the Dreyfus Affair, Brisson's Ministry accepted the necessity of avoiding a naval war which they were in no state to undertake, even with Russian help. By the Anglo-French Declaration of March 1899 France was excluded from the entire Nile valley. In return she received the central Sudan from Darfur in the east to Lake Tchad in the west. This decided the Egyptian question in a way that the Anglo-French *entente* of 1904 merely ratified. With that settled, the drawing of lines on maps might have ended as it had begun, with Egypt; but it was too late. By this time there was no more of tropical Africa left to divide.

VIII

This central struggle for Egypt and the Nile had produced a series of side-effects elsewhere in Africa, collateral disputes which had twitched into a life of their own. Of these much the most virulent was the Anglo-French rivalry over the middle Niger. During the early 1890s this affair was as hollow as it had been during the first decade of the Scramble, with tempers on the Niger still blowing hot and cool according to the state of negotiations over the Nile. Until Kitchener invaded the Mahdist Sudan and Marchand struck towards Fashoda in retaliation there was little substance in the West African quarrels. But after 1896 they were more fiercely contested, as Lugard and the other filibusterers scuffled around the chiefdoms in the Niger bend. From London's standpoint, this flurry of claims and expeditions was a tiresome business, for it had little bearing on the crucial question of the Nile except as a way of marking up bargaining points for the inevitable settlement there. But the struggle for the middle Niger had much more meaning for the official mind in Paris, since its connection with France's Nile strategy was direct. If the Fashoda operation were to succeed, there would have to be solid communications from the West African bases across the Bahr al-Ghazal to this new position on the Nile. As usual, such calculations decided that all roads must lead to Lake Tchad. 'Our chief requirement', wrote the Minister for Colonies, 'must be to bind together our possessions in [French] Sudan with those in the Ubanghi, and the latter with the Nile. Between the Nile and the Ubanghi matters seem promising . . . between the Ubanghi and the Sudan we must rely on [fresh] missions if the desired result is to be won.'[30] Two ways were tried of carrying out these directives. Pushing up from the Congo, one force strove to come to terms with Rabih, still the man in possession of the eastern and southern sides of Tchad. But they found him far from placable, and in any case the French Congo was too poor to throw much weight behind the thrust. On the other axis of advance, Cazemajou was sent from French Sudan to make his way across the Niger bend to the west side of the lake. But this line of march took him into Sokoto, trampling down the paper barriers erected in 1890 between the French and British spheres. At the same time, a support group from Dahomey threatened to pull Nikki and Borgu out of Goldie's ramshackle empire in northern Nigeria.

Briefly, the long line of British surrenders in West Africa was now to be interrupted. At the Colonial Office, Chamberlain was one of the few powerful politicians anxious to build an African empire for the sake of a new imperialism. Whereas the old school approached the partition on the principle of limited liability which governed all their foreign policy, Chamberlain believed that a bankrupt rival should be hammered. To push forward on the Nile, they were ready to fall back on the Niger; but Chamberlain played for everything or nothing. Having annexed Ashanti in 1896, he jostled the French for possession of the Volta chiefdoms beyond. It was not long before this new forcefulness was warming up the quarrels on the Niger. To defend Borgu and Sokoto, he screwed up Goldie's company into a belligerence as damaging to its dividends as it was distasteful to the diplomats. Cazemajou was to be thrown out of Sokoto by force—a work of supererogation this, since the explorer was already dead. But for all this fire-eating, there was a treaty. Both sides had their eyes cocked elsewhere. Salisbury overruled his Colonial Secretary with the argument that 'if we break off negotiations . . . it will add to our difficulties in the Nile Valley'. Hanotaux calculated that an agreement would stop Britain employing 'a policy of grievances and compensations to block our claim over the Egyptian question'. So

[30] Colonies to Commissioner-General, French Congo, 15 April 1897, AEF 3 D.

on 14 June 1898 they came to terms, France gaining the Upper Volta and Borgu, while its neighbours, Ilorin and Sokoto, were reserved to Britain.

So far as London was concerned, this was the end of the West African affair. Brought to life at the onset of the Egyptian crisis, it could now be tidily buried before the consummation of that crisis. For Paris, however, West Africa remained unfinished business, and its consummation was a necessary part of keeping the Egyptian issue alive. The Lake Tchad strategy had gone all awry. Settling with the British offered a chance of securing the Timbuktu–Fashoda route without the interference of Chamberlain's West Africa Frontier Force. While the Anglo-French negotiation was in full swing, Paris was already organizing a force to settle the Tchad business once and for all: with a certain felicity of timing, this group sailed for Africa the day after the agreement had been signed. Organized on a larger scale than the Marchand mission itself, the Voulet–Chanoine mission was to move east from Timbuktu to Tchad, where they would at last give Gentil and the Congo Government the chance to impose their will on Rabih. Another expedition, led by Foureau and Lamy across the Sahara, was also converging on Tchad: it was no part of the main scheme, but as things turned out, this group was to decide the issue.

Marchand's fiasco on the Nile knocked the heart out of these plans. After Fashoda, French opinion was far from favourable to more adventures in the African bush. Fearing trouble with the Chamber, the politicians were now inclined to leave Rabih to stew in his own juice. Even less inclined to take risks, the Commissioner-General in the Congo recommended that France should make a loose agreement with him, leaving him to do 'whatever he likes on the left bank of the Benue'.[31] The news that Voulet and Chanoine had gone mad and shot it out with their brother officers and then wandered off to found a private empire in the wastes of the western Sudan made Paris even less anxious to try conclusions with their Muslim enemy. But it was the local situation, not the calculations of Paris, which decided the matter. There was no way of coming to terms with Rabih; one by one he attacked Gentil, the Sahara mission and the remnants of the Voulet–Chanoine party. On 21 April 1900 the three groups joined forces. The following day they fought the battle which settled the Tchad issue, which overthrew Rabih, and which clinched the union of Algeria, the French Sudan and the French Congo. It was the end of a long story.

[31] Commissioner-General, French Congo, to Colonies, 24 November 1899, AEF 3 D.

In Morocco, Libya and the Congo there were to be further adjustments; but these were part of the prelude to the First World War, not of the scramble. By 1900 the directors of the partition had done with tropical Africa. It remained for the administrators to make sense of their paper-work and to make their conquests pay. There could be no going back now. They had embroiled the nations of Europe and the peoples of Africa in such a fashion that their destinies were not to be disentangled.

In the 1880s the policy-makers had intended nothing more ambitious than building diplomatic fences around these territories and hamstringing their rulers by informal control. But such methods would not work with the proto-nationalists of Egypt and Ethiopia, the Muslim revivalists of Tunisia and the Sudan, the Arab slavers of Nyasaland and the Congo, the large animist kingdoms of Buganda and Dahomey. They would not collaborate. They had to be conquered. Once conquered, they had to be administered; once administered, they had to be developed, to pay the bills for their governance. Slowly this development was translated into the idiom of progress and trusteeship, as the new tints of blue or red or yellow or green on the African map awakened feelings of pride or shame among the European voters.

The conversion of the paper empires into working colonies came about from nothing so rational or purposive as economic planning or imperial ardours. The outcome of Salisbury's Nile-valley strategy was as strange as it had been unforeseen. To pay for the occupation of Egypt and its Sudan in the early twentieth century, government had to spend public funds in damming the river and developing Gezira cotton. To recover the money spent on the Uganda railway, government had to provide it with payable loads, and this was the sharpest spur for bringing white settlers into Kenya, as it was for turning the Baganda into cash-crop farmers. Elsewhere the sequence was the same. The development of French West Africa under Roume and Ponty did not come until the Government-General was reorganized to attract capital from France. The German colonies, acquired as by-products of Bismarck's tacking towards France, remained derelict until Dernburg after 1907 carried out a total reconstruction.

So African territories were launched into a development which had not been envisaged at the time they were occupied. What was more, government itself was forced to take the lead in this. Businessmen were still unwilling to plunge into African enterprises, and so most of the capital and the technical services had to be drawn from the public sector. By now the manoeuvres and blunders of the partition had been rationalized into apologias for African empire. But the crux of this imperialism lies in its sequence. It was not businessmen or missionaries or empire-builders who launched the partition of Africa, but rather a set of diplomats who thought of that continent merely as a function of their concerns elsewhere. But once started off, this paper partition was turned into occupation and colonization by the clashes between the Europeans and the proto-nationalists, the religious revolutionaries of Africa. Only at the end of the process did the businessmen arrive—when Europe had to foot the bill for having dealt with Africa as though it was uninhabited. The sequence is quite the reverse of that postulated in the traditional theories. Imperialism was not the cause of the partition. It was the result.

IX

As the Egyptian crisis was giving rise to the devious geometry of partition, an independent process of expansion reached a climax in the southern sub-continent. Unlike the rest of Africa, the temperate south was being settled by white men who since the Great Trek had pushed their homesteads northward from the Orange and the Vaal to the Zambezi and beyond, subjugating the Bantu as they went. Here, moreover, during the last quarter of the nineteenth century investors and merchants were bringing the industrial energies of Europe to develop the colonial economy on a scale unknown elsewhere in Africa. Colonization grew dramatically deeper and wider after the gold discoveries, which brought a swift inflow of new capital and settlers. Hence the crisis in the south stemmed from the rapid growth of white colonial society and not, as in the rest of the continent, from the decay of an oriental empire and its concatenation of effects. Moreover, it arose from conflicting national aspirations among the colonists, not from rivalry between the powers. The Anglo-French quarrel over Egypt, so fateful for the rest, hardly affected this part of Africa. Occasionally the Germans made as if to intervene, but at most their contribution to the crisis was marginal. This partition was essentially an affair of Boer and Briton in South Africa—even more than it was a matter between the imperial government in London and the colonists—with the silent Bantu looking on. Yet the South African and Egyptian emergencies were alike at least in this: neither was set off by new imperial ambitions; in both the late-Victorians, striving to uphold an old system of paramountcy against a nationalist challenge, fell almost involuntarily into conquering and occupying more territory. Between their vision and reality, between the intent and the outcome of their actions, fell the shadow of imperialism in South, as in North and Central, Africa.

Until the 1870s official London had been content to secure the Cape route to India through colonial control of the Cape and Natal, leaving the inland republics of the *Trekboers* in the Transvaal and the Orange Free State their ramshackle independence. But with the diamond discoveries at Kimberley and the beginnings of investment and railway-building, the British aim became specifically imperial, as it was not in Egypt or tropical Africa. Colonization, which the Colonial Office had tried first to prevent and then to ignore, had gone so far that there was now nothing for it but to bring the dependencies and the republics together into a self-governing dominion. There were successful models for this kind of imperial architecture in the Australian responsible governments and the Canadian Confederation of 1867. Once united under the Union Jack and relieved of formal Downing Street control, surely the South African colonists' community of interest with Britain in trade and freedom, if not in kinship and culture, would keep them also loyal to the empire. Certainly this technique of collaborating classes worked well in the case of the Cape Dutch who, as the most anglicized and commercial of the Afrikaners, were given responsible self-government in 1872. It might have worked with the Boers of Transorangia. Those of the Transvaal proved far less amenable. Their trading and cultural links with Britain were of the slightest. As they had moved farthest to escape imperial rule in the Great Trek, so were they the most anti-British and inveterately republican of the Boers; and they had a propensity for inviting foreign powers into South African affairs. Happily, or so it seemed to Disraeli's Colonial Secretary, Carnarvon, these twenty thousand Calvinist frontier farmers from seventeenth-century Europe, bankrupt and ringed round with hostile Bantu, were too few to hold up the march of nineteenth-century progress. In 1876 he annexed their country in an attempt to force them into an imperial federation dominated by the far wealthier, more populous and more reliable Cape Colony. But like the Egyptians and Tunisians, the Transvaalers rose three years later to fight the invaders for their independence; and the illusion of federation was consumed in the smoke of the first Boer War of 1881. More than that, the image of imperial aggression awakened among the Afrikaans-speaking South Africans a feeling of racial solidarity with their brothers beyond the Vaal. Gladstone's ministry realized that 'the Boers will resist our rule to the uttermost . . . if we conquer the country we can only hold it by the sword . . . the continuance of the war would have involved us in a contest with the Free State as well as the Transvaal Boers, if it did not cause a rebellion in the Cape Colony itself'. Colonial loyalty had been shaken. Afrikanerdom seemed to be uniting behind Kruger's rebellion. To avert a 'race war' between Boer and Briton, the Liberals wisely swallowed the humiliation of Majuba and gave back the Transvaalers their republic.

Out of these reactions of Carnarvon's rough-hewing emerged the modern Afrikaner national movement, with the annals of the Great Trek as its myth and 'Africa for the Afrikaners' as its slogan. Hofmeyr's Farmers' Protection Association at the Cape coupled with the spread of the Afrikaner Bond in the Free State and the Transvaal showed how the Boers' political consciousness was solidifying. Similarly, the Afrikaans language movement of S. J. du Toit and the predicants of the Dutch Reformed Church showed how they were preparing to defend their cultural heritage against anglicization. Afrikaner nationalism, faced with an empire whose liberality toward the Bantu threatened the colonists' position as a white aristocracy, was bound to be anti-imperialist; yet its leaders were for the most part moderates, by no means unwilling to collaborate with the British authority. But in the Transvaal after the foiled annexation there developed a nationalism more self-assured and much more extreme. Increasingly, the Transvaalers turned from the need of South African unity to the assertion of a romantic particularism, from building a new nation to wrecking an old empire.

It was not going to be easy for British statesmen to turn this balkanized South Africa with its militant nationalists into another Canada. There was no United States on its borders to persuade the Boers that the empire was the best guarantee of their national identity, as the French Canadians had been persuaded. And whereas it was the English-speaking majority who were carrying Canadian colonization westward to the Pacific, it was the Afrikaans-speaking majority which was expanding into South Africa's hinterland. Downing Street had so much to do in upholding paramount influence over three Afrikaner-dominated, autonomous governments that it could only make haste slowly toward making a dominion. Until 1895 it waited for its colonial collaborators, helped by the inflow of British capital and immigrants, to bring about an imperial union from within. It accommodated its policies to the Cape Ministry's views, so as to avoid offending its chief ally. The Transvaal was handled with kid gloves lest open quarrels with its nationalists should unite Afrikanerdom against the empire, as it had threatened to do in 1881. In conciliating the colonies and republics alike, the 'Imperial Factor' in South Africa was progressively dismantled in favour of the politics of 'moral influence', in all respects but one: London intervened to help the colonies' expansion and to hinder that of the republics, so as to ensure a preponderance of imperial elements in the ultimate federation.

Everything therefore depended on keeping the South African balance favourable to the Cape Colony's future. When Bismarck disturbed it in 1884 by proclaiming his protectorate over Angra Pequena, the British listened to the pleas of Cape Town and quickly brought Bechuanaland and St Lucia Bay under imperial control, thus blocking a German junction with the Transvaalers. Ironically, however, it was not German diplomacy but British capital, pouring into the Transvaal to exploit the gold rushes on the Witwatersrand, that turned the balance against the Cape in favour of the republic. Toward the end of the 1880s the turn was already visible. As the centre of South African prosperity began to shift from the ports to the republic's gold-mines, the colonies frantically pushed their railways northwards to catch the new Eldorado's trade. It was plain that their revenue and their farmers would soon depend mainly upon the Transvaal market. Kruger's government on the other hand preferred to apply its new economic power to the strengthening of republicanism throughout South Africa. At the cost of antagonizing the Afrikaner Bond at the Cape, he shut the Cape railway out of the Rand, while using his new riches on building a line to Delagoa Bay that would release the republic from the thraldom of colonial ports and dues. Out of this economic revolution, there followed the long struggle for survival, fought with tariffs, railways and territorial claims, in which the Cape financial and mercantile interests extended their system northward in search of a future. Encircled with colonial railways and new English-speaking settlements, the Transvaal was to be forced or cajoled into a favourable commercial union.

It was this surge of colonization and capital, this commercial civil war in the south, that drove the scramble for territory northward to the Zambezi, and onwards to Lake Nyasa and the southern boundary of the Congo Free State. Here was empire-building with a vengeance, whose like was to be found nowhere else on the continent. Yet if not cyphers, the men of Whitehall were little more than helpless auxiliaries in it. They were denied by Parliament the price of a protectorate or a colonial railway. The idea, the millions, the political fixing in London and Cape Town, in short the main impetus, was supplied from the craggy genius of Cecil Rhodes. With the impregnable credit of Rothschild's, De Beers and the Consolidated Gold Fields at his back, he knew as well as Leopold II himself how to put big business to work in politics and politics to work for big business—without putting off the shining armour of idealism. He thought big without thinking twice, and yet carried out schemes much larger than his words. A financier with no time for balance sheets but with time for dreams, awkwardly inarticulate, but excelling as a politician, passing as an Afrikaner in South Africa, an imperialist in London, his passionate belief in himself and the destiny of South Africa left him innocent of inconsistency.

When his prospectors told him in 1887 that the gold of Matabeleland would prove as rich as that of Johannesburg, he set about acquiring it—as a way of 'get[ting] a united S. Africa under the English flag'. 'If', he decided, 'we get Matabeleland we shall get the balance of Africa.' That was characteristic. And he persuaded Salisbury's Government of it. That was characteristic too. Hope of another Rand and a strong British colony in Lobengula's kingdom which would offset the rise of the Transvaal moved ministers to charter Rhodes's South Africa Company in 1889. Part of the bargain was that he should extend the Cape railways through Bechuanaland and relieve the burden of this pauper protectorate on the Treasury; its essence was that Rhodes under one or other of his twenty different hats should do and pay for everything. Fearful of an anti-imperialist Parliament, suspecting the loyalty of Cape ministries under the shadow of the Bond, the imperial authorities saw no alternative but to play the King of Diamonds. Only Rhodes could make the imperial counterpoise in the north: he alone, first as Hofmeyr's political ally and soon as Cape Premier, could keep the Bond faithful in the struggle for supremacy in South Africa. The intransigence of Kruger and his nationalist burghers forced Rhodes to pay the piper but it allowed him to call his own tune. At his insistence Salisbury elbowed aside Portugal's claims and Queen Victoria's protests, taking northern as well as southern Rhodesia for the South Africa Company in 1890, instead of letting it go as he first intended. Moreover, it was Rhodes's cheque-book that enabled Salisbury to throw a protectorate over Nyasaland in 1891 and save the land of Livingstone from the Catholic Portuguese advance. Henceforward Whitehall clung to the coat-tails of the Colossus who had become almost an 'independent power' in southern Africa. For them the problem was not one of promoting British trade and investment, but of shaping to their fixed imperial design the intrinsically neutral movement of colonists and capital. The danger of provoking Afrikaner nationalism stopped them from doing this directly, even if they had had the money. Rhodes not only had the purse, he was the leading Cape Afrikaner. He must do it for them.

But by 1895 all the Cape Premier's projecting looked like failing. The fabled gold of Matabeleland had not materialized, but in the Transvaal the deep levels had proved profitable and practically inexhaustible. The settlers who might have colonized Rhodesia were joining the Uitlanders of Johannesburg instead. For a long time to come, the counterpoise across the Limpopo would be a mere featherweight in the imperial scale. Shares in the Bechuanaland railway and the South Africa Company slumped, while Witwatersrand issues boomed. After forty years in which the empire-builders had been working for a dominion founded upon Cape colonial supremacy, it was now certain that the real stone of union lay out of reach in the Transvaal republic. In 1894 Kruger opened his Delagoa Bay railway and, though the Cape now had a line running to the Rand, the Colony's share of the traffic and trade dwindled, as the lion's share went increasingly to the Transvaal and Natal. A year later, the battle of railways and tariffs almost brought the Colony and Republic to blows in the Drifts crisis, but no threat could force the Transvaalers into a commercial union on Rhodes's terms. Kruger held every advantage and he knew it. The true Rand together with the Delagoa Railway was raising him to be arbiter over the colonies' commercial future. Rhodes and Chamberlain suspected that he would arbitrate for a republic of South Africa. They set out to topple him.

Toward the end of 1895 Rhodes organized a rising of the Uitlanders in Johannesburg. It was a fiasco. Worse than that, Dr Jameson's Raid exposed the conspiracy and implicated the imperial authorities. Throughout South Africa, Afrikaner nationalists came together once more against British aggression. At Cape Town, Rhodes fell from office and the Government came into the grip of the antagonized Bond. In the Free State, the moderates were replaced by sterner nationalists who soon made a far-reaching alliance with the Transvaal. Afrikaners in the Cape, the Orange Free State and the Transvaal stood united in defence of republicanism. Germany was giving Kruger cautious diplomatic support, hoping to lever Britain closer to the Triple Alliance. If the Rand had turned the economic balance, Rhodes had swung the political scale against an imperial future.

This cataclysmic view was not that of Rhodes alone. The High Commissioners, Robinson and Milner, and the Colonial ministers, Chamberlain and Selborne, shared it. Early in 1896 the latter were persuaded that the Transvaal must be absorbed quickly into 'a Confederacy on the model of the Dominion of Canada . . . under the British flag'; otherwise it would 'inevitably amalgamate [the Colonies] . . . into a [republican] United States of South Africa'. About this vehement thesis the rest of the cabinet were highly sceptical. Recalling the reactions of Afrikaner nationalism to the first Boer War, they suspected that, however low colonial fortunes had fallen, a second war would lose the whole of South Africa for the empire. Such a struggle, moreover, would be extremely unpopular in Britain. The Salisbury ministry resolved to bring Kruger to reason through external pressure alone—perhaps by obtaining possession of Delagoa Bay; perhaps by squaring the Germans; perhaps by using threat and bluff to get the vote for the Uitlanders; by any means short of war to bring the Rand into a South African commercial union. Their efforts to avert a crash repeated Gladstone's over Arabi. But once more events took charge, and the outcome belied the intent. In using the severer weapons of 'moral suasion' called for by Rhodes and the extreme colonial party in South Africa, whose loyalty as their last remaining collaborators they dared not lose, the British Government followed them over the edge of war. And like Arabi before him, it was Kruger who finally declared it. Gladstone's Ministry had not realized their blunder in Egypt until after the event; unhappily Salisbury's knew theirs in South Africa before-hand. Hicks-Beach protested: 'I hope Milner and the Uitlanders will not be allowed to drag us into war.' Ruefully the Prime Minister admitted that they had. He foresaw with pitiless clarity the vengeance that Afrikaner nationalism would take upon the imperial cause. On the eve of the second Boer War in August 1899 he predicted: 'The Boers will hate you for a generation, even if they submit . . . If they resist and are beaten, they will hate you still more. . . . But it recks little to think of that. What [Milner] has done cannot be effaced . . . and all for people whom we despise, and for territory which will bring no profit and no power to England.'

Hence the taking of the Rhodesias and the conquest of the Transvaal came about from a process of colonization in which the struggles between Afrikaners and British nationalists had receded beyond imperial control. Once economic development had raised the enemies of the imperial connection to preponderance over the colonial collabora-tors, the government in London attempted diplomatically to switch back South Africa on to imperial lines. But in trying to make it into another Canada, they only created another Ireland. From this standpoint it was a case of mistaken identity. But the mistake went deeper than this: in the end they went to war for the obsolete notion of imperial supremacy in a Dominion—for a cause which was already a grand illusion.

X

Despite the astounding games of partition it played with the maps of

Asia and Africa at the end of the nineteenth century, the so-called new imperialism was merely a second-order effect of the earlier work of European expansion. Colonizing the Americas and the other white dominions had been a durable achievement, constructed out of the manpower, the capital and the culture of the lands on the Atlantic seaboard. By this time their growth in self-sufficiency was throwing them outside the orbit of European control, whatever relics of that overlordship might still exist on paper, or might still be fleetingly reasserted by force of arms. Yet far from this being a period of decay for Europe, its energies were now developing their maximum thrust. The potential of the old colonies of settlement had matured so far that they were generating local expansions of their own. The Canadians and Brazilians had organized their backlands. The Americans and Australians had spilled out into the Pacific. The South Africans had driven north of the Zambezi. Whatever the flag, whatever the guise, the expansive energies of Europe were still making permanent gains for western civilization and its derivatives.

None of this was true of the gaudy empires spatch-cocked together in Asia and Africa. The advances of this new imperialism were mainly designed to plaster over the cracks in the old empires. They were linked only obliquely to the expansive impulses of Europe. They were not the objects of serious national attention. They have fallen to pieces only three-quarters of a century after being thrown together. It would be a gullible historiography which could see such gimcrack creations as necessary functions of the balance of power or as the highest stage of capitalism.

Nevertheless, the new imperialism has been a factor of the first importance for Asia and Africa. One of the side-effects of European expansion had been to wear down or to crack open the casings of societies governed hitherto by traditional modes. Towards the end of the nineteenth century this had produced a social mobility which the westerners now feared to sanction and did not dare to exploit by the old method of backing the most dynamic of the emergent groups. Frontiers were pushed deeper and deeper into these two continents, but the confident calculus of early nineteenth-century expansion was over and done with.

It is true that the West had now advanced so far afield that there was less scope for creative interventions of the old kind. The Russians had as little chance of fruitful collaboration with the Muslim Emirs of Khiva and Bokhara as the French and British were to have with the theocrats of the Sudan. When the time of troubles came to the peoples of China or

Tong-king or Fiji, their first response was to rally around the dynasty, just as in Africa the Moroccans and Ethiopians were to group under the *charisma* of the ruler. Movements of this sort were proto-nationalist in their results, but they were romantic, reactionary struggles against the facts, the passionate protests of societies which were shocked by the new age of change and would not be comforted. But there were more positive responses to the western question. The defter nationalisms of Egypt and the Levant, the 'Scholars of New Learning' in Kuang-Hsü China, the sections which merged into the continental coalition of the Indian Congress, the separatist churches of Africa—in their different ways, they all planned to re-form their personalities and regain their powers by operating in the idiom of the westerners.

The responses might vary, but all these movements belonged to a common trend. However widely the potentials might range between savage resistance and sophisticated collaboration, each and every one of them contained growth points. In cuffing them out of the postures of tradition and into the exchange economy and the bureaucratic state, western strength hustled them into transformation. One by one, they were exposed to rapid social change, and with it came conflicts between rulers and subjects, the rise of new élites, the transforming of values. All that the West could hear in this was distress signals. But just as its ethnocentric bias has obscured the analysis of imperialism, so its Darwinism has stressed the signs of decrepitude and crack-up in these societies at the cost of masking their growth points.

In dealing with these proto-nationalist awakenings, Europe was lured into its so-called age of imperialism; from them, the modern struggles against foreign rule were later to emerge. But the idiom has hidden the essence. Imperialism has been the engine of social change, but colonial nationalism has been its auxiliary. Between them, they have contrived a world revolution. Nationalism has been the continuation of imperialism by other means.

The Decline, Revival and Fall
of the British Empire

JOHN GALLAGHER

I

EDWARD Gibbon said of the Roman empire that 'the causes of destruction multiplied with the extent of conquest; and, as soon as time and accident had removed the artificial supports, the stupendous fabric yielded to the pressure of its own weight'. 'Time and accident'. We might look at the fall of the British empire in a briskly functionalist way, and conclude that it was simply the damage of the Second World War which brought the British empire down. But I shall be arguing first, that the British world system was perilously fragile and had been showing signs of decay long before 1939; secondly, that important sectors of that system were decaying fast after the First World War, when it was moving away from a system of formal rule towards a system of influence; and thirdly, that a result of the Second World War was (temporarily) to reintegrate the system, reversing the trend and turning it back from influence towards empire before the downfall.

Arguments of this sort will commit me to a general position. In examining the breakdown of the British system, I shall be taking for granted that the causes of that breakdown must be sought further back in time, that the collapse had its origins in small sparks eating their way through long historical fuses before the detonations began. But imagery alone will not take us far. 'Pretty words and they mean nothing', as the great Lord Salisbury might have said. Behind them lies a central problem: if the system broke down or fell in, then why did it do so? And why did it break down when it did? One advantage of grappling with these questions is that there has not been much effort to grapple with them hitherto. One has not read so many treatises on the subject that it spoils one's nerve. Colonial resistance movements, a romantic term, are not going to help us through our problems. We need have no truck with the view that the downfall of this empire was brought about by colonial freedom-fighters because, except in some Pickwickian sense, these processes involved next to no fighting. We have no Dublin Post Offices in

73

our story, although there are plenty of disillusioned Indian Gandhians who were once non-cooperative and twice shy, and plenty of Africans who knocked and it was opened unto them. We shall find we can be helped by colonial politics, but for the time being let us put that argument on one side.

In seeking some general cause of downfall, then, we seem to be left with a choice between two main types of explanation. The first states that the system lost its freedom of action as it became more and more clogged by changes in domestic politics in Britain, that social democracy, broadening down from precedent to precedent, with noises off stage from Great Turnstile and the academic groves, finally dished the British world system. The second states that what destroyed the system was chiefly international pressure. It argues that there were too many bets to be covered by British resources. As international competition grew more intense, the British, like the Republic of Venice, had to rely on diplomacy to camouflage their weaknesses; and like the *Serenissima* they found that palavering was no substitute for power. It also points to the heavy punishment the British received during the wars of the twentieth century, in particular the new strains on them once the European civil war of 1939–41 became a world war, when the contestants were joined by the super-powers, both of which believed that the British empire was an outdated technique for running a world system.

Domestic or international causes: which, then, should we pick as the more important? I suggest that we should pick neither, that we should have nothing to do with this historical card-trick. All theories to explain the growth of imperialism have been failures. Here and there on the mountain of truth lie the frozen bodies of theorists, some still clutching their ice-picks, others gripping their hammers and sickles. All perished; and most of them because they believed they could find some single cause or factor which could satisfactorily explain imperialism's efflorescence in the later nineteenth century. We may expect a similar fate for those who want a monocausal explanation of its fall. They may climb hopefully, but they will not arrive. The task when considering domestic constraints and international pressures is not to rank them, but to join them up, to identify ways in which one set of forces worked on the other in critical situations. To do this, we shall have to bring into the argument other factors which cannot be properly seen from the annals of diplomacy or from the history of the voters' choice. There remains one other preliminary remark. In considering the downfall of the British empire, we shall be mainly concerned with the eastern limb of British power in Asia, and then with the African territories. That has to be so, since there was never any question of amputating the white colonies or dominions from the empire, however tenuous, even metaphysical, their connection with it seemed to become, turning as it did on such questions as Kevin O'Higgins's comma and treaties about halibut. We shall be much more exercised by the fact that the fall of the empire as a system of power comes from the cracking of its backbone in the Middle East and in India.

Since we are committed to the doctrine of long historical roots, let us start by looking at British expansion in its heyday, so as to observe what were the reasons and the conditions for that expansion. I speak of British expansion, rather than of the British empire, in order to estimate more realistically the nature and extent of British interests in the world. Many of those interests, including some of the largest of them, did not need to be secured by a colonial bond; some of them could not have been; others of them were to be tied to Britain by annexation and formal rule later on. This is not merely a haggling point about jurisdictions and status. What I am contending is that the 'empire', as a set of colonies and other dependencies, was just the tip of the iceberg that made up the British world system as a whole, a system of influence as well as power which, indeed, preferred to work through informal methods of influence when possible, and through formal methods of rule only when necessary. This viewpoint is important to our argument. That becomes clear when we examine the epochs of British expansion.

Let us begin by considering British expansion in the nineteenth century from about 1800 until 1880. In that period, the necessary domestic conditions for that expansion were satisfied. It fitted the interests of the political nation, which included the needs of the expanding economy and its increasing dependence on foreign trade, the value of emigration as a palliative for domestic difficulties, and the growth of capital investment abroad, which by 1880 stood at £1,190 million. Of course these types of growth demanded expansion. This was quite compatible with a vociferous scepticism in some sections of British opinion about the need to acquire any more colonies, especially among non-Europeans. There were two main reasons for scepticism. First, there were always powerful metropolitan interests ready to defend the possession of colonies. For example, the humanitarian interest voiced the concern of the Saints about the African slave trade and slavery in the West Indies. This was mainly Evangelical; the High Church, and *a fortiori* the Oxford Movement, thought little of Borrioboola-Gha. The strength of organized Christianity is one of the great political facts of mid-nineteenth-century England, as the Corn Law agitation shows. Then there was the professional political interest. In the nineteenth, as in the twentieth century, controversy over the British empire was frequently engineered or orchestrated by domestic political groups in their own factional interest. Thus many of the anti-imperial comminations during the period, whether of Cobden, Bright or Joseph Hume, father of Allan Octavian Hume, founder of the Indian National Congress, had less to do with the rights and wrongs of colonies than with doing down the gentry and the service families; and many pro-imperial campaigns were designed for winning a point in the faction fights of domestic politics, as for example Disraeli and the agitation of 1869 to 1870, a tendency which became more marked in the twentieth century. The second reason is that whatever may have been the reservations about colonial rule, the Victorians had no reservations about the expansion of their influence in the world outside Europe. After all, it increased their trade and enhanced their power. It allowed them to disseminate the truths of their civilization, and this in turn dovetailed into the advantage of further influence and further trade. They did well by doing good. One of the good fortunes of an expanding society is that its self-interest so often coincides with its sense of duty. Hence the arrogance of the Victorians, a quality faithfully shown by their descendants, the Edwardian and Georgian intellectuals, in both their lauding and their lambasting of empire. In the nineteenth century, whether the technique of expansion through colonial rule was liked or disliked, the desirability of expansion through one mode or another was generally accepted. So in the event there were few domestic constraints upon expansion. What of international pressures?

When we look to international factors, here again there were not many obstacles standing in the way of an advanced western state and society which was committed to expansion. The argument does not need much development. Of course there were some blockages to expansion. In the western hemisphere, the growth of the American republic blocked the growth of British influence along the St Lawrence and the Mississippi. From time to time, it also thrust the British position in Canada into jeopardy; and its Monroe Doctrine worked to limit British expansion in Latin America to the technique of mere influence. In the eastern hemisphere, occasionally there was friction with the French, for example in Syria and West Africa, not to mention altercations in Madagascar and Tahiti. And there was a more continuous friction with Russia, conspicuously, of course, over the Ottoman empire, Afghanistan, Central Asia and Sinkiang. From 1840 the Afghan problem was linked with the Turkish question; the 'Great Game' in Asia opened in the eighteen-forties and grew sharp from the eighteen-sixties, and Sinkiang became an issue from the eighteen-seventies. But so far these Russian pressures were little more than inhibitions, matters for Indian army generals to write books about. Although the Tsar and Queen Victoria were the only potentates who were as yet seriously committed to expansion in the East, yet in Asia there was room for both. Not until later in the century was it to become standing-room only. So there is not much in that aspect of the international factor.

But let us note another aspect. During this period, the main thrust of British expansion was pushing eastwards. These moves were not hampered by serious local resistance. The growing decentralization in the vilayats of the Turkish polity, the beginnings of the breakdown of the Qajar dynasty in Persia, the crack-up of Rangoon and Mandalay, the collapse of Spain in Manila and Johore in Malaya, and the distraught condition of the Ching Government in Peking, faced with the threat of breakaway by the Chinese provinces, all these processes worked to make British expansion in the East remarkably free of local resistances, just as the Portuguese irruption had been in the sixteenth century. There is yet another aspect: the head and centre of British expansion eastwards lay in India. India was the nucleus of the eastern empire, the battering ram of empire, the base where the need for security was so great that its British rulers were compelled to protect all the routes thither whether by way of South Africa or by the Mediterranean, the Red Sea and the Gulf, and were compelled to secure its frontiers, whether with Afghanistan, Persia, or Burma. India was the imperial loss-leader, where the British cost and commitment had to be reimbursed by expansion in South-east Asia and in the Far East. India then is pivotal in any explanation of British advances between Cairo and Peking. And, as we shall see later, India will be pivotal in any explanations of British withdrawals between Cairo and Peking.

So far we seem to be finding that neither domestic constraints nor international pressures worked to hold back British expansion in the mid-nineteenth century; and indeed that domestic demands and international opportunities thrust it forward, and that it would not meet hard resistance from those who came into its grip. But these findings do not really amount to more than a set of *nihil obstats* to British expansion in general. They do not give us much help in thinking about colonial rule in particular. What then were the features of colonial rule which made it acceptable and even attractive to metropolitan society? What brought colonial governance under the rules of the game of British expansion during the middle of the nineteenth century? Here we begin to touch upon other factors which may help with the puzzle of decolonization in the next century. We must now bring into play the factor of imperial rule. When we look at the actual workings of imperial rule in colonies, we are struck by the ease with which they fit the requirements of domestic opinion. Consider first the methods by which colonial rule could be shaped so as to fit British requirements. In India, the Raj was worked in the service of interests far larger than India herself. Here the British were more intent on pulling resources out of the country than in putting their own resources into it. The administrative and military systems had to be paid for out of Indian, not out of British, revenues. These Indian revenues had to meet much of the cost of using the Indian army to defend or to expand British interests outside India, in China, in South-east Asia and in the Middle East. Indian revenues had also to guarantee much of the British investment in India, especially for the building of railways. To argue that Indian resources were siphoned off for British ends is not to revive some banal theory of the 'drain', but to point to their being used to strengthen and extend the British system of power and profit in the world at large. To this end the system of rule in India was shaped. The Acts of 1833 and 1858 formally vested London with 'the final control and direction of affairs in India'. That meant control of affairs not only of the supreme government in Calcutta, but also of all the provincial governments as well. London controlled the revenues of Calcutta, and through Calcutta it controlled the revenues of the Indian provinces. Indeed, one reason for the autocratic and rigidly centralized government of India lay in the British need for a system of rule which would give them the greatest degree of control over Indian resources for their global aims.

Much the same points apply to the methods of rule. It was characteristic of British expansion during the mid-nineteenth century that both in its formal colonial mode and in its informal mode of working through mere influence it relied heavily upon local collaborators. We can readily see how the colonial government could win the support of local notables, how, say, the rais, the rajah, the landholder and the urban magnate in India could be enlisted to work for the Raj. But we have had enough of India for the time being. So let us note how the British rulers in humbler regions could utilize the mudaliars of Ceylon, the sultans of Malaya, the creoles of Sierra Leone, the bewildered kings of Lagos, and the even more bewildered kings of Fiji. One of the fruits of collaboration was cheapness. It cut down administrative costs. It avoided the need for sending out crowds of British quill-drivers. It did without British garrisons. Already in the nineteenth century, we can see the emergence of that characteristic feature of British colonial outposts, the lonely quartet of district officer, engineer, doctor and policeman, playing endless games of cards and telling very plain tales from the plains. We are not concerned here with the *accidie* of colonial society. But the cheapness of the system of loose administration working through native agencies is very much our concern, since that was a feature which fitted well into the conditions imposed by British domestic opinion for a tolerable system of colonial rule. It had to be self-supporting and must not burden the taxpayer at home.

There was a third condition imposed by domestic opinion for accepting colonial rule. The system was intended to damp down discontents, or still worse uprisings, in the dependencies. There were uprisings, of course: the rebellion in India in 1857, the troubles with the Afrikaners in the eighteen-fifties and the eighteen-seventies and so on and on. But in the nineteenth century Britain did not have to make large use of force to hold down her formal colonial empire, except in India between 1857 and 1858. Force may have been used to make an entry; but other forms of persuasion were preferred for staying on inside. Generally, the divisions and rivalries inside colonial societies were enough to stop their peoples taking up guns or lathis or spears in any collective way. But the matter goes deeper than that. Colonial questions, as we have seen, were sometimes stoked up by special interests in Britain. Yet these were enthusiasms of a day. No colonial or overseas issue could command continuous attention or exert a continuous effect on British politics. Nothing blows back in the unending and devastating way that, say, the Irish question could do, upon domestic politics. Was it not notorious that debates on India would find members of parliament rushing away for refreshment, leaving the chamber to those few who could pronounce these sesquipedalian Indian names? Neither John Bright nor Mrs Jellyby, neither Hawarden Castle nor Exeter Hall, could breath lasting life into the scandals, follies and crimes that colonial adventures might bring. The political nation of Victorian England was self-absorbed, of course. It soon cut down to size pro-consuls from Calcutta or businessmen from Singapore when they returned home. Moreover, it had too many irons in the fire throughout the world to fix its attention for very long on any one of them. And yet again no colonial issue could remain locked into domestic politics because there were more continuous issues nearer home for the factions to fight about, and because colonial issues very seldom at this time proved expensive to the taxpayer, whose attention was riveted on his pocket. This was not the age of colonial development. It was only very reluctantly the age of grants-in-aid. There was no way in which colonial politicians could *demand* a change in the system whereby their rulers took resources from their countries, rather than put them in. You will observe that if this state of things were to alter, then the possession of empire might begin to look less appetizing to the voter at home.

Next, let us consider the course of British expansion and of the British empire between 1880 and the First World War, in the light of the categories we have employed for the earlier part of the nineteenth century. First, there is the Age of High Imperialism down to about 1900 for us to look at, in some ways the Age of High Camp Imperialism. The conditions of the epoch we have been studying so far fitted most elegantly the wishes of a power with propensities towards expansion. Between 1880 and 1900 these conditions became slightly less favourable, although there was much more overt expansion. But the change in conditions seems not to have been large. Indeed, it was much smaller than is assumed by those anxious to make something portentous out of late nineteenth-century imperialism. Rather it is the continuities which ought to be stressed. Let us briefly review these changes and continuities in the context of domestic British circumstances. Many writers have assumed that imperial expansion became more popular during these years; indeed that this enthusiasm had much to do with the growth of empire. But this cannot have been so. Most of the important steps forward were taken during the eighteen-eighties. The second Gladstone Government was the real founder of Britain's East African empire; the second Salisbury Government decided the strategy of selling West Africa to buy East, and also concluded the vital agreement of March 1890 with Germany. But the Gladstonians quaked with the fear that opinion would spurn them; and Salisbury lamented that opinion was so queasy and unstable. It hardly matters how ardent for expansion opinion may have become in the eighteen-nineties, because it was certainly in the eighteen-eighties that the large expansion was brought about.

We may concede that there were some changes during the eighteen-nineties, whether a penchant for dramatizing the confrontations when rival pro-consuls glared at each other, for example Kitchener at Fashoda; or a growing tendency by interested parties to try to orchestrate opinion, for example by the well-synchronized petitions that flew into the Foreign Office at the news that the British might quit Uganda; or an increase in political log-rolling over imperial issues, for example by the Liberals, between 1899 and 1902. But in these affairs we see simply the herald angels of twentieth-century politics, where everything is held to be dramatic and momentous. But now, by the eighteen-nineties, we are moving—are we not?—towards a new structure of politics in Britain. Here comes Demos carrying his vote. Yet it does not seem, from the evidence of Working Men's Clubs and Trade Councils, that Demos had any decided view about the South African War of 1899 to 1902. Indeed, he does not seem to have had a steady view about anything. But parliamentary candidates in London were now finding that it took talk of social reform to get the voters out. By 1902 Herbert Samuel remarked that what divided Progressives in the constituencies was 'usually . . . the question of labour representation'. So it was clearly on the cards that domestic politics would one day come to turn on the question of the sharing of resources at home. But as yet this was irrelevant to the question of empire. Empire was not competing with Demos for British domestic resources. It was not likely to do so until colonial politics had reached a point where the colony could demand that resources be pulled out of, rather than be put into, Britain.

It would be foolish to deny that there were important changes in the international situation: the tendency of all the powers to block, to pre-empt, to demand payment for the colonial flutters of the others. Certainly, there was a wider rivalry. But was it a sharper rivalry? People write about international competition because this makes vivid subjects for theses. But we would do well to think of international cooperation as well. None of these rivalries led to war between the powers except in the Far East. Africa, the Pacific, South-east Asia, all were partitioned peacefully, even elegantly. Nor could we say that in the British case there was a greater preoccupation with the security of India. Admittedly, the care for Indian security brought about the large, the preposterously large, insurance of founding an empire in East Africa. But the self-same care for Indian security had been a dominant factor in British world policy since the days of Pitt and Palmerston. So neither domestic constraints nor international pressures suggest evidence of radical changes in the context of later nineteenth-century British expansion.

This brings us to the third factor, the factor of imperial rule. During this period, the impact of events outside Europe upon British policy became more marked. There was the impact of what might be seen as the 'colonial nationalisms' of Egypt and South Africa. In Egypt it provoked a crisis, and a military *putsch* by the colonels; the British occupation of Egypt in 1882 was a direct result. In South Africa, by the eighteen-eighties, there was already the spectre of a Pan-Afrikaner alliance which might drive the British out. Ultimately this impelled

Chamberlain and Milner to go to war against the Afrikaner Republics in 1899. Indeed a good deal of what is commonly described as imperialist aggression during this period should rather be seen as imperialist counter-punching; or, to put it more demurely, as reactions by British policy-making to developments outside Europe. But here and now we are not discussing what led to the scrambles and partitions of the late nineteenth century. We are more concerned to look at their impact on British politics.

There is no doubt that this impact was increasing. The occupation of Egypt upset the Liberals. After all, it was Gladstone himself who had excoriated imperialism. What about all the village Hampdens around the Nile? Indeed until the eighteen-nineties it was Liberal orthodoxy that Britain was getting ready for the day when the redcoats would sail away on the troopships from Alexandria. The war in South Africa brought even wider splits. Was it not a war fought against small peoples? (The Afrikaners were popular among the Left in those days.) Was it not enormously expensive? (It cost £223 million.) Was it not fought for the benefit of the Mining Corporations? Was not all the money going to prop up Eckstein and Farrar and Beit? The war split the Liberal party—with most of the men who were to dominate the next ministry on the side of imperialism. Here we can see a good example of the exploitation of colonial issues for reasons of domestic British politics, and of the irruption of colonial issues into these politics. One more case—trivial at the time, but important later—might be mentioned. In December 1885 the Indian National Congress was founded. As the Old India Hands never tired of showing, its claim to speak for the peoples of India was preposterous. But that was not the point. The reason for founding the Congress was to create a body which could appeal over the heads of the Government of India to parliament in Westminster. That is why Frank Hugh O'Donnell, the Irish MP, became interested in Indian politics, and why English Radicals such as Bradlaugh (who became President of the Indian National Congress) lent a hand. Indeed the issue was symbolized by the election to parliament of an Indian, Dadabhai Naoroji. None of these tentative moves came to much before 1900. But the strategy of putting the Condition of India question squarely before Westminster was to have a great future. So we can conclude that whatever the continuities between the mid-nineteenth century and the Age of High Imperialism, the greater effect of colonial questions upon British national politics is a marked change.

Now let us consider the changes for the period between *circa* 1900 and the outbreak of war in 1914. By now, both the domestic constraints and the international pressures on British expansion were clearly to be seen. There were abundant signs of change, but hardly of crippling change. One interesting sign of the times, hinting at the new domestic constraints, was the Radical reaction against imperialism which burgeoned into a systematic critique, in the hands of such writers as J. A. Hobson, Mary Kingsley, E. D. Morel, Ramsay MacDonald, and L. T. Hobhouse, together with the renewed attacks upon land policy and white settlements in Africa. Some of these critics derived from Cobden; others from the sentimental humanitarians of the nineteenth century. All of them carried on the essential Victorian desire to push ahead with expansion. What they were quarrelling with was the methods by which it was being conducted. None of them (that I know of) wished to dismantle the British empire, merely to conserve it by judicious alteration. All of them transmit into the twentieth century that characteristic Victorian arrogance of *Gesta Dei per Anglos*, that God's Englishman should do his duty, that it will profit him to do so, that he should not only set an example to foreigners but should also castigate them for their sins. These people were not opposed to British expansion; they simply wanted it to operate on their own terms. Like the writers who came after them, such as Gilbert Murray and A. D. Lindsay, they were, in this sense, imperialists to a man.

But aside from these articulate critics, there were other forces—the inarticulate forces which had listened in 1900 to the talk about Labour representation and social reform, which in 1906 had elected those Liberal backbenchers who harried Elgin and Churchill in the Colonial Office and which in the elections of 1910 showed that some parts of the north of England were now becoming permanently hardened against the Unionist party. The statistics of government expenditure reflect the outcome: in 1900 the percentage of British government expenditure on social services was eighteen per cent; by 1913 it had risen to thirty-three per cent. This reflects a successful demand by the voters for a larger share of domestic resources. As yet there was small demand on those resources for overseas commitments. We are still far before the age of colonial development. Few people resent the possession of an empire until they have to pay for it. They did not have to pay for it before the end of the First World War, although the fate of tariff-reform suggests what might have happened to empire if they had had to pay. So there was change in the air, although it had yet to come.

Turning now to international pressures, we are on familiar ground. By now the British world system was under strain. It had been so since the Far Eastern crisis of the late eighteen-nineties—perhaps earlier, if we consider the extraordinary over-reaction of the British to the scramble for Africa which endowed them with a huge and rather pointless empire in tropical Africa. Britain's empire was over-extended, and in the years before the Anglo-Russian Agreement of 1907 the strain was manifest. It showed in the gloomy calculations and the papers of the Committee of Imperial Defence about the defence of India. Moreover, there was by now an undeniable loss of appetite for more territory; the British were not interested in abetting a re-partition of Africa over the Belgian Congo or the Portuguese colonies. In the more strenuous fields of the Middle and the Far East the British were similarly inert. Imagine how Palmerston or Salisbury might have exploited the chances offered by the Persian revolution of 1906 and the *putsch* by the Young Turks in 1907. London deplored what a British diplomat called 'the predatory bureaucracy of Russia' (words oddly reminiscent of Lenin), but chose to split its Persian interests with that bureaucracy; and London allowed Turkey to fumble for the embrace of the Kaiser. Britain by now was a satiated power, a *status quo* power, or in the words of another Foreign Office man, 'a huge giant sprawling all over the globe, with gouty fingers and toes stretching in every direction, which cannot be approached without eliciting a scream'; a power, too, which was peculiarly vulnerable because of its multiplicity of lands, peoples, hopes, fears and grievances, all of which would encourage an enemy to try on it the crowbar of *Revolutionierungspolitik* (to speak in the language of the power which tried to do so).

So the international pressures were mounting against the British world system. But so, too, they were mounting against all the other world systems. We must not write the history of power in the first half of the twentieth century in the terms of the British empire *contra mundum*, as it so often looks in the records of the Committee of Imperial Defence (and of the Chiefs of Staff Committee after 1923). Against the new insecurity and instability of the period between 1900 and 1914, we must place the successes of British diplomacy. Perhaps there was something Venetian about being forced to use diplomacy to cover the bets which power itself could not win; but diplomacy was able to do so. The British world system was growing insecure. But so were the other world systems. World systems are always insecure. In any case, whatever the long-term effect of these changes, the British empire was to come through the First World War unscathed—or, at least, ostensibly unscathed.

We shall now look at forces arising from colonial rule. As we might expect during a period where the grievances of the world were becoming unified, the operations of the nation of shopkeepers were now having effects in the non-European world which boomeranged on them. But the boomerang was still mostly falling in the sphere of policy-making. More and more, British policy was losing its old autonomy; more and more it was reacting to situations which were unfolding in non-European regions, instead of creating them, as it would once have done. The impossibility of governing the Transvaal with the Afrikaners led to the policy of magnanimity which gave the Afrikaners political control over South Africa. In other ways, the revolutions in Persia, in Turkey, and the Revolution of the Double Tenth in China, all had the similar effect of narrowing the options for British policy. But we are less concerned with policy-making than with politics. Political development in non-European régimes was beginning to throw up challenges to British political groups, which might divide them over the ultimate question of how British resources should be re-allocated between home and abroad. Well, this was coming. While John Morley was Secretary of State for India and meditating about constitutional change there, he thought it expedient to consult Gokhale, the representative of the Indian National Congress. Gokhale's credentials were impeccably Edwardian—he even stayed at the Reform Club—but the Morley-Minto constitution that emerged in 1909 was the precursor of those later Indian reforms which were to do so much to upset the imperial applecart. This was a formative period in the growth of politics in some of the dependencies, in India, Egypt, Ceylon, the Gold Coast, Rhodesia and so on. Nonetheless, none of these developments was able to impinge firmly upon British politics. The blow-backs and the boomerangs were yet to come.

This steeplechase through a century of British expansion suggests some conclusions. First, that the conditions for its success which were easily met during the nineteenth century became somewhat harder to meet after that. But not much harder. By 1914 the system was far from being in disarray. There were many continuities from the earlier period. Moreover, pushing that pole hither and yon, politicians and diplomats were able to keep the imperial punt drifting along the twentieth century. Now there was a certain fragility about this success. It continued because it had not yet run into serious trouble. The conditions had not yet arisen which were to make the rulers of Britain or their electorates ask whether colonial rule was an outdated method for operating their world system. Nor had the conditions yet arisen which were to allow other powers to wrest colonial rule from the British. Secondly, we have not yet found any way in which these domestic and international factors were to combine to end the system. Nor was there, by 1914, any political leverage from the colonies themselves which might work to do so. And yet quite soon the system began to decline. How this took place will be the burden of what follows.

II

In our steeplechase over a hundred years of history one suggestion at least has emerged: the history of British involvements outside Europe has not been an unbroken movement in the same direction. If there have been continuities, they have been in aim, not in performance. There is a general notion that this empire rose, flourished, declined, fell, and that in its fall lay its fulfilment. But this is a sentimental view, arising from a banal teleology. In fact, the movement towards decline was reversible and sometimes was reversed. So far from showing some steady trend towards decolonization, the period between 1919 and 1945 might be described as the decline and rise of the British empire. But there were active elements of decline. In three important respects the empire was proving to be fragile. First, it was fragile because another great war was quite likely to knock it to pieces. Secondly, it was fragile because of the demands of the voter at home. Thirdly, it was fragile because, in terms of imperial power, there were large parts of the so-called dependent empire which were hardly under British control at all—parts of East Africa and Rhodesia and much of the administration of British India. Consequently, the whole system sometimes swung and lurched about during the nineteen-twenties and nineteen-thirties. There were comas punctuated by fits, stops which glimmered into go, flips which were corrected into stability.

I want now to look at the years between 1916 and 1922, in the light of this argument. These were years when there was a large expansion of British rule, followed by a falling back. That falling back was in no immediate sense fatal to the system, merely a shrinking of imperial corpulence. Yet it looks like the first step towards decolonization, and so deserves to be examined in a little detail. In the summer of 1916, Lloyd George formed his War Cabinet. The presence of Milner and Curzon in that Cabinet showed that the strains of war had brought to power two of the old Adams of imperialism, men who had seemed to be finished and out-of-date, figures denounced by one of the politically-minded newspaper owners of the time (C. B. Scott of the *Manchester Guardian*) as 'men whom no one would tolerate before the war as members of a Government, and essentially reactionary'. It was true enough. War had brought back to power obsolescent imperialists, as it was to do again in May 1940. Indeed it would be hard to find any more imperially-minded government in British history than Lloyd George's—not Chatham's, not his son's, certainly not Salisbury's. Hence, if war were to throw up the chances, it was likely enough that the coalition ministry would take them up.

The needs of the war put growing pressure on the internal régime and its policy of *laissez-faire*. The government had to take control over capital issues; the Munitions of War Act brought in a greater control over labour and there was more control over the railways. All this was done by Asquith. And with the Lloyd George Government came the control of imports and the search for import substitutes as well as the device of bulk-buying abroad by government agency. By 1918, ninety per cent of all imports were bought by the state. As Addison said, 'heaven knows we have been Socialists enough'—well, more correctly, State Socialists. But our concern is not with the decline and fall of *laissez-faire* or the name and nature of its supplanter, but with the immense addition of power that this gave to the British state as it organized the military transactions of a nation of shopkeepers, not merely for siege warfare on the western front, but also for its efforts to break the Turkish empire in the Middle East and to block first the German thrust towards south Russia and then the Turkish thrust between the Black Sea and the Caspian, with its threat to northern Persia, Afghanistan and even India. When prefabricated ships were overlanded from the Black Sea and reassembled at Krasnovodsk for service on the Caspian, when Indian infantry pushed towards Baghdad or their cavalry jingled towards Damascus or into the Caucasus, nearly all these efforts relied on the armourers in Britain. And this support relied on the ordering of the war economy in Britain. Moreover, the military and naval strength built by that war economy was still available when that war ended; and it seemed to be available for imposing British imperial solutions when Germans and Turks and Russians had all stopped resisting them.

The First World War provided a vast bargain basement for empire builders. The downfall of Hohenzollern Germany placed African, Pacific and Chinese territories on the market; some of the vilayats of the old Ottoman empire, Syria, Palestine, Iraq, Cilicia, as well as Anatolia, seemed disposable and awaited a take-over. So did the old Russian interests in Persia, Afghanistan, China and Turkey. Here, then, was the opportunity for a new partition of the world. Partitions are interesting to the historian, because they tell him about the priorities of the partitioners, and sometimes about the resistance of the partitioned. So far as the British were concerned, it seemed more urgent to slice up the Middle East than to slice up Africa. There they would not have been averse to placing an American presence in someone else's colony, but in the event they fell back on their old preference for East Africa, and sold West to buy East. But in the Middle East there were higher stakes to play for. British armies controlled from Cairo had conquered Palestine and Syria and helped to liberate the Hejaz. British forces controlled from Delhi had conquered Mesopotamia [henceforth Iraq], had overawed Persia and encouraged Ibn Saud. To contain the last Turkish offensives in 1918, other British forces controlled from Delhi had struck northwards from Persia so as to hold a line between Batum and Baku, and the arrival of another force east of the Caspian stimulated the growth of the new independent Republics of Georgia, Armenia, Azerbaijan and Daghestan.

The Lloyd George Government were clearly minded to retain some of these options. Indeed most of the victors were forming queues—British, French, Italians, Greeks in the Middle East; South Africans, British, French and Belgians in Africa; and, half a world away, Japanese, Australians, New Zealanders in the Pacific. All these twentieth-century politicians thought that non-European peoples could be flipped about like coins, just as eighteenth-century politicians had thought they could dispose of European peoples. All these dealings seem eighteenth-century in another sense as well. In British eyes, the main value in scrambling for the Middle East lay in strengthening the security of India, in the time-honoured belief that security lay in the control of huge territories beyond the frontiers of the Raj itself.

By 1919 this approach was, at best, obsolescent. The Cabinet itself was divided about it. Milner, Curzon and the fire-eaters on the Eastern Committee were strongly for it. Montagu, however, took up the new India Office thesis and argued that it was poor policy to look after the external security of India by methods that would risk the internal security of these new possessions and also of India itself. Balfour was worried about the effect on American opinion. H. A. L. Fisher, like a good academic, had philosophic doubts. The Prime Minister, who was an abler imperialist than any of them, saw the international hazards. Disembowelling the Russian empire might drive the Bolsheviks into the arms of Berlin. Gouging too much out of the Ottoman empire might drive the Turks into the arms of Moscow. Another complication was the decision taken at Paris in January 1919 to place all the Turkish territories under the supervision of the League of Nations. Technically they were to become 'A' Mandates, territories, that is to say, where there must be an Open Door for trade. The Americans protested against British violations of this understanding, although some of them were demanding a mandate without an Open Door on Yap Island (which lies between the Philippines and Waka Island) giving rise to the memorable lines:

> Give us Yap!
> Give us Yap!
> The Yanks have put it
> On the Map!

But what was mainly at stake in the dispute about the Open Door in the Middle East was the future of the oil concessions which the British had won from the old Turkish empire (we shall return later to the oleaginous diplomacy of the Iraq Petroleum Company and of Standard Oil in Saudi Arabia).

But in spite of these uncertainties the British plumped for expanding their role in these regions, and getting territory. Their war aims had already been defined: Palestine was to be British; southern and central Iraq were to be British also, and Kuwait was to be ruled from Iraq; British influence was to be dominant in Persia; Britain was to have spheres of influence on the southern and western coasts of Arabia. Then they decided that it would be inconvenient to have the French in northern Iraq. How could the French be bought off? The policy-makers pored over their maps. Why not give them Armenia? Unluckily, Paris refused the offer of that pious but astute race. Why not something in Africa then? The shorthand report of the Eastern Committee shows the outcome:

Chief of the Imperial General Staff	Cannot we bribe France in some other way?
Lord Robert Cecil	I know that if Mr Balfour or myself makes any proposition with regard to Africa, we shall be told that there is an aeroplane station, or a submarine base, or that it is the oldest colony, or that it will offend some New Zealand politician if we do it, or, something of that kind. It is always the same.

It was to go on being always the same. Exactly the same thing happened in the period between 1936 and 1938 when the British were rummaging through their African title deeds to find something to give Hitler.

But elsewhere the prospects for British expansion of influence, if not expansion of rule, looked bright. In August 1919 Curzon pressed the Shah into signing an agreement, 'to assist Persia in the rehabilitation of her fortunes'. In Arabia, the ruler of the Hejaz was to have all his foreign relations controlled by the British. In Asia Minor, Lloyd George and the

Foreign Office were minded to install the Greeks whose own weakness would guarantee their loyalty to the power which had put them there. They would be a safe sentinel for the Dardanelles—and so the Foreign Office welcomed the Greeks.

Beyond the Middle East lay even more effulgent dreams. In south Russia the British General Staff were happy to discover that all its races 'have their own national aspirations'. Curzon saw Great Britain as the Prince Charming who could awaken these Sleeping Beauties. Britain had pushed the imperial redoubts as far forward as the Caspian; 'in the future it may do the same with the Caucasus. . . . I think that it must come to us.' Later Curzon said: 'You ask why should Great Britain push herself out in these directions? Of course, the answer is obvious—India.' So one of the prizes of victory in the First World War was to be an immense, an almost definitive, guarantee of the security of India. The Indian Ocean would become a British lake. So would the Persian Gulf. So would the Red Sea. From Egypt to India a vast new spur of territory would be under British rule, or a British Monroe Doctrine. In south Russia and across to Sinkiang, other clients would assure the defence in depth of the north-western approaches to the Raj.

So we have here another huge expansion of British rule and influence. Just as care for the security of the Indian empire had led to the creation of an East African empire, so now the renewed search for the safety of the Raj was building another empire in the Middle East. As in 1763, so in 1919, the result was to leave the British desperately over-extended. This vast new system had been thrown together largely by default of opposition. That was soon to become plain, when the opponents revived. In the second place these plans meant the overburdening of a world system which the British economy was already under-engined to propel. And thirdly, the new situation meant an extension of what were becoming out-of-date methods. Direct colonial rule was to incur heavier burdens, greater political troubles, higher strategical risks. The future was to lie with the expansion of influence not with the expansion of rule.

The history of British imperialism between 1850 and 1950 can be summarized as a system predominantly of influence turning into a system predominantly of rule and then trying, unsuccessfully, to return to influence. The argument is that between 1918 and 1922 we are witnessing the last fling of a technique which would not for much longer be fitted to the conditions of modern power. Look at it. Here was an elaborate recasting of the Middle East, primarily for external reasons of Indian security. Middle East oil did not need colonial rule. Yet at the same time internal security inside India was failing. It is like a householder seeking fire insurance while his house is beginning to burn down. This is not merely to be wise after the event. Already in 1919 the Permanent Head of the Indian Office could write to Arnold Wilson in Iraq: 'the idea of Mesopotamia as the model of an efficiently administered British dependency is dead (the same thing is dying in India and decomposing in Egypt)'.

Within a year of their apogee, the new plans were thrown into disarray. The Russian schemes were the first to go. Balfour had always thought it wiser to leave the Russians to cut each other's throats (his phrase). Lloyd George knew that the schemes were a folly. The new south Russian Republics lacked support. Britain lacked the troops to prop them up. Moreover the condition of British domestic politics could not sanction the intervention. Lloyd George knew that it would probably cause 'trouble at home' (his phrase again). The new Republics turned out to be expendable; and under Bolshevik pressure, they were expended. By June 1920 the last British troops had left. One of Curzon's telegrams writes the epitaph: 'HMG are not indifferent to fate of Georgia, but other burdens are such they cannot say what practical form their sympathy is likely to take. We can therefore only express close sympathy.' It is obvious what was going wrong with that part of the plan. It was reconquest under new management from Moscow. British expansion had come by default of Russian power; with the reorganization of that power, British power had to fall back.

Much the same thing happened in two other spheres where Russian influence had temporarily departed and now returned. The first of these spheres was Afghanistan. During the war the British had boxed up Afghanistan, always regarded as a threat to India's security. They had done so by putting a force into northern Persia (NORPERFORCE was the acronym of the period) and by the good offices of the Tsar. His disappearance knocked a hole in the box. How could it be plugged? Curzon thought he could do it by casting the Afghans for a role in what he called a 'Moslem nexus of States' north of India, sworn-in and paid-up as sentinels of the Raj. Perhaps they could be encouraged to reconquer Pendjeh from a fortunately distracted Russia? Or perhaps they could be wheedled into an alliance with Bokhara, a people struggling rightfully to be free from Lenin and his saturnine Commissar for Nationalities? Or perhaps, so the General Staff hoped, they could at last be bundled into a formal alliance with Britain? Not a bit of it. Once the Moscow Government, the heirs of St Petersburg, were strong enough to reoccupy the Russian seat at the Great Game, this British gambit in Kabul was blocked. The Amir signed a treaty with the USSR.

Now a Soviet representative coexisted in Afghanistan with the representative from New Delhi. That was on 28 February 1921. The following day the Turkish Government of Mustafa Kemal also signed a treaty with Russia. Lenin had succeeded Tsar Nicholas as Britain's chief rival in the east. He had inherited the Tsar's advantages of being able to bring greater weight to bear in the Central Asian power struggle than the British could. But incidentally he did so with less knowledge. Lenin held the singular belief that the majority of the population of India was Muslim. Later the Bolsheviks were to throw away their geographical advantages when they decided that trade with Britain was worth more than Kabul and when Stalin went chasing moonbeams in China. Still all this meant a crack in the defensive line round India.

And there was another. During the war, Persia had been a prostrate satellite of New Delhi. Here, too, the October Revolution in Petrograd had been of great value to British interests by clearing the Russians off the scene. In 1919 Curzon pressed, persuaded and bribed Persian ministers into signing an agreement which riveted British influence over Teheran. These ministers were mayors of the palace for the broken-down Qajar dynasty, but unlike their Merovingian predecessors, they were unable to deliver the goods. So greatly did the Persian political nation dislike having been hustled and administered by the British during the war, that their ministers did not dare submit the agreement to the Persian House of Representatives. Ministers came and went. All were pressed by Curzon. None would confront the Majlis. The Foreign Secretary in London huffed and puffed. But there was nothing doing. Meanwhile Russian influence in Persia was stirring again. In June 1920 the ominously named Persian Soviet Socialist Republic was proclaimed in the north. In Teheran this cleared the mind of ministers wonderfully. On 26 February 1921 they concluded a treaty with the USSR while denouncing the draft agreement with Britain. It is significant that on 26 February the Russians had signed a treaty with Persia, on 28 February a treaty with Afghanistan, and on 29 February a treaty with Turkey. What a good month for Chicherin and the Commissariat for Foreign Affairs in Moscow. Incidentally, all this shows how those diplomatic historians, who are parochially obsessed with western Europe, err in thinking of the USSR as being clampled into isolation until the treaty of Rapallo in April 1922. Here, then, was another hole knocked in the grand new perimeter of defences that had been constructed around India. The attempt to put Indian security above any peradventure, to a degree of certainty, where moths could not corrupt nor thieves break in and steal, had left the system more uncertain than at any time since the Anglo-Russian agreement of 1907.

The new expansion was blocked by diplomatic pressures. But furthermore it was shaken by troubles from subject peoples. Egypt was the *arcana imperii* of the new policy, the western wing of the new empire, the armature of the Suez Canal which the Admiralty declared to be more important than ever to the safety of the empire after the end of the war. In 1917 Milner had predicted that 'Egypt will in future be as much a part of the British Empire as India or Nigeria'. Yet in March 1919, Egypt, the candidate for colonial status, dashed his prophecy by rebelling against British rule and thus opening great incertitudes until 1936. With the bewildered efforts of Austen Chamberlain, Uncle Arthur Henderson and Anthony Eden to read the hands of the Egyptians—of the crafty King, the shifty politicians, the ambiguous minorities—I shall deal later. But for the time being let us simply note how British policy towards its new Middle Eastern empire blew up in the face of its makers when a quite unexpected colonial resistance brought them into another Egyptian bondage.

In 1920 Britain was finally awarded what was to be the deadliest of gifts, a Title 'A' Mandate over Palestine. The British hived off trans-Jordan and put Palestine under a civil administration controlled, improbably and parsimoniously, by the Colonial Office. The Colonial Office set to work forming a Legislative Council to represent all the communities. But by 1921 Arabs and Jews had been set by the ears over immigration questions and by May they were knifing each other. That discouraged the Colonial Office and finished the plan for a Council. By August the British Cabinet was facing the first of its many cross-roads on the way to Israel, when it held the first of its many discussions whether or not to pull out of Palestine. When the French pitched the Amir Faysal out of Syria and allowed the Lebanon to avoid closer union with Damascus, Syrian resentments turned to making trouble for the Europeans elsewhere, that is in Iraq. In April 1920 there was a local rising in Iraq. By July, while General Headquarters, Iraq, were taking perfect rest in a Persian hill-station, this burst into a full-scale rebellion against the British occupation.

> Half a lakh, half a lakh
> Up to the Persian hills
> GHQ wandered.
> Think of the water laid
> On, and the golf links made,
> Think of the bills we paid,

Oh! The wild charge they made!
Half a lakh
Half a lakh squandered.

Here, then, was another setback for the new expansion. In Arabia, from 1919, Cairo's candidate for pre-eminence was coming under pressure from the Wahhabi leader, Ibn Saud, who was to evict him in 1924. Here was another link in the chain of disasters.

To all these shocks to the system, we ought to add rebellion in Burma, the riots in China from 1919 (the May Fourth Movement), the disasters of Lloyd George in Turkey and, of course, shaking British power in India, the Punjab rising, Gandhi's capture of the Congress and his non-cooperation movement in 1921 to 1922. Here we have (to borrow a phrase from the historians of the seventeenth century) six contemporaneous revolutions—in fact a baker's half-dozen of them. The post-war world was showing that while the imperialists could still chop the map about, they now had to pay for their pleasures. All this is to overdramatize a little. The eastern arc of empire was to survive these difficulties and what was to pull it down was not the pin-pricks of the Bolsheviks but the hammer blows of the Japanese, not the nibblings of freedom-fighters but the push of American influence, added to the fragility of the British economy and, perhaps, other forces we have not yet brought into the argument. During the years 1919–22 the challenges to empire were ominous, but they were not yet formidable. The riots orchestrated in Egypt, the punch-ups in Palestine, the siege of a few garrisons in Iraq, the insubordination of Persians, Afghans and Turks, the temporary alliance in India of Hindu opportunists and Muslim zealots, all had been solved by the mid-nineteen-twenties. But surely most of these difficulties could have been swept away by a whiff of grapeshot? Why then were they able to put the calculations of the Lloyd George ministry seriously out of joint? Let us consider this first, in terms of international pressures and of domestic constraints, those two jaws of the nutcrackers.

As I read the period between the two world wars, there was a sense in which every British Government realized that the empire was now a fragile system which might be smashed to pieces if it again collided with strong powers. There was an overriding British interest in keeping out of war, not merely because British appetite for territories was now satiated, but because war might rip them away from her. In the eighteen-nineties Lord Salisbury had wondered whether his warships were made of porcelain; after 1919 ministers suspected this might be true of their empire at large. Lloyd George knew this, of course. 'In 1914' as he told the Committee of Imperial Defence in 1920, 'the resources of the British Empire were greater than the resources of our opponents. Today, this is not the case.'

By 1921 the Admiralty began those gloomy predictions which they were to make until 1941, that a war in the Pacific and in the Indian Ocean would be extremely hard to sustain. Admittedly, there were consolations. The disappearance of the German, the Russian and the Turkish empires was an easement. But all it did was to give the British empire a spurious air of strength, just as it gave a spurious air of importance to the goldfish bowl of European diplomacy during the nineteen-twenties. Hence, for the guardians of that empire, that colossus stuffed with clouts, the revulsion from war on the part of the electorate fitted powerfully into their own construct of the national interest. Certainly they should not fight America; possibly they should not fight Japan; probably they should not fight Russia. In any case, could they fight?

Turning to domestic constraints, we begin with the formidable constraint of economic failure. The volume of British exports from 1919 onwards was well below its pre-war volume. This remained true of all the inter-war years. This dwindling of exports was linked with the slump in industries which had been the traditional export staples, textiles, coal, ship-building, iron and steel. Between 1920 and 1925, their workforce dropped by one million. During the nineteen-twenties the unemployed from these industries came to amount to nearly half the total of unemployed. To begin with, the political implications of these trends were very dramatic indeed. During the railway strike of 1919 the Government detailed forty-three infantry battalions and three cavalry regiments to keep watch and ward. During the coal strike of 1921 they called on fifty-six infantry battalions and six cavalry regiments. By the winter of 1921 when one and a half million were out of work, this was clearly not the pre-war kind of unemployment because these were not the pre-war kind of unemployed. As a Cabinet Committee noted, 'They are largely people who all their lives have been used to regular work and good wages.' Moreover, many of these unemployed were skilled workers from the traditional export staples who tended to be bunched in the north and north-east of England, in Scotland and in Wales.

These trends threw up new possibilities for British politics. The regional bias of unemployment worked to turn parts of the country into Labour strongholds (although they seemed to be parts that had started to turn their faces and their majorities against the Unionists before 1914). Moreover, political futures were unsure in any case. At the end of the war at least seventy-nine per cent of those now entitled to vote had never voted before. In 1924, 5,800,000 more voters turned up at the polls than at the Coupon Election of 1918. No one knew which way these new recruits to the political nation would jump. But there is a great deal in the contention that the chief theme in politics at that time was the impact of Labour. The Conservatives and Coalition Liberals both admitted impediment to a marriage of minds. There was to be no Centre party. But nonetheless the strategic need to counter Labour called for a tactical recourse by the old parties to moderate politics. The discontents of the working-class (or more precisely some of the working-classes) could not be solved by bayonets and sabres. All the same there were ways of damping them down, and by 1922 expenditure on social services had climbed to nearly thirty-six per cent of all government expenditure.

But the old parties also needed to look after their own supporters. Taking care of the poor did not mean that the taxpayers would look after themselves. There was pressure from the Anti-Waste League, a contrapuntal composition played on the strings of the public purse by the *Daily Mail* and Horatio Bottomley. No case of government extravagance offered a better political target than spending on armaments and on the new Middle East empire. They were castigated as severely by the Anti-Waste League as by any coal-miners' MP. Asquith, too, spoke of 'our already overburdened shoulder'. Retrenchment was an electoral necessity.

In 1919, Hankey, as Defence Remembrancer, had been arguing that in the event of war, Britain could not beat the Americans; so she should join them in a common disarmament. Accepting this position, the Cabinet on 15 August 1919 had ratified the Ten Year Rule. This was to make very deep cuts in all three armed services. But we are interested in empire. In those days it took infantry to hold empires. Consider then the course of expenditure on the army:

1919–20	£395 million	1921–22	£95 million
1920–21	£181 million	1922–23	£45 million

In other words, expenditure on the army was cut by a half each year. Now we can clearly see one reason why the new empire was faltering. In July 1920 the General Staff made a gloomy survey of the military liabilities of the empire. Before the war those liabilities had called for sixteen and two-thirds infantry divisions and three and one-third cavalry divisions. Now they called for twenty-nine and two-thirds infantry divisions, five and two-thirds cavalry divisions and thirty squadrons of aircraft. Then there was the need to check strikers in England and the IRA in Ireland. 'In no single theatre are we strong enough', wrote the Chief of Imperial General Staff, 'not in Ireland, not in England, not on the Rhine, not in Constantinople, nor Batoum, nor Egypt, nor Palestine, nor Mesopotamia, nor Persia, nor India.'

During 1920 it was British generals who did more than anyone to pull British soldiers out of Russia and Persia. In 1921 the pressures grew all the greater with the Chief of Imperial General Staff talking of the need to find one hundred thousand troops or more for Ireland (this indeed was no new thing; in 1914 it was estimated that Ireland might require the entire British Expeditionary Force). In 1922 when the British were forced to sell their alliances with Japan so as to buy naval disarmament from America, the Geddes Axe could fall, slicing still more of the Service Estimates. Policy had to fall in line with weakness. Retrenchment meant contraction. Curzon's extravaganzas of 1918 had to give way to Bonar Law's announcement that Britain could no longer be the policeman of the world.

These decisions were taken by Conservative or Conservative-dominated governments. The Labour ministry of 1924 did not establish a new trend. It followed an existing trend. The so-called 'anti-imperialism' of the intellectuals, in which they felt themselves to be pathfinders, perfectly mirrored the views of the politicians. When Gilbert Murray wrote of 'that lust of power and expansionist imperialism which were to have but a brief reign in England, but which in other nations had proved a menace to civilisation', he was quite close to the position of Field Marshal Sir Henry Wilson, although he would have been puzzled to learn it. Well, have we solved our question? Not really. We have gripped it between the jaws of international pressure and domestic constraint but it is not yet cracked. The fragility of empire was to become an important factor, but not yet. The military poverty of Britain was more immediately important. It came from economic weakness at home when the economy was finding it hard to sustain an empire. European imperialism might have had a longer future if Ludendorff had won the First World War. But Britain's shortage of troops was merely a symptom of the underlying trouble. After all, the local difficulties which the British ran into were awkward, because they were unexpected, not because they were unmanageable. Once the Bolsheviks rejoined the Great Game, then the British had to fall back from the new outer defences of India. But the other perimeter of Indian defence, stretching from Egypt to Palestine, to Iraq and on to the Gulf, could still be held, whether the troops were overworked or not. So, too, could India itself.

But the central problem was not military at all. The heart of the matter was not external, but internal security: how to keep or to win political support among its subjects. Let me illustrate what I mean by an excursus. Consider for a moment the history of Ireland between these years. The Irish troubles are useful to us because they form a kind of intersection between the problems of empire and the problems of domestic British politics. Why, then, did the Irish issues lead to the 'treaty' signed at ten past two in the morning of 6 December 1921? Here, too, we can see international pressure working on Lloyd George, in the form of Irish–American pressure on the American Government to put pressure on the British Government to sign the treaty. At most, we can say that the Irish question circumscribed the limits of Anglo-American relations. What of domestic constraints? The historian of English and Irish troubles has concluded that the Englishmen who were stirred into protest by the Black and Tans were mainly middle-class liberals and journalists. No English dockers ever refused to load supplies for the Tans in Ireland. There were no 'Jolly Georges'. As J. R. Clynes said, 'Irish troubles would not provoke English strikes.' But what brought Lloyd George to his agreement was that the Irish war had gone on and on. That did not depend on freedom-fighters. Michael Collins estimated his real fighting force at only about three thousand. What it depended upon was not the resistance of freedom-fighters but the non-cooperation of sleeker and tamer men whose support would have been vital for the British to work Anglo-Irish relations as they desired. It is the local political situation in the twenty-six counties which made the question insoluble without a new basis of accommodation.

With that judgement in mind let us return to our imperial question proper. Consider next the disposal of the Indian army. In 1920 there were forty-five British and one hundred and five Indian infantry battalions, and eight British and twenty-four Indian cavalry regiments in India. Of the forty-five British battalions, twenty-six were detailed for internal security. Over and above this, the Raj maintained its garrisons abroad: ten Indian battalions in Iraq, nine in Egypt, seven in Palestine, and six in south Russia, and smaller formations in north China, Hong Kong, Malaya, Aden, Ceylon and the Persian Gulf. There was nothing new about this. Throughout the nineteenth century the Indian army had been the enforcer of Britain's will in Asia, an attractive arrangement for the British taxpayer, since more often than not it was the Indian taxpayer who met the bills when his army was used abroad for British purposes. Here was the real balance-sheet of imperialism.

We need to notice two sides of the position in 1920. First, despite the scarcity of British battalions throughout the world, it was still necessary to keep twenty-six of them for internal security in India. The local political situation had thus an important effect on the world imperial situation. Secondly, during the time when British military scarcities were compromising the position throughout the Middle East, it would have been highly agreeable to have been able to use Indian troops instead. But these days were over. On Christmas Eve 1920, Edwin Montagu, Secretary of State for India, told the Committee of Imperial Defence:

So far as India is concerned, all idea of initiating as a normal peace measure a scheme, whereby she is to become the base for vast military operations in the middle and far east, must be definitely abandoned. . . . In short we must definitely get out of our heads the . . . idea . . . that India is an inexhaustible reservoir from which men and money can be drawn towards the support of imperial resources or in pursuance of imperial strategy.

So India would no longer cover Britain's bets.

As the British army was deflated and pulled back, the Indian army could no longer be inflated and pushed forward. As Britain retrenched, India could no longer be compelled to spend. Why should these changes be coming? Not because of the bomb-throwers, not because of Gandhi, but because of Britain's growing dependence in India on those men prepared to work the Indo-British connection. Their price was to insist on bringing the Indian army back to India. Lloyd George now stood to lose the use of troops paid for by people other than his own electorate. And what was bringing this about? Obviously changes in the political balance in the dependency, not merely international pressures or domestic constraints. Lloyd George used to remark that all he needed to get his own way was five allies around the Cabinet table. It was becoming clear that by this time a British Prime Minister needed more than that.

III

Half a century forward from the nineteen-twenties, we can see that British imperialism during the decade stood betwixt and between. In the past lay the expansion of mid-Victorian Britain which had relied so heavily upon what was demurely called 'mere influence', upon the cutting edge of trade, the seductive force of literature and of the useful arts, and upon the ultimate sanction of the navy whose arm did bind the restless wave. In that age, the strategy of expansion had been that British control should be extended 'informally if possible, formally if necessary'. During the last years of the century there had appeared the phenomenon which I shall term (since there is no reason why we should leave all the best phrases to the medievalists) 'Bastard Imperialism', although the British took on rule over tropical Africa only on the assumption that it would be harmless and non-committal. After 1918, as we have seen, came the extravaganza of the Middle East empire. Then during the nineteen-twenties, *nobilmente* was followed by *diminuendo*; there were clear signs that in some regions the system was beginning to edge its way back into the earlier, the safer, the cheaper, the more elegant technique. We have identified some of the forces which were working to point the empire in that direction. There were domestic pressures aplenty on Britain to drop her baton and refuse to be the policeman of the world. Presently we shall see how this refusal was worked in party political terms. International pressures had little to do with the retreats of the nineteen-twenties. It remained generally true that war with a great power might wreck the empire, but the American challenge was limited to the *fausse bonhomie* of Socony-Vacuum and Standard Oil in Iraq and Saudi Arabia. And Japan was ruled by a series of prim constitutionalists such as Kato and the patrons of Rotary Clubs. But another force was now beginning to press hard against the empire.

When we surveyed the century of British expansion after 1815, we found that political change in overseas regions affected the course of that expansion. But it did so only spasmodically and occasionally. From the nineteen-twenties until the end of empire, it was to put an increasing pressure upon the operations of the British system. Now this is either rather obvious or rather arcane. So let us be clear about what we mean. When we look at the course of colonial nationalism between the nineteen-hundreds and the nineteen-fifties, we are impressed, of course, by its diversities, by the great differences in organization, in composition and in timing between the nationalism of one region and another. Demands for political change erupted much more swiftly in some places than in others. At no time before the nineteen-fifties were these demands made generally throughout the entire system. Before the nineteen-fifties, these movements had their ups and downs, just as their supposed antagonist, British imperialism, was having its own ups and downs. Indeed, we might say that by the nineteen-fifties imperialism and nationalism can be seen as a brace of old and battered boxers each clinging to the other to avoid sinking to the floor. I shall return later to this piquant theme.

But amid the diversities of these nationalisms, we can find a common factor at work upon them. It lies in the growing weight of government intervention inside the colonial society over which it ruled. Generally the reasons for this intervention lay in financial stringency (as in later nineteenth-century India) or in economic crisis (as in Africa in the late nineteen-forties). It had always been one of the rules of the game of colonial administration that there were many areas of social life in which it did not meddle. When the British Raj in India started hunting for new sources of revenue, it invaded these old franchises and immunities. The notables, who had hitherto controlled them without much let or hindrance, now found it necessary in self-defence to organize on much wider bases than they had done hitherto. Any colony could be held for ever, so long as its politics remained localized. But any colonial government faces trouble once the politics of its subjects expand out of their old immunities and into a wider arena, as these colonial Geoffrey de Mandevilles climb onto a larger stage. This is not a central theme in this argument, so perhaps I may leave it in this simple form. But it will help in the exposition of what I have to say from now on if we keep this process in mind as we consider the ways in which colonial political development increasingly affects the course of an empire.

The case of India plainly shows how far political growth overseas could set limits to policy-making. The Government of India Act of 1919, the outcome of the Montagu-Chelmsford reforms, had been planned as a way of diverting Indian political attention from the national, the all-India stage, and directing it to provincial affairs. There were to be Indian ministers in the governments of eight of the nine provinces, under a system which Lionel Curtis insisted should be known as dyarchy, although not all that many Indians knew Greek. Indians were also to be the majority in the Legislative Assembly in Delhi. Somehow or other, this constitution had to be worked. 'A reversal of policy in India', Montagu, the Secretary of State wrote to the Viceroy, 'would mean the end of the Indian empire.' But who was to work the reforms? Clearly the British would have to rely on the grace and favour of Indian politicians. But which Indian politicians? Broadly, we can group them as either constitutional or agitational politicians (although many men crossed back and forth between these two groups). In part because of the Christian and Quaker influence upon British thinking, it has been fashionable to bid up the prestige of the agitators. But although it was Gandhi and not the Indian constitutionalists who stayed in the Master's Lodge at Balliol, it was the latter group who were much the more important during the nineteen-twenties. They were the men who were now covering the British bets for retaining India. Accordingly they had to be given a hand to play. Accordingly, too, they could make their terms with the British.

By 1920 military costs were more than forty per cent of the total expenditure of the Government of India. There were urgent political reasons in Delhi for cutting these costs (just as there were in London). Under the new constitution the centre had to transfer about £6 million a year to the provinces. If provincial politicians were to work the reforms, they needed the money; the more of the army, the less for them. They looked on the use by Britain of Indian troops abroad, not only as exploitation but also as a frittering away of resources which would help to turn out the voters at home. In 1921 the Legislative Assembly resolved that the Indian army 'should not as a rule be employed for service outside the external frontiers of India'. The following year it tried to cut the army's size. These pressures could not be shrugged off. In January 1923 the British Cabinet had to approve the view of the Committee of Imperial Defence that 'The Indian Army cannot be treated as if it were absolutely at the disposal of HMG for service outside India . . . except in the gravest emergency the Indian Army should be employed outside the Indian empire only after consultation with the Governor-General in Council'. If Indian troops were still to be used as colonial garrisons, then their whole cost should be borne by the colony which needed them, or, if the worst came to the worst, by HMG. This did not entirely strip the Indian army of its tasks as a colonial fire-service. In 1927 it sent a mixed brigade to Shanghai. There were contingency plans for sending troops to protect the Persian oilfields, for sending a division to Iraq and two brigades to Singapore. But the old days of getting the support for next to nothing had gone. Now the Indian army was a fire-service which worked on contract, which turned out only in emergency, and which was bound first to its own ratepayers.

That was not all which was lost. Financial pressure pegged the Indian army to just over 200,000 men, in the rather Byzantine ratio of one British soldier to 2.41 Indians. Moreover the main operational task of the army was still seen as war against Afghanistan, a peculiar insight since Afghanistan was the only one of India's neighbours which did not give her trouble during the Second World War. Consequently the equipment of the army was allowed to run down until it became a force of screw-guns and mules, incapable of taking on any serious opponent.

We saw how the checks on the use of this army helped to weaken the new British empire in the Middle East. Now we can see how this army's dwindling role as the enforcer of British wishes was linked to political change in India itself, how a shift in the basis of British rule, leaving that rule more dependent upon its Indian collaborators, could act to weaken the British grip on other countries far away. Could this weakening have been checked? As usual it was Lloyd George who saw most clearly into the dilemmas of British imperialism. He knew, as Cromer had known before him, that the secret for successful imperial government of the east lay in low taxation. But he saw, too, that:

the tradition of government in India with regard to finance and development has been the over-cautious one of an old family solicitor. We must increase the wealth of India if we are going to make a success of the new system of government. To attempt progress on the basis of the present revenue must be to march straight towards turmoil and failure.

An admirable insight. But increasing the wealth of India meant more trade and investment and the British economy was too small to provide them. Not until 1941–45 was the Indian economy to be driven full blast and then it was done through heavy government intervention. For that there would be a heavy political price.

We seem to be emerging with the view that most of the forces working against vigorous imperialism during the nineteen-twenties can be traced back to domestic constraints and the fragility of imperial rule as a result of the growth of colonial politics. Certainly these forces were not working to destroy the system but at least they imposed various circumscriptions around it. All this was happening in a period when there was little international pressure against the system. Russia had come back into the Great Game in central Asia, but that had not been taken very seriously except by Lord Birkenhead, Political Intelligence in New Delhi and by Dr E. H. Carr at Trinity. So during the nineteen-twenties we can study the system as it worked in the luxury of freedom from international danger, a luxury which was to disappear during the nineteen-thirties.

What I wish to consider next is the way in which these factors worked their way through British domestic politics. After the fall in 1922 of Lloyd George's Ministry of All the Talents, British politics began to move towards a system of consensus. Of course consensus is a cant term; let us gloss it as a system of broad agreement at the limits of difference. That was quite compatible with public expressions of illimitable difference, but these were rhetoric intended to recruit Demos to one side or the other. In fact we shall find that when these politicians did agree their unanimity was wonderful. Once the Conservatives had wrested control of their party from Austen Chamberlain, Balfour and Birkenhead, the new leaders chose to dish the Liberal rather than the Labour party. Even when the rejected Talents were re-admitted to office in Baldwin's second Government (with the exception of Sir Robert Horne whose talents were thought rather too gamey), they were mainly kept out of the making of domestic policy. That policy was intended to show the Conservative party, not the Liberal party, as the bulwark against Socialism. 'The future', said Baldwin in the Commons in 1924, 'lies between Honourable Members opposite and ourselves.' It was the Labour MPs he was looking at. Asquith shook his white head; but Baldwin was right. Such a strategy meant that Labour could not, should not, be beaten into the ground. By and large, Baldwin hoped to check them. After his fiasco over Protection in 1923, after the fracas with the House of Cecil and with 'Genial Judas' (Lord Derby) and Lancashire, he would now play the card of speaking for 'undogmatic average opinion' extending far beyond Villa Toryism and the playing-fields of Tunbridge Wells. But if this was to be resistance against Socialism, it would be resistance of a supple and accommodating sort. After all, by the new rules of the game, the honourable members opposite were bound from time to time to be the government.

These easements from the Conservative side were matched by easements from the Labour leaders. MacDonald might have been elected leader with the help of the Clydeside MPs. But he was eager to form a ministry, for all that it would be a minority government—'this High Adventure', as he called it in the blowsy prose style of the nineteen-twenties. By doing so, the Labour politicians were committing themselves to upholding the policies which they found were already established in their departments. The same harmonies were heard when the parts were transposed. In 1924, and between 1929 and 1931, Baldwin was very far from being a costive or relentless Leader of the Opposition. Between 1924 and 1929, the Labour leaders were accommodating too. It is characteristic of the period that in 1926 Baldwin had warned J. H. Thomas that 'a general strike would throw back the Labour party's chances of coming into power for many years', and that in 1929 MacDonald should have appealed to all MPs to 'consider ourselves more as a Council of State and less as arrayed regiments facing each other in battle'. It is no less characteristic that both sides should have joined in commination of Lloyd George's Keynesian plans of 1929, on the grounds that they would be expensive.

Many of the explanations of these harmonies are banal; the Manichean School of historians has always been influential in this country, whether among our provincial Robespierres on the left who see MacDonald diverted from the moral grandeurs of Lossiemouth just for a ribbon to stick on his coat, or among our latter-day Straffords who see Baldwin lured into fantasies about pastoral unity by the tunes which Mary Webb grated on her scrannel pipe of wretched straw. None of this is very interesting. We shall do better to look at this as a period when the leadership in both parties was set upon ditching its own dissident factions so as to bring about a sort of interpenetration between the majorities on either side.

Throughout his career, Baldwin worked to conciliate the Trade Union leaders. Had they not vetoed a coal strike in 1921 when the miners had balloted in favour of striking? Was it not the Trades Union Congress in 1926 who rejected the miners' request for an embargo on the transport of foreign coal? Then again they were more powerful than the Labour politicians. Was it not Bevin who snubbed their plan for a National Industrial Conference? One of Baldwin's tasks was to detach this broad-bottomed group from the Labour left whose strength lay in the constituencies and who tended to be spokesmen of the party and a far from silent minority. But if this were to be done then Baldwin had to free his own party from the power of its unreconstructed right wing, a view expressed later by his adjutant, Davidson, 'that the dyed-in-the-wool Tories, although the Praetorian Guard of the party, were a wasting asset, and . . . unless we recruited from the Left we would die'.

It was much the same on the other side of the hill. MacDonald could deliver his own patter to the faithful, saying that politics was a show-down between 'the capitalist parties' and 'the Labour and Socialist party'. But his own leadership did all that it could to free his party from the power of its unreconstructed left wing. As he warned them in 1929, this time there was to be 'no more monkeying'. What it came to was that each side was set on breaking its own minority factions, so as to appear more trustworthy to the electorate. In this task, both parties were helped by the structure of politics in the nineteen-twenties. At that time, the power of the constituency parties over the Conservative Central Office was still weak, for Central Office was still regularly financing electoral campaigns. After the 1929 elections when Labour held 287 seats, 114 of their members were openly sponsored by Trade Unions (fifty were miners), while many of the other constituencies had also sponsored manual workers. The result was that if faction was not suppressed then it was dampened, because on both sides the majority faction remained in control.

How does this conclusion affect our general enquiry? It affects it considerably. In the Conservative party, the dominant group were able to respond to the pressures of domestic politics and of colonial political developments. They could tack towards a 'moderate' policy on issues of overseas expansion, and they were safe in doing so, because their own right wing had been tied to the mast. In the Labour party, the dominant group were able to accept the fundamentals of the policies they inherited when they came to office. The imperial system might need pruning or its workings might need de-emphasizing and stressing in a different way. But they had no wish to throw the imperial system away. Hence both parties could broadly concur. Both were minded to jib away from the imperial commitments accepted after 1918. Both of them, too, were inclined to fall back from the risky and rather seamy imperialism of the later nineteenth century, and to revert to the safer, the less compromising, strategy of the middle nineteenth century. It would be hard to decide whether Austen Chamberlain or Arthur Henderson was the more eager to return to the British position in Egypt before the eighteen-eighties or to the British position in China before the eighteen-nineties. Perhaps a truer way of putting that would be to state that in these overseas questions, both sides were equally willing to listen to their professional advisers. Lloyd George had paid next to no heed to the promptings of the official mind in these matters. Nor was Neville Chamberlain to do so. Between 1919 and 1922, and between 1937 and 1939, the answers to the big questions do not lie in the files of the Foreign Office; they do not lie in the files of the Colonial Office; they lie in the files of the Prime Minister. But during the years in between, the age of Baldwin and MacDonald, the official mind came back into its own.

But let us note how fragile and how conditional was the area of broad agreement between the parties. A great deal of it rested on their success in stifling their own minority voices. But this success was to vanish. From 1929 the Conservative right wing was to raise its head once more against Baldwin's leadership. From 1931 the Labour party was to be aligned against its own leadership, and to find itself spread-eagled between the Pacifists, the Trade Unions and the Radicals in the constituencies. In both cases there was to be a similar result. Inside each party, issues of the greatest importance—the future organization of the imperial system, the devising of policies towards Nazi Germany—were pounced upon by factions which hoped by simplifying them to overthrow their opponents, whether in the other party or in their own, and to shin up the greasy pole into power. But during the nineteen-twenties, the rivalries inside parties and between parties were not sharp enough to cause sudden changes in policies towards world issues. In foreign policy their difference lay chiefly in rhetoric. In essentials there is little to distinguish between the diplomacy of MacDonald, Austen Chamberlain and Henderson. All of them saw that peace was the great British interest, that war would be the great British disaster; 'the aim of every statesman in the British Empire', said Chamberlain, 'is, and must be to preserve peace'. In much the same vein, the MacDonald Government stated that 'no solution of the unemployment problem is possible until normal conditions have been re-established in the world'. But how was peace to be preserved? Both sides saw the usefulness of the League of Nations to a *status quo* power. But both could see dangers in the League unless it was kept in swaddling clothes and prevented from causing any dangerous extension of commitment. In 1923 the zealots for the League had produced a Draft Treaty of Mutual Assistance which would have authorized its Council to identify an aggressor and to determine which powers were to supply armed forces to stop aggression. The Labour Government would have none of it. It might add to armaments. It might lead to military alliances. It might seem that the party was ready to hand the navy over to foreigners. MacDonald preferred a scheme which would not lead to enforcement. International disputes could be arbitrated out of existence. He suggested instead the Geneva Protocol, a pact of mutual non-aggression extending right across the world: if someone attacked someone else, the Council would arbitrate and could *ask* members to apply sanctions. This rather limp plan certainly respected national sovereignty, but it still contemplated very wide alliances. The dominions were against it. A majority of the Labour Cabinet was against it. Austen Chamberlain destroyed it. 'Great Britain', he wrote, 'is not prepared to accept a universal extension of her covenanted liabilities.' Separate pacts on a regional basis would be safer and better; the only boundaries Britain should guarantee were those between Germany, France and Belgium, a policy which led to the Locarno Pact in 1925.

Side by side with the question of the League was the question of disarmament. As we have seen, one of the objections against ambitious guarantees was that it might demand the strengthening of the armed forces. The Labour Government of 1924 cut the naval estimates but announced that they were ready to build five new cruisers, so as to relieve 'the serious unemployment'. Labour back-benchers protested, but the government got the decision through the Commons with the help of Conservative votes. Between 1924 and 1929 the Baldwin Government took over the torch. Its domestic constraints were the same. Its attitude towards disarmament and the League were much the same. At home, direct taxes had to be cut to conciliate the Conservative voter. They were cut. That meant that defence spending had to be held down. Hence the dispute in 1925 over building the new cruisers. The Admiralty insisted. Churchill at the Treasury refused. Only after threats of resignations and the now standard argument that the cruisers cut down the dole queues was the building programme approved. The same government in 1928 adopted a more restricted version of the 'Ten Year Rule', making it automatically extensible from day to day. Every morning a new ten years began. And it was the same government which tried another bout of negotiation with the United States over naval disarmament. After 1929 Labour followed suit. MacDonald weakened the new Ten Year Rule ('a change for the better'). In 1930 he was active in another conference for naval disarmament (this time successful), and his government smartly rejected French plans for a regional pact in the Mediterranean and a scheme for European federation.

Were there, then, no zig-zags of policy between the parties, at least over the naval base at Singapore? At first sight the vacillations over Singapore looked like a difference of approach. When the future of the Anglo-Japanese Alliance became doubtful in 1921, the defence planners argued that Singapore must be turned into a fortress to secure British interests against Japanese attacks. In March 1924 the Labour Government stopped its construction; in November 1924 the Conservative Government decided 'in principle' to resume its construction; in July 1929 the Labour Government halted it again. Is this a case of a large imperial interest chopped about by changes of ministry? Yes; but again only in headline terms. The continuities are impressive. By 1924 the Conservatives had done little to build the base in Singapore. Between 1924 and 1929 they went on doing little. Balfour, speaking like Philip Snowden or any other Labour Little Englander, thought it might be wiser to spend the money at home. Churchill, like Lansbury, or any other Labour pacifist, suspected that the Japanese danger was a turnip ghost rigged up by the Admiralty. When the next Labour Government once more held up work on the base, not much had been done. As late as 1933 Hankey was castigating the National Government for not taking seriously the defence of Singapore.

So throughout the nineteen-twenties, there is a pattern in the carpet. All the politicians were determined to avoid another war. At the League of Nations they enjoyed talking about peace. They found in the League a high-style façade of internationalism. But they meant it to cover an interior of minimum commitment. Instead they would put home considerations first. Domestic constraint and economic weakness had forced them to do so. Each of these governments subsided into a Little England position. Labour said so outright, the Conservatives implicitly. When the economy refused to come right, then both were ready to play the imperial card. The Conservatives said so outright, Labour implicitly. But the new-fangled interest in colonial development lay in the hope that it could assist the domestic economy.

How, then, did domestic politics affect the operations of British expansion overseas? The general primacy given to domestic interests could not mean the jettisoning of overseas interests. There were too many of them for that, because of the world-wide activities of the British and because so many British jobs depended upon them. No one demanded that the country should clear out bag and baggage from its overseas possessions and positions. All that can be said of the nineteen-twenties is that in this transitional period there were moves designed to lighten the loads carried by the British Atlas, to cut the bills paid by the British taxpayer and to accommodate the demands emerging out of colonial politics. Here the trends of Britain's policy towards her eastern empire are interesting, for they reveal a falling-back of imperial power, carried out in a variety of modes, yet so as to conserve British interests. If we like, we can look at them as early sketches for decolonization, but only if we remember our earlier conclusion that there were to be no straight roads to decolonization, and that most of these tentative slackenings of control in the nineteen-twenties were to be followed by tightenings of control in the years that followed.

One obvious technique for lessening commitments lay ready to hand from the experience of the nineteenth century. Faced with the growth of colonial politics in Canada, the British had renounced any effort to rule the country in detail; they had pulled out of local government in the provinces and had fallen back upon the centre. Ontario was no longer their concern; now it was Ottawa. And even when they lost formal control at the centre, they still preserved vast influence over the affairs of Canada, not least through their control over its foreign borrowings. In India, as we have seen, the Montagu-Chelmsford reforms made a beginning in these tactics by trying to attract Indian politicians towards provincial matters, while checking their intervention in all-India affairs. We shall have more than enough to say about India later, so for the present let us confine ourselves to saying that after the collapse of Gandhi's campaign of non-cooperation in 1922, the steam went out of Indian politics for the rest of the decade. Neither the Labour nor the Conservative Government was minded to move towards further concessions; the talk of dominion status for India in 1929 which so excited *The Times* and All Souls was quite spurious, or at best a post-dated cheque. Olivier, the Labour Secretary of State for India in 1924, had a felicitous turn for light verse, but was not a man to get things done. Nor was Wedgwood Benn, Indian Secretary in the second Labour Government. He had no felicitous turns; his letters to India were spoken into a dictaphone in the small hours, and they read like it. In fact his policies were dictated to him, by the Viceroy, Lord Irwin, the later Lord Halifax.

Indeed, it was not India which bothered the policy-makers in London during the nineteen-twenties, so much as Egypt and China. Egypt illustrates vividly the use of the second technique of British detachment from a commitment. Since the political development of so many of these eastern territories hampered British rule over them, why not contract that rule by abandoning detailed administration and falling back on the essential British interest? Already in 1919 Milner, of all people, had seen this: 'Egypt is truly the nodal point of our whole imperial system. But is it therefore necessary that we should own it? Is it not sufficient if we have a firm foothold there?' The corollary was to give up the British protectorate over Egypt and concentrate upon interests, not upon territory. In 1922 London recognized the independence of Egypt, but it was only in a Pickwickian sense, because four subjects were 'absolutely reserved to the discretion of H.M.G.': the security of the Canal, the defence of the country, the protection of foreign interests and the integrity of the Sudan. But this was to pull all the plums out of the Egyptian cake, leaving the King and the Wafd to scramble for the stodge. They would not. Here we find the countervailing forces of colonial politics at work again. The Court and the Wafd were both more intent on doing the other down than on uniting against the British. Neither group would lay itself open to the attacks of the other by signing an Anglo-Egyptian treaty on these lines. Soon the War Office was noting with irritation that they had more troops in independent Egypt than there had been during the Protectorate. The Foreign Office yearned to cut clear of Cairo and its seedy politics. They longed 'to rally the solid elements in Egypt', so that someone could be cajoled into signing the treaty. Just as Cornwallis had combed the Carolinas for Tories in 1780, and as Reading was even then scouring India for moderates, so did Labour and Conservative Foreign Secretaries look for collaborators in Egypt who would shoulder the burden of ruling the country while leaving the British in possession of the Canal. To MacDonald in the nineteen-twenties, as to Anthony Eden in the nineteen-thirties, the only alternative was to annex Egypt outright, an unpalatable option.

But how were the Egyptian politicians to be lured into snapping at the flies which the British kept throwing over them? One solution might be by not meddling in the domestic politics of that country. Lord Lloyd, the High Commissioner, could not resist doing so. Chamberlain castigated this strenuous and obsolete imperialist:

It is not in the interests of His Majesty's Government to intervene in the internal affairs of Egypt further than is necessary to secure our political objects. Since in certain cases it is essential that the wishes of His Majesty's Government should prevail, their influence must not be frittered away on other and less important matters.

Chamberlain was minded to dismiss Lloyd. Chamberlain's successor, the Labour Foreign Secretary, Arthur Henderson, did so. Lloyd was the third High Commissioner in succession to be retired abruptly from Egypt. Incidentally, his dismissal was a perfect example of the power of the official mind, for the men who ejected him from Cairo were really the civil servants in the Foreign Office.

But the British Government was ready to go further than dropping their High Commissioner through a trap-door. They were also ready to overrule their Chiefs of Staff. In 1929 and again in 1930, the Egyptians seemed about to nibble on the hook. Now they wanted a guarantee that British troops would pull out of Cairo and Alexandria. The Chiefs of Staff Committee would have none of it. The Citadel and the Abbasia barracks in Cairo were the ark of the covenant. Now perhaps they were, but the British Government was ready to give them up for the sake of a treaty, especially with the Oxford graduate, Muhammad Mahmud, who negotiated with Henderson in 1930. Yet on both occasions the Egyptian spokesmen were choked off by the court and excoriated by their fellow-countrymen for trying to arrange a sell-out. So nothing came of it. In 1882 the British shot their way into Egypt so as to secure a vital imperial interest, the Suez Canal and the route to India. During the nineteen-twenties, they tried to talk their way out of the country while holding on to the vital interest. But Egypt's political development meant that the country could now block them from compelling Pharaoh to be free.

With the third of these new techniques of propping up the imperial load, I shall be brief. We saw how the reappearance of Russian power, under new management but studying the same maps, forced the British to pull back from the outermost perimeters of Curzon's pipe-dreams on to the old fortifications of the Raj as they had existed before the Anglo-Russian Agreement of 1907. The result was a drawing back of British control from Afghanistan, Turkey and Persia, and a sullen recognition of the parity of Russian influence. In each case that meant settling for the rule of a strong man who could at any rate ensure stability, even if the strong man was less than ideal. Hence the British came to acquiesce in the rule of Mustafa Kemal in Turkey, of Amanullah in Afghanistan and of Reza Khan (later Reza Shah) in

Persia. This was not only a policy of pulling out but also of propping up. For example in Persia (Iran in modern parlance), already by 1922 Reza Khan Pahlevi was clambering upwards, and in that year the British representative was urging that he was the man to keep the country together and so was more important 'than the local supremacy of any one of our particular protégés'. Hence step by step, the British relaxed their support for their old clients in the Gulf and allowed them to fall under the control of the revived Teheran. By 1926, when Reza, emulating an earlier military *arriviste*, placed the crown upon his own head, it was clear that the British had backed the right horse.

It was not always so clear how to do so. Pulling out was one thing; propping up was another. Who should be propped up? In China both the Conservative and Labour Governments vied with each other in making concessions. During 1926 and 1927 Austen Chamberlain stated that Britain was ready to revise the 'Unequal treaties', especially the restrictions on Chinese tariff autonomy. Even during the turmoil of 1927, the British Government was careful to impose only a graduated protection of British interests in Hankow and Shanghai. The Labour Government took concession further, handing back Wei-Hai-Wei and Amoy, and establishing Chinese courts in Shanghai (the British ark of the covenant in China) and preparing to surrender British extraterritorial rights generally in China. But the question was to whom to surrender these rights and which group to support in China. Chiang Kai-shek and the Kuomintang had the merit of having dished (that is to say shot) the Communists. But Chiang Kai-shek was an unsatisfactory ally. Much water has flowed under the bridge in China since 1930 and it is easy to forget how much of the programme of Chiang and the Kuomintang was based on opposition to western imperialism. In any case the whole British policy of proffering easements to China stopped on the night of 18 September 1931 when the Japanese army struck at China. That put all the plans for concessions to China into abeyance, because from now on in China, unlike in Iran or Turkey, it was uncertain which was the right horse to back.

We turn now to the fourth technique: staying in the country and relying on collaborators. In Iraq and in Palestine, British governments of both parties decided to hold on to rule. During the war, Iraq enjoyed the singular distinction of being the only country in the Middle East which all departments of state were determined to bring under British control. But the effort to rule it by Indian methods led to the rebellion of 1920. The Turks had left the people alone. The British had invaded the franchises of the local notables, and in Iraq, as in India, these interventions had provoked a strong political backlash. If British control was to continue in Iraq, the Arab façade would have to be redecorated. Moreover the cost of running the country led to strong demands in London that it should be given up. Labour back-benchers said so, very strongly. So did some Conservatives. Bonar Law was far from ardent about holding on to Iraq. His Cabinet was divided on the subject. Reluctantly, they decided to remain, since departure would mean that King Faysal would tumble and perhaps that the Turks would come back. But there were to be heavy cuts in British spending, one of which was made by making the Royal Air Force, not the soldiers, responsible for holding the country. Moreover, a constitution had to be forced on to the new country. As usual the British had one of their off-the-peg constitutions ready for King Faysal. They insisted at first that nearly half the revenues of Iraq must be spent on holding its own peoples down; even by the end of the nineteen-twenties twenty per cent of those revenues were going to the Iraqi army and another seventeen per cent to the police. Now to what end was all of this being done? Certainly it was useful to control Iraq, since Iraq assisted in the defence of India and of the Gulf and of Persian oil, besides possessing oil of its own. But oil companies did not need colonies, as Standard Oil was soon to show. Still less would they help to pay for them. Nor was Demos in Britain minded to pay for Iraq. The only alternative for the Cabinet was to place more of the load on Faysal and to trust that he would be ready and able to carry it, first as ruler of a mandated territory, then after 1932 as ruler of a nominally independent state. But no collaborator lives for ever; and after Faysal's death, the system ceased to yield to the British what they wanted from it. In 1936 came an army *putsch* in Iraq, the first in a series which has gone on from that day to this.

In Iraq the technique of collaboration worked well enough for some fifteen years. In Palestine it did not work at all. After the riots of 1921, the Cabinet had discussed whether to leave or to stay in Palestine. In 1923 the question was raised again. The Conservative right wing, exactly like the Labour left wing, was strongly against 'commitments' abroad, especially when they were costly. The same men who had denounced surrender in Ireland now advocated it in Palestine. The question was whether to rule or to quit. The General Staff dealt a blow against staying: 'Palestine is not of strategic importance for the primary task of defending the Suez Canal', they reported. But as against that, there was always the last refuge of imperialism, the argument, Curzon's favourite argument, that if Britain withdrew from a territory, who could tell which malignant power might come creeping into it? With a bad grace, it was decided to stay. There was not even the hope to nurse, as there was in Iraq, that the mandate would soon expire. The Arabs were deemed too feckless to run an administration, the Jews too unbending to waive a comma of the Balfour Declaration. There was nothing for it but to plod indefinitely on, hoping to keep some sort of balance. The Jews had to rely on support from the fox-hunting English Jews and their friends in high places, the Arabs on the support of the rackety politicians of the Middle East. The Jews were anxious to be Britain's collaborators, but the offer was too dangerous to accept; the Arabs would not collaborate at all. So there could be no final solution. Of course the very words 'final solution' carry an eerie ring of *Die Entlösung*. But the nineteen-twenties did not raise the hard questions of the nineteen-forties. During the nineteen-twenties, Palestine, it seemed, could not be abandoned, but it was not yet an insupportable commitment.

There are other examples of the British tendency to work with collaborators, such as Kenya and Rhodesia, where white settlers repeatedly humiliated the British, but could not be repudiated. We shall deal with them in their place. During the nineteen-twenties much of Britain's eastern empire seemed to be quietly fading away. It might be sound policy and sound business, this slow reversion to the methods of the mid-nineteenth century, but it came to show that disillusion was in sight. All this had been brought about by domestic constraints and the pressures of colonial politics. By the nineteen-thirties there was to be a new and imperious threat, the danger of a violent end through international attack. Yet for all this, the imperial Lazarus was to rise again.

IV

We have already noted some of the reasons why the Labour Government of 1929 to 1931, like its predecessor under Baldwin, thought it necessary to muzzle its own *enragés* in the interests of general harmony. This was especially to be seen in the Colonial Office, those specialists in parsimony, those imperial Micawbers, or Oblomovs, or Messieurs Bovary. With Sidney Webb as Colonial Secretary, policy was made by the official mind of the civil servants in the Colonial Office, perhaps because he had himself been one of them before he married the woman who had almost become the wife of Joseph Chamberlain. This subservience to official advice was especially marked in African policy. It was the Labour Government which sanctioned the Land Apportionment Act in Southern Rhodesia, which was not averse to a proposed union between Southern and Northern Rhodesia (Zimbabwe and Zambia on modern maps), and which was saved by a whisker from being confronted by a closer union between the three East African territories of Kenya, Uganda and Tanganyika. The pattern is clear. Since white settlers had been embedded in Rhodesia and Kenya, their political position had been strong enough for them generally to get their own way against London. After the grant of semi-responsible government to Rhodesia in 1923 there was no gainsaying them. Until the aftermath of the Mau-Mau rising, it was still a fact in Kenya. In both territories the settlers continually humiliated the British Government, and the Colonial Office, who generally disapproved of them, had come to acquiesce in their demands. So it was under the second Labour Government.

There was obedience to official thinking over Iraq as well. Iraq was scheduled to shed the mandate and become an independent state in 1932. In return, the Colonial Office wanted to shackle Iraq into an alliance. Sidney Webb agreed and he persuaded the Cabinet. Iraq was vital for a British air route to India. It was a guarantee for security in the Persian Gulf. It would be a base for the Middle East air reserve. Curzon might have written that. Admittedly Curzon might have had his doubts about the new India policy which set a goal of Dominion Status and called for a Round Table Conference, but then again he might not, because the policy was forced on the Labour Government by the Viceroy, Lord Irwin (the later Lord Halifax), hardly a turbulent radical. Carrying out the policy, the Viceroy remarked, 'will take a long time'.

There were some signs that the MacDonald Government was thinking about imperial solutions to its economic problems. Emigration had dropped. In 1913, 285,000 souls had shipped out of British ports into the empire. After the war, far fewer people migrated to the empire, but emigration picked up again in the mid-twenties with government subsidies. The Baldwin ministry began to take it seriously, significantly, because of pressure from the Cabinet Committee on unemployment policy. In 1929, Oswald Mosley, a member of the Labour Government, and Walter Citrine of the TUC were sympathetic to it. J. H. Thomas liked it very much. But it broke against the opposition of the Labour parties in the Dominions. Of course it was the troubles of the British economy, especially the rise of unemployment, which brought about this interest. Exactly the same anxieties brought about an interest in the possibilities of developing empire trade. On 26 June 1930, the TUC gave the government a memorandum calling for the empire to be turned into an economic bloc. Isolation was played out. The British economy had to merge into a larger unit. Common marketing with the USA and with Europe were ruled out. But why not merge the economies of the empire? Why not issue tied loans? Or make block purchases? On 24 September, the TUC and the Federation of British Industries joined in sponsoring such a policy. It set the Cabinet by the ears. J. H. Thomas liked it. A positive policy might help employment, and that would mean 'our position in the country would be strengthened'. Another Cabinet minister, Oswald Mosley, thought it was bound to fail, since only heavy investment at home could right the economy. Snowden would have none of it, for it would erode Free Trade. MacDonald probably liked it (insofar as he knew what he liked) but the opposition of Snowden at the Treasury scared him off. This is an instructive affair, Thomas echoing Joseph Chamberlain, Mosley echoing Hobson, Snowden echoing Cobden and MacDonald echoing Lord Liverpool. It is instructive to people who believe that the Labour party and the Trade Union leadership were the herald angels of decolonization. It is instructive again as a case of continuity. The Baldwin Government had earlier launched the Empire Marketing Board, assuring working-class house-wives that empire goods were produced under idyllic conditions for the colonial workers. Ernest Bevin went one better. He wanted a richer empire to save British workers from their own economy. It is also instructive because the impulse towards a new policy sprang entirely from domestic circumstances, not from any solicitude for the men growing sugar in the West Indies, but from solicitude for Jack Crankshaft standing in the dole queue in Burnley; and after all Jack Crankshaft had a vote.

All these judgements apply to the other new departure, the new interest in colonial development. This had been canvassed by both parties when they were in office earlier in the nineteen-twenties, significantly in Cabinet committees on unemployment. When he went to the country in 1929, Baldwin's election programme promised to set up a Colonial Development Fund. Labour was not averse to this sort of thing. Loans to India might help British engineering. Even Snowden saw merit in helping Indian peasants, because that might help them to buy Lancashire cotton. J. H. Thomas picked up the torch; as the minutes record, 'he attached great importance to stimulating develop-ment projects . . . within the Empire and other indirect ways of providing employment at home'. To this end, the Colonial Develop-ment Act was passed in 1929, and there was much fine talk of building railways in east Africa, roads in Nyasaland and harbours in Ceylon.

By the end of the nineteen-twenties, when the problems of British economy had turned out to be long-term, both parties were minded to play the imperial card in the hope that it might turn the economic game. But as matters turned out, it did not even win a trick. What defeated it was first the stunning effects of the slump and then the revival of faction. The slump and the atmosphere of economic crisis in 1931 soon ended the concern with overseas affairs. It was puffed away by a whiff of devaluations. By 1932 the net long-term movement of British capital was £21 million *back* into Britain and the net movement of migration was 32,000 *back* from the empire. The experience of negotiating at Ottawa showed the Conservatives that imperial markets offered wealth considerably less than the dreams of avarice. Citrine was also at Ottawa, and he was shaken by the huckstering that went on, so much so that the TUC quickly signed off its imperial programmes until they were revived again after 1945. It was the same with the Labour party. Lansbury, the new leader, who did not have clear views about anything except Hyde Park, thought that all countries—meaning Germany—should have free access to British colonies. The fact was, as a speaker at the Labour Party Conference in 1933 pointed out, that the colonial issue was 'not one that would fire the enthusiasm of the electors at a general election'. After the Communists had tried, and failed, to blow up India, left-wing interest in colonial questions was now restricted to the Socialist League, the Friends of Africa Committee (designed to help Labour in South Africa), the India League (Krishna Menon) and the International Africa Service Bureau (George Padmore).

These were generals without troops; and without quartermasters too, for they were usually short of money. The best hope lay in working on the Labour Party Advisory Council on Imperial Questions, a body run by Leonard Woolf, for he, too, favoured opening up the colonies to all the powers. British freedom-fighters for the colonies were never in short supply in London. Some wrote books, some became peers, and some there be that have no memorial. But at this time they were more articulate than influential. The fact was that the slump blighted colonial issues. Once the bottom had fallen out of world commodity prices, there was no chance of developing the economies of the African or the Caribbean colonies, except by a strong capital investment which it was out of the question for the British economy to make. Any future development of the colonies, so a government committee reported in 1934, must pay heed to 'industrial and commercial interests of the United Kingdom'. Even development of this sort, however, would have to be put off for the present.

Thus as we move into the nineteen-thirties, we seem to be in a period when the grip of domestic constraint was tighter than ever before. By now it had squeezed almost out of being whatever impulse had earlier existed towards colonial development; at the same time, the growth of colonial politics had continued, leading to more efforts by the British to loosen their commitments overseas. But now there were new factors in the situation. The first of these was the breakdown of the general agreement between British political parties about these overseas issues, along with the revival of factions inside each of them. The second was the resurgence of international pressures upon the empire. The breakdown of agreement between Conservatives and Labour followed the crisis of 1931, which was itself a consequence of the slump. It thrust the Labour leadership into the hands of Lansbury, whose total, and loudly proclaimed, pacifism, put him at odds with the National Government, although privately their pacifism was not much less than his. Labour also opposed government policy over the India Bill, with Attlee attacking its safeguards, so that the Bill was the first proposal for Indian constitutional reforms since 1784 which did not go through Parliament on the nod. And the Labour party, perhaps under the influence of the Jewish Socialist Labour party of Britain which was affiliated to it, also opposed the Government over Palestine. Behind the new hostility between parties lay the revival of faction inside them. For Labour, the faction fights at first turned on the issue of pacifism versus collective security. But there were other voices in other rooms. When the Ethiopian crisis erupted in 1935, Fenner Brockway, for the Independent Labour party, would have nothing to do with the League of Nations, a capitalist thieves' kitchen. Nor would the Socialist League, which campaigned against sanctions since they did not mean to fight on behalf of 'Medieval Abyssinia'. After 1936 some of these factions, especially the Socialist League, switched their attacks against the Labour National Executive to the issue of Spain. This new campaign from the left—from the European left too—*avions pour l'Espagne*', diverted their attention from colonial issues. It has been remarked that Stafford Cripps, supposedly the most active friend of Indian nationalism, made hardly any reference to Indian affairs in the late nineteen-thirties. Aneurin Bevan spoke on India once. Faction inside the Conservative party also seized upon external issues. After the defeat of 1929 it was first evident in the campaign for Empire Free Trade, launched by Beaverbrook with the connivance of a number of Tory MPs and peers and the ambiguous counsel of Neville Chamberlain; then in the campaign to defeat the new plans for constitutional reform in India, directed by Churchill, with the support of Lord Lloyd, Sir Henry Page-Croft and others; and then in the attacks against the government's foreign policy, by Churchill from 1935 and from 1938 by Eden's group, the 'Glamour Boys' who included Amery, Cranborne and Duff Cooper. What interests us about these struggles is that each of them was really an attempt to knock someone out of power, sometimes an attempt to win power for oneself. They all tried to exploit a general disgruntlement inside Conservatism by focusing it upon a single issue which could be simplified or turned into a question of right and wrong for the benefit of Demos. Most of those who supported the Empire Crusade or denounced India Reform really had other things in mind, and their public statements are in a code which has to be broken into its true meaning: concern to hold power for the party and to win power in the party for the authors of the statements. Perhaps this judgement seems too sardonic for the great debate in Britain about Hitler and his demands which opened after 1933. Perhaps it is. But the historian of the British press and the German question during the nineteen-thirties has concluded that Nazi demands were like a funnel into which British attitudes on every conceivable question were poured. Until March 1939, most of those who denounced appeasement did so during the safe periods when there was comparative calm in Anglo-German relations. Whenever there appeared a danger of war, they were quick enough to preach appeasement's virtues.

Now let us turn and look at the working out of some of these trends during the early nineteen-thirties—the tighter domestic constraints upon overseas affairs, the growth of colonial politics, the influence of faction. First, let us take Beaverbrook's Empire Crusade, but only at a tangent, in terms of some of its implications and consequences. The campaign was made possible by the growing freedom of Conservative constituencies from the control of Central Office, encouraged in this case by subsidies to his own candidates from Beaverbrook. It was also helped by its good timing, by the disgruntlement of many Conservatives and the electoral consequences of Baldwin's leadership. Its programme for economic integration of the empire was never on—it would have been electorally impossible, both in Britain and in Canada. But it is a mark of the Conservative demoralization that the leadership treated it with so much deference until the by-election in St George's, Westminster. Beaverbrook, of course, was pressing for the full-strength version of Imperial Customs Union, food taxes and all; his campaign picked up support from Conservative constituency parties—'there exists', reported Topping, the Chief Conservative Agent, 'an air of uneasiness and unrest that alarms me'. Beaverbrook intended the Customs Union to extend over the entire empire, not merely the white dominions. 'The non-self-governing colonies', he declared in *My Case for Empire Free Trade*, 'are entirely controlled . . . by the British Parliament . . . these colonies, if they were brought into fiscal union with Great Britain, would be brought in by the decision of our Parliament . . . not of Parliaments abroad.' This remark shows an almost stupendous ignorance of how the imperial system worked. It totally neglects the political developments in these territories. It shows, too, how even the most sweeping form of Empire Free Trade was merely an extreme form of imperialist exploitation, designed above all to help the British domestic economy. If Beaverbrook had triumphed, then Rosa Luxemburg's theory of imperialism would have been proved right. But he did not triumph. For us the most interesting aspect of this example of faction, as Miss Gillian Peele has recently written, is that if it had succeeded, the next outbreak of Conservative faction, the revolt against Baldwin's India policy, would probably not have taken place.

Now let us turn to the complexities of the eastern sector of empire. The British empire, like the Roman, possessed both its western and its eastern wings. It had been the western segment of Diocletian's partition which had gone down first, while the eastern empire flourished. In the British case it was the other way round. Already in the early nineteen-twenties, it had seemed that the imperial system east of Cairo was failing. It had been reprieved by the petering out of agitation in India, which allowed the British to concentrate upon lessening their imperial load elsewhere and to bargain with punier forces such as King Fuad in Egypt, King Faysal in Iraq and the Grand Mufti and Dr Weizmann in Palestine. By 1929 the Indian question was becoming insistent again. Upon the reasons for this revival we cannot elaborate here, but one of the most telling was the impossibility of unifying Indian politics and of preventing splits between the politicians working in the local arenas who then opened cracks in the higher political arenas as well. There was faction in the districts, in the provinces, and at the national level. Gandhi and the high command of Congress were driven into a new challenge to the Raj, whether they liked it or not. Indeed, the great Government of India Act of 1935, which has so enthralled the constitutional historians, can be more realistically seen as a combined operation between the factions of politicians in India and the factions of Conservative politicians in Britain. It is usual to discuss the making of the Act in terms of irreconcilable communities and unobtainable federations. But it is at least as instructive to look at it in terms of power and profit. Throughout Irwin's term as Viceroy, his chief tactical aim was to cut off the

Gandhians, the agitational wing, from those Indian politicians who were willing to work the constitution. Of course that meant political concessions, so as to give the constitutionalists a good hand to play. His chief strategical aims were two. First, he strove to keep India in the empire, so he had to settle 'the real question, whether all this Indian nationalism that is growing and bound to grow, can be guided along imperial, or will more and more get deflected onto separatist lines'. Secondly, he was willing to give Indian politicians control over the provinces. But the British had to keep control over the central government, so as to ensure command over defence, foreign policy and internal security. After all, these were the keys of the political kingdom. Hanging on to New Delhi was worth a few declarations about dominion status in the sweet by and by. India had been the battering-ram of British expansion in Asia; it would still be the protector of those gains. So the plans for political change which Irwin imposed upon the Labour Government in 1929 and which were continued by the National Government in 1931 were meant to revise the workings but not to weaken the realities of British power in India.

But this advantage had to be paid for. During the nineteen-twenties, there had been a fiscal autonomy convention that Britain would not intervene in fixing the Indian tariff. At first it had been gingerly applied. But the world slump forced the Government of India to try to raise the duties on imported cottons in 1929, 1931 and 1933. In these commercial matters, New Delhi was trapped inside its political calculations. Needing all the help it could get against agitational politics, it did not dare to embitter the Bombay millowners, who might hit back by financing the agitators. But, awkwardly enough, the duties fell on British cottons. What was sweet for Bombay was dire for Lancashire, and measures which brought easement for New Delhi brought agony to Whitehall. For Lancashire was not without defences. It had more than sixty MPs. Hence the anguish with which British Cabinets, Conservative, Labour and National alike, heard of each new Indian tariff demand. In 1929 there was 'a general feeling of consternation' in Baldwin's Cabinet; in 1931 'another tiresome tussle in the Cabinet this morning', reported Wedgwood Benn, the Labour Secretary of State for India; in 1934 Hoare, his Conservative successor, was deep in the dumps—'if the moderates in Lancashire go off the deep end ... I shudder to think of the results on my Party in the House of Commons'.

Here is a spectacular case of how developments in colonial politics could now impinge upon domestic politics in Britain herself. It is striking to see that both Labour and National Governments pushed the reform plans ahead, in spite of Lancashire's political leverage. The plans were much disliked both by the employers and the Trade Unions, but the politicians were resigned to the need to finesse their opposition. Why? It made trouble in domestic politics. But it made sense in imperial terms. Indeed it was in these terms a necessity. British Governments were dragged into the risks and tedium of Indian constitutional reform by the need in India to round up politicians who might otherwise stray along separatist trails. There were still higher risks, in the forms of the factions in the Conservative party. At the most, thought Hoare, in his morose way, only thirty Conservatives liked the India Bill; as for those who were dragooned into voting for it, what struck his Under-Secretary, R. A. Butler, was 'their attitude of boredom'. On the other side, there were at least eighty Conservatives against it. Some of this opposition was grounded on the desire that the meteor flag of England should still terrific burn above the citadels of India. The party still contained 'imperialists of the Second Jubilee', as Baldwin remarked. But there were other grounds for opposition. Some Conservatives joined in because they disliked the party's captivity inside the coalition of the National Government. Others, especially in the constituencies, joined it out of a dissatisfaction over entirely different issues. At the Annual Conference in 1934 the Indian reform proposals just scraped through by 543 votes to 520, but many of the opponents were much more irritated at the fiasco over the Unemployment Assistance Board and the result of the Wavertree by-election than by half-naked fakirs standing on the steps of Viceregal Lodge. Joined to the strictures of three Dukes, Deaf Jim Salisbury, the Old India Hands, Page-Croft and some of the Courtauld family were others whose oppositions offered a teasing correlation: Churchill himself, Lord Lloyd and some of the spear-carriers in the later campaign against the appeasement of Nazi Germany, such as Sir Roger Keyes and Brendan Bracken. But the connection is more tantalizing than exact, because this group also contains Lady Houston, whose spear was to point in the opposite direction.

From another point of view, the India Bill was a monstrous load upon British domestic politics. It was under consideration from 1931 to 1933, and was on the stocks from 1933 to 1935. Between 1934 and 1935 the Government had to fight through parliament a gargantuan bill of 473 clauses and sixteen schedules. Its passage was embellished by six hundred speeches by Hoare and his answers to fifteen thousand questions. This war of attrition wrecked the time-tables of Westminster and delayed the course of British politics. So long as the Bill's fate was uncertain, so was the leadership of the Conservative party. Until it became a statute, the government could not call a General Election. The growth of colonial politics was exacting a revenge upon the development of British politics.

For those in the councils of state, the romantic imperialism of Churchill now looked obsolete. 'Sensible men of all Parties', in the prim judgement of Lord Irwin, 'do not any longer think along these lines.' Certainly they did not do so about Middle East oil. In 1901 W. K. D'Arcy won a concession to look for oil over five-sixths of Persia. In 1909 D'Arcy's interests were taken over by the Anglo-Persian Oil Company, and in 1914 the British Government bought a controlling interest in the Company. We are not much concerned with the operations of the Company in Persia, except to note that the British conquest of Iraq was related to the security of the oilfields in southern Persia. But we are concerned with the fact that after the war their security was not jeopardized by the new assertion of Persian independence by Reza Shah. British control of Persian oil did not require Britain to rule over Persia. The Shah could look after British interests. What does concern us is the Company's efforts to extend its holdings in the Middle East proper, first of all in Iraq.

The greatest authority on Middle East oil has instructed us about the origins of the Iraq Petroleum Company. It was, wrote Calouste Gulbenkian, 'a unique Company born of prolonged and arduous diplomatic and economic negotiation'. During the days of the Turkish empire, Gulbenkian had reported so sanguinely about oil prospects in the Turkish vilayats of Mesopotamia that the Sultan Abdul Hamid had deftly transferred ownership of large tracts to his own private account. Both the Germans (through the Antolia Railway Company) and the British (through the Anglo-Persian Oil Company) tried to get concessions, and in 1914 they fused their interests into the Turkish Petroleum Company [TPC] in which Gulbenkian, for services rendered, was given a five per cent interest. Defeat in the war locked out the German claim. In 1920 the British reluctantly agreed to transfer it to the French in return for the right to build a pipeline from Iraq through the new French sphere in Syria to the Mediterranean.

The French were one thing, but the Americans were another and the British kept their prospectors out of Persia. But the American demand for an Open Door policy, reminiscent of the old western slogans in China, could not be resisted for long. Next to demand admission were Standard Oil who lay behind the American demand. It was hard to resist. After all, Iraq was a mandated territory. Moreover, all countries, including Britain, were still dependent on the United States of America for most of their oil. There were long negotiations. On 27 June 1927, the oil flowed 'wild' from the well spudded in at Baba Gurgur. This showed that the geologists had hit a jackpot in Iraq and it speeded matters up. Where diplomacy had failed, the gush of oil succeeded. Hence the agreement of 1928 by which the stock of the Turkish/Iraq Petroleum Company was readjusted. Anglo-Persian, Royal Dutch Shell, the Compagnie Française des Pétroles and the Near East Development Company (which was Standard Oil of New Jersey and Socony) were each to have 23.75 per cent leaving five per cent to Gulbenkian.

This agreement contained two very important clauses. The Americans did not want such a big conglomeration as the Iraq Petroleum Company to go into competition with other oil companies, and they did not want to pay taxes on its earnings. So the Company was turned into a non-profit making concern, each of the shareholder companies taking its proportion of the oil produced by the group as a whole. Thus the Iraq Petroleum Company became a sort of charity, doing good to its members by stealth, very much by stealth. The second clause has had an enormous effect on the later history of the Middle East oil concessions. The groups comprising the Company agreed to a so-called 'self-denying clause'. All their activities in oil production were to be carried on collectively under the umbrella of the Company and not by individual firms, at least that was to be so in those territories which had previously belonged to the Turkish empire. These were the so-called 'red-circle' territories, including Iraq, Saudi Arabia, Bahrein, and Qatar and many of the other sheikhdoms in the Persian Gulf, except Kuwait. Persia itself was also excluded.

The agreement was kept secret. It had been made because the partners in the cartel had different interests, not easily reconcilable. On the one side stood the Big Three (Anglo-Persian, Royal Dutch Shell and the American Group, Standard Oil of New Jersey and Socony–Vacuum). On the other side stood the Smaller Two, the French and Gulbenkian who stood to lose if individual firms in the group were allowed to scramble for oil. They insisted on the clause in self-defence. Their formula was simple: no self-denying clause, no consent to the general agreement. The importance of the clause soon became clear. In 1932 Standard Oil of California found oil in Bahrein. They were not members of the consortium, and they were separate from Standard Oil of New Jersey. In 1933 Standard Oil of California won a large oil concession in Saudi Arabia in rather shady circumstances, abetted by St John Philby, a renegade Indian Civil Service officer, a former Trinity man, and father of Philby the spy. These invasions alarmed the Big

Three in what had now been renamed the Iraq Petroleum Company. But Bahrein and Saudi Arabia were both red-circle territories, to which the self-denying ordinance applied. They could hardly bargain with the invaders without the consent of all the members of their group. France and Gulbenkian were not inclined to agree. Could they then redraw the red-circle so as to exclude Saudi Arabia and Bahrein? Again France and Gulbenkian would not agree, or only on condition that they could charge sky-high prices for their own oil. Hence there was no way of buying out or buying in to the concessions obtained by Standard Oil of California. The result was that Standard Oil of California, father of Caltex which was father of Aramco (the Arabian American Company which was father of King Faysal and Khalid and Sheik Yamani of Saudi Arabia) kept the concessions in Saudi Arabia and Bahrein. But the Iraq Petroleum Company did not do so badly, winning concessions in the Gulf States of Qatar and Abu Dhabi.

What is the point of all this peering into the family trees of Middle East oil? Well, in the first place, the subject is deeply interesting and under studied. I have discussed it without mention of governments. Yet by the nineteen-thirties oil was an important national interest. In fact, the British Government's role had not been large. It had been instrumental in securing the main concession from Iraq in 1925. It wanted the pipeline to the Mediterranean to include a fork-line going to Haifa. But it would not pay for it. In 1929 and in 1930 the Labour Government would not spend or guarantee a shilling (Snowden's words) towards it. In the event, it was Faysal, no lover of the French, who insisted that a branch of the line must go to Haifa (in that way, a rather longer stretch of the pipe would go through Iraq territory). Iraq Petroleum Company had to pay. But throughout, the British Government would not pay, in spite of the strategic arguments for having a Mediterranean oil outlet in British hands.

Secondly, let us note that despite all the political power it had amassed in the Middle East, the British Government was quite unable to prevent the Americans from obtaining a share in the Turkish Petroleum Company. Thirdly, despite Britain's political power in the Middle East, her Government had no strong agent for protecting its own oil interests. Her agent had to be the Anglo-Persian Oil Company, holder of less than one quarter of the Turkish Petroleum Company and the performance of that Company showed how disunited a large consortium could be, a fact worth remembering when we inveigh against multi-nationals today. Because of this the British Government could do nothing to stop other American companies from moving into Saudi Arabia and Bahrein.

What all this shows is how obsolescent imperialism had become for the pursuit of national interest. Caltex and Aramco did not need an American political presence in order to walk out with the biggest prizes in Middle East oil. Of course from one point of view, the British did well out of these oleaginous scrambles. Yet they did not need to rule a country to suck out its oil, as Persia shows. But from another point of view, the British were maintaining a vast system of security throughout the Middle East in which various brands of Standard Oil could operate free of political expenses. None of this made a convincing argument for the retention of the Middle East through the old techniques of rule. On the contrary it offered new arguments for cutting the imperial commitments.

Like all the arguments between the wars for disengagement, for lessening the burden, for taking the cash and letting the credit go, this line of thinking rested on the major premise that no great power threatened to overthrow the British system. By 1942 the security of British oil supplies was to look very different when Field Marshal von Kleist's First Panzer Army was driving through the Caucasus. The British world system entered the nineteen-thirties with the bland assumptions of the nineteen-twenties: that there were severe constraints in domestic politics against her costly commitments overseas, and there were stirrings in the subject territories. Hence there ought to be some easements in the system. But the nineteen-thirties, the first of the two iron decades, revived a factor absent since 1918, the challenge from great powers. Thus the nineteen-thirties also revived the terror that a new war would knock the empire into smithereens.

The Far Eastern Crisis of 1931 to 1933 dashed into emptiness the hopeful outlook of the nineteen-twenties. By the end of that decade the British had only seven British battalions and one Indian battalion in China, although there were 22,000 British subjects and large interests to be safeguarded there. Yet the government saw no risk in procrastinating over the Singapore base and in denying reinforcements to China itself. Once the Japanese attacked in Manchuria, and still more when they moved against the Treaty Ports, all this optimism smashed into hard facts. At the Foreign Office Vansittart noted:

If Japan continues unchecked, our position and vast interests in the far east will never recover. This may well spread to the middle east. . . . By ourselves, we must eventually swallow any and every humiliation in the far east. But if there is some limit to American submissiveness, this is not necessarily so.

Much of British opinion was agitated by the Japanese attacks. It was not, however, prepared to do anything difficult or dangerous to repel them. Nor was the government. 'We have to remember', wrote the Foreign Secretary, Simon, to the Prime Minister in 1932, 'that although America expresses great surprise if we do not work with them . . . if we do, they will leave us with the brunt of the work and of the blame'—a view repeated by Neville Chamberlain who had always thought it a mistake in 1922 to free the Japanese bird in hand so as to grope for the American bird in the bush. It was in official thinking that the effects of Japanese aggression were mainly felt. In 1932 at the insistence of the Chiefs of Staff the Ten Year Rule was scrapped, and a Defence Requirements Committee was set up. But the Treasury said there was no money for weapons and Ramsay MacDonald talked about his conscience, because the War Office wanted to prepare an expeditionary force for war on the continent.

Now begins the period well described by General Pownall in his diary as 'the financial disintegration of Cabinet decisions'. By 1933, it was clear that the Disarmament Conference was a failure. Now the Chiefs of Staff announced that Britain's defence priorities must be, first, the Far East, then Europe, and thirdly the defence of India. But there was not much money available from the Treasury, which under Neville Chamberlain and Warren Fisher continued to sigh for the old and cheaper policy of an understanding with Japan, a more reliable ally than the USA. Still the priority given to the Far East now compelled government to press ahead with equipping the Singapore Base. Since 1921 the Admiralty had planned a strategy which would compensate for Britain's weakness in the Far East and the chances of a Japanese attack by converting Singapore into a fortress and by sending the Main Fleet there, so as to destroy the Japanese navy. The Main Fleet was to go to Singapore; but how was it to get there? In 1935 British opposition to the Italian onslaught on Ethiopia had a disastrous effect on British security in the Far East. Once sanctions had been clapped on Italy, Mussolini's resentments drove him towards an alliance with Germany. This was compounded by the outbreak of the Civil War in Spain in 1936, when Italy and Germany supported Franco, whose victory would tilt still further the balance in the Mediterranean. By 1936 the British Government was reluctantly forced by the Committee of Imperial Defence to consider the strategic case that all these troubles would cut British communications in the Mediterranean. In that event, British communications with the Far East would have to be re-routed. But what would happen to the strategy of Main Fleet to Singapore?

By 1937 the problem was tighter still. In that year, Eden was arguing that Italy should be classed as a potential enemy, especially if she could gain German support. In that case, reported the Chiefs of Staff, all British reinforcements for Egypt would have to sail around South Africa. By that year, 1937, all the crises in different continents were beginning to interlock to Britain's disadvantage. In that year the Chiefs of Staff were contemplating a war in which 'we, with France and her allies, might be involved against Germany, Italy and Japan'. It was essential for Britain to 'support France and the Low Countries against German aggression'. On this argument, because of the continental commitment it postulated, Britain must strive for European security, but how could the fleet be spared from European waters if Britain was to fight Germany? In any case, if the Mediterranean was blocked, how could the Main Fleet sail to Singapore in time to check the Japanese? Less far afield, how was Egyptian security to be assured? Sending reinforcements there would provoke the Italians. It might also irritate the Egyptians. It would weaken the defences in western Europe, and that might encourage the Germans. In other words the task of containing Germany for European reasons greatly complicated the task of containing Italy and Japan for imperial reasons. By 1937, it seems, Britain lay trapped in a set of interlocking problems which were insoluble in the event of the worst possible case, a war which from its outbreak would have to be waged simultaneously against Germany, Italy and Japan. Of course this did not happen in 1939, but the possibility of the worst case could not be ignored.

It is characteristic of any power which works a world system that it cannot isolate any one situation and decide it on its own individual merits. Every possible solution squeezes the trigger of another problem. Every strategic case modulates into another. Every local security nurtures the blood-red blossom of war with its heart of fire. No world system has provided such spectacular evidence of these interlockings than Britain's did by the second half of the nineteen-thirties. Too few resources, too many commitments; not enough friends, too many enemies. Not since 1779 had Britain been faced with danger from three powers at once, and that was not an inspiring precedent. During the nineteen-twenties Britain's imperial interests had taken second place to her domestic concerns; by the nineteen-thirties, they were put at risk by her European imperatives. Amid this confusion, the government did not get much help from its military advisers. In 1936 Montgomery-Massingberd, the Chief of Imperial General Staff, gave the impression that his chief care was to keep out of the war. His successor, Sir Cyril Deverell, together with his three Directors of Military Operations, of

Staff Duties and of Military Training, wanted to send an army across the Channel but with no clear idea of what it was to do when it arrived there.

This would not do and it could not go on. One way to cut the knots lay in appeasement. Appeasement meant seeking diplomatic easements in Europe and trying to lessen commitments there. Appeasement in Europe was to begin a renewed imperialism outside Europe. And so, too, was the war which broke out in 1939. Now in 1937, we have Hitler on the move. That was the end of an old song and the start of a new opera.

V

At the Foreign Office in 1938 Cadogan noted gloomily that 'we are faced at the other side of the world with a situation not unlike the one that confronts us here. . . . It is as difficult to find the answers to the Far Eastern problem as it is to the European one.' But over and above the strategic problem lay the apparent obsolescence of empire as a method of exercising influence in the world. As a system of direct colonial rule over other peoples, it offered too many hostages to propaganda. During the nineteen-thirties, political warfare preceded armed warfare, just as it was to follow it in the later nineteen-forties. All over the Middle East the British positions were vulnerable to German and Italian propaganda. In India, again, there was Japanese propaganda to be reckoned with. In 1942 a poster celebrating the fall of Singapore shows an Asian delightedly waving the Japanese and the Chinese flags.

Our first task is to look at the situation between 1937 and 1939. The policy of appeasement has now produced its own revisionist school of history, and much of its case rests on the insoluble problems for British policy which were produced by the interlocking of crises half a world away from each other. The extraordinary richness of the Cabinet Papers, the records of the Committee of Imperial Defence and of the Chiefs of Staffs Committee, now show us that the British system was a sort of imperial Laocoon, writhing as it was pulled hither and yon by those who sought to squeeze it out of existence. The best argument for appeasement is that one way for Laocoon to try to simplify his problems was by squaring one or other of the serpents. But here there is a danger that we may be led by our material into looking at these issues of world politics from the British viewpoint alone. Laocoon has his problems; but we should also pay heed to the problems of the serpents. Neither Germany nor Japan was running a world system as the British were doing. They clearly stood to gain by coordination. Yet the Anti-Comintern Pact of 1936 to 1937 was only rodomontade, a speculation in futures. Efforts in 1938 and 1939 to convert these futures into spot cash were failures. And the Tripartite Pact, which was signed in September 1940, never served to coordinate the actions of the Three Powers. They could never agree about the right moment to raise the Arabs or the Indians against the British; those behind cried 'Forward!' and those before cried 'Back!'.

With that reservation, let us now consider how these inter-continental crises interlocked to Britain's disadvantage. We have already seen how the British position had come to be challenged by German rearmament, Italian resentments about Abyssinia and the Axis help for the rebels in Spain. After July 1937 the incident at the Marco Polo Bridge brought on the undeclared war between Japan and China. And by August, the Japanese were fighting in Shanghai, which put vast British interests at risk. That summer London heard that a German move was imminent in central Europe, while Italy put two armed divisions into Libya and stirred up the Middle East Arabs against the British. By 1937, the Chiefs of Staff were studying a case in which Britain would soon be at war simultaneously with Germany, Italy and Japan.

Everyone knows how the British used diplomacy between 1937 and 1939 to get either the German or the Italian burden off their backs. But not everyone is as aware that the appeasement practised in Europe was not matched by a similar appeasement in the Far East. Appeasement of Japan had been tried in 1935–36 in a diplomatic attempt to win back some of the benefit of the old Anglo-Japanese Alliance. This had been a failure. But after 1937 Britain was very far from caving in to Japan. Her opposition had to be cautious because of military and naval weakness. But a number of financial moves were made to help the Chinese: for example, granting them export credits and making them a currency stabilization loan. Now why was this? Chamberlain took the view that British economic interests in the Far East were too great to allow the Japanese a free hand, that appeasement would alienate the Americans and that the Japanese were sticking their heads into a bag with their China war which they were unlikely to win outright. If China was saved, Britain's economic interests would flourish again.

All this shows us that there was more in Chamberlain's world policy than meets the eye. As usual, the diplomatic historians let us down. They concentrate on the origins of the war which broke out in September 1939. But until the end of 1941, that war was no more than a European civil war. We should not copy Hitler's mistake of confusing European policy with world policy. There was a good deal in the argument that the Japanese army had taken on more than it could manage in China; after 1937 General Kita was busy organizing régimes of collaborators in China. They were rather more interested in growing opium in Jehol and getting their cut from the gambling casinos in Shanghai than in running the country in Japanese interests. And the army replaced them with the famous régime of Wang Ching-wei at Nanking, collaborator *par excellence* of Chinese historiography. This reliance on a kind of Chinese Marshal Pétain in Nanking while they went on struggling to crush the Chinese de Gaulle in Chungking shows that the Japanese were not so strong as they made out. Therefore the cautious resistance of the British was justified, but only up to a point, because the rival régime of Chiang Kai-shek in Chungking was not minded to look after British interests either.

This policy meant that what the British were playing in the Far East was a long, slow game. But suppose their opponents kicked the table over? What if the Japanese navy, which was not tied up in the Chinese bag like the Japanese army, decided to swoop upon South-east Asia? In the official mind of the British Chiefs of Staff the answer to these dire questions was 'Main Fleet to Singapore', the plan elaborated from 1921, that a Japanese attack would be contained by moving the bulk of the British fleet to the fortress that was to be built at Singapore. Procrastination throughout the nineteen-twenties, dilatoriness through-out the nineteen-thirties, meant that the Singapore base would not be ready until 1940. But worse than that, it became harder and harder to see how the Main Fleet was to get there. In reply to the anxious Australians, Chamberlain assured them that Britain would send a fleet to Singapore, even if she were at war with Germany, Italy and Japan. But the size of that fleet could not be settled in advance. Behind the cloudy phrase lay some hard thinking in secret by the official mind. By the spring of 1939 Britain possessed fifteen capital ships, only ten of them immediately serviceable. If there was to be war against Germany and Italy, the Admiralty planned to station seven of these ships in Home Waters, three in the eastern Mediterranean.

But say Japan joined the war? The Main Fleet to Singapore might come from the eastern Mediterranean. But if the Mediterranean were to be stripped of sea power, what could happen to the new policy of offering guarantees to Greece, Rumania and Turkey? Something would have to give. Chamberlain ominously told the Committee of Imperial Defence on 2 May 1939 that 'should this country be defeated, the fate of the Dominions would be sealed'. So naval charity would have to begin at home and the Far East and the Pacific would have to take their chance.

The Committee concluded that they could not say how soon reinforcements could be sent to Singapore or how large these reinforcements would
be. Of course this alarmed the Australians. They claimed that only the
previous November (1938) the Admiralty had spoken of sending seven
capital ships to Singapore. Chamberlain was dubious. If there were a
war with Japan alone, then 'the temptation to the Axis Powers to take
advantage of the situation would be almost irresistible'. The Australians
pressed for a plain answer. Inskip told them on 11 July 1939 that 'no
definite decision has been reached and no definite plan formulated'.
This could hardly be called a plain answer. But its implications were not
very obscure. In fact, five days earlier, the Committee of Imperial
Defence had concluded that relief for Malaya must not be expected
before ninety days after a Japanese attack, and it might take as long as
six months.

Just as the Singapore base had been the touchstone of imperial
indecisiveness during the nineteen-twenties, when the going was good,
so its reinforcement was an indication of imperial weakness during the
late nineteen-thirties, when international pressure had now appeared as
the chief threat to empire. There are many other instances of weakness
before the new threat. Two cases need to be mentioned briefly. The first
is in Africa. Perhaps there was a role for appeasement to play in tropical
Africa? In 1937 the Cabinet discussed the transfer to Germany of her old
colonies in West Africa (not in East Africa, which was, as always in
British thinking, considered much more important from a strategic
point of view than the West). In 1938 the Prime Minister went further,
suggesting that the Germans might administer 'certain territories' in
Portuguese and Belgian Africa; it is always more attractive for sacrifices
to fall on the territories of other peoples. All this fell flat in Berlin. As
Goering said to the British Ambassador: 'if you offered us the whole of
Africa, we would not accept it as the price of Austria'.

The other case is Palestine. In the open forum of politics, the question
of Palestine was often discussed in a sense favourable to the Jews.
Chamberlain's Cabinet contained two ministers devoted to Jewish
interests, Ormsby-Gore and Walter Elliott, both of them gentlemen-in-
waiting at the salon of Baffy Dugdale, niece of Balfour and an upholder
of his declaration. Labour, too, as we have seen, was sympathetic to
Zionism. All this benevolence grew more strained as Hitler, like some
Malthusian devil with a pitchfork, chased Jews out of Germany. Many
came to Palestine, especially in 1936. Hence the Arabs rose in 1936. The
chief recommendation of the Royal Commission in 1937 was devised by
the Beit Professor in the University of Oxford. Professor Coupland

suggested that Palestine should be partitioned into Arab and Jewish sections which were both to remain connected to Britain. In effect this plan would have furnished Britain with a loyal colony in the eastern Mediterranean, garrisoned with what we may call Jewish Gurkhas and providing two million defenders for Haifa, the terminal for the Iraq pipeline and a potential naval base. Weizmann was attracted by the plan. And from today's perspective, we can see how it might have altered the history of the Middle East. But official thinking argued against this. The Arab rising tied up British troops in Palestine, which would be needed in Egypt when war came. So the rising had to be ended. But the Palestine problem affected more important Arabs than the Palestinian Arabs; it affected Egypt, Saudi Arabia and Iraq. By January 1939 the British Chiefs of Staff saw that the goodwill of these states was 'of great importance to our imperial strategy'. This was a question not only of communication, but also of oil. The Saudis, for example, could threaten the pipeline from Iraq to the Mediterranean, or they could make trouble in Kuwait or along the Gulf. How, then, was Arab goodwill to be kept? The Committee of Imperial Defence in February 1939 approved the view that when war started 'the necessary measures would at once be taken . . . to bring about complete appease ment of Arab opinion'. The British White Paper of May 1939 announced that land sales and immigration in Palestine were henceforth to be restricted, and promised an independent state of Palestine within ten years. Here again we can see the tribulations that are inevitable in a system of world power; here again, crises in different continents interlock; here again, decisions are made for extraneous reasons. Policy in Palestine has to swing about because of the Italian threat to Egypt, because of the diplomacy of oil, and because of German and Italian propaganda all over the Middle East.

From 1937 it was fairly plain to the official mind that Britain would soon be at war again. This was not to say that it was plain to Chamberlain. Some of the historical revisionism about appeasement relies on strategic appreciations which it does not appear the Prime Minister accepted. Chamberlain, as it seems, resembled Hitler in that they both tended to believe that will-power could overcome facts. To both of them we might apply the judgement which Mommsen made of Caesar—'Insight into what is possible and impossible is what dis- tinguishes the hero from the adventurer.' But if the essence of appeasement lay in simplification, then Chamberlain and the military advisers were in good agreement. From 1935 professional advice kept on warning government against the risk of colliding with Germany and

Japan at the same time. It called for an expeditionary force for the Continent which should be reinforced by a further twelve divisions within eight months of the first embarkation. Chamberlain doubted the wisdom of these plans and repeatedly opposed them in Cabinet on much the same grounds that Liddell Hart opposed them in the press. They would end, as they had ended in 1914, with an unlimited liability for a land force in France or Flanders. This was an eventuality which terrified public opinion. And in any case, the plans rested upon a silly dogma. What was needed was a rational distribution of resources.

Once he became Prime Minister in May 1937, Chamberlain pressed for his own policy. In December, the Chiefs of Staff urged the need 'to reduce the numbers of our potential enemies'. Later that month the Minister for the Coordination of Defence persuaded the Cabinet that the order of defence priorities ought to be, first, 'protecting this country from attack'; secondly, safeguarding imperial connections; thirdly, the defence of imperial possessions; then 'our further objective, which can only be provided after the other objectives have been met, is cooperation in the defence of any allies we may have in war'. The Regular Army should now define its primary role as that of imperial defence. The Territorial Army should also abandon the thought of fighting on the continent. It should now be responsible for anti-aircraft defence and for supporting the Regulars in Imperial Defence. Hore-Belisha, Secretary for War, summed up the new course for the army: 'to organise it with a military prepossession in favour of a continental commitment is wrong'.

So much for Europe; and to make sure, it was decided that the Regular Field Force should not be equipped on a scale for European warfare. Clearly, this strategic policy meant a return to imperialism. It was an attempt to struggle back to the classical strategy of British expansion which had deployed her resources to help her interests outside Europe rather than to break windows with golden guineas in the Low Countries. So we find that the empire, and the imperialism whose weakness and obsolescence since 1919 we have been assiduously noting, was now reviving once more. The decline of the British empire had been followed, not by its fall, but by its rise. As dying, yet behold it lived. Now the coma is ended and the fit begins anew. Put more drily, we can say that the strains upon the British world system, both in the Middle and the Far East, seemed too great for the European commitments to be shouldered as well. Therefore defence now appealed to diplomacy to call off the European bets which Britain could no longer cover. But the imperial bets were to be doubled.

This argument is very helpful to my general case, that the decline of empire was a discontinuous process and that its fall has been dated far too early by persons with more ideological than political sense. At the same time, we can push the antithesis between a continental and an imperial commitment too far. To some extent, they were bound to fit together. When Britain decided to reactivate the Indian army in 1938–39, its modernization could obviously be helpful to either commitment. Again, it was all very well to old-soldier the French by saying that 'perhaps' the British would send two divisions, but there were political limits to these tests of French diplomatic virtue.

These are obvious arguments. Now let us try one from technology. Weapons speak louder than words. The new emphasis on the air defence of Great Britain was possible because of the greater capacity of fighters. Spitfires and Hurricanes were born out of some rather tepid requirements in 1932. But aircraft engines were rapidly being improved, and the specifications were quickly rewritten to exploit the new technology. By 1930 an aero-engine could develop four hundred horse-power; by the mid-thirties, six hundred horse-power; by 1939, one thousand. The Hurricane first flew in 1935, the Spitfire in 1936. Let us add that the first radar station was set up in 1936. Very well; technology aided air defence. But it also aided the air offensive. The development of the immediately obsolescent Wellesleys and Harrows did not help, but the Wellingtons, Whitleys and Hampdens were also made possible by the new technology. These twin-engined bombers were designed to fly 1,500 miles and they were meant to bomb Germany. Perhaps we should add that the B17, the Flying Fortress, a four-engined plane, first flew in 1935. The new technology then allowed the British to bomb western Germany, and obviously they could fly further and bomb harder if they took off from France. But perhaps the most telling comment on the strategy of limited liability was made by General Ironside at an army conference in 1938. 'Let us make imperial plans only. After all, the politicians will be hard put to it to refuse to help France and Belgium when the 1914 show begins again'—shades of Sir Henry Wilson.

In any case, the policy of limited liability in Europe was soon rushed off the scene by new fears of Germany, not long after the would-be peacemakers had met at Munich. By January 1939, the British Chiefs of Staff were again resigned to the probability that Britain would have to send large land forces to Germany. On 1 February, the British agreed to defend the Dutch and the Swiss against what was suspected to be an imminent German attack. Then, as everyone knows, the shock of the German occupation of Prague provoked the British into their guarantees of Greece, Rumania, and Poland, together with their efforts to hook the Turks, and into a Ministry of Supply and into conscription, both of which obviously assumed a large land army and the end of limited liability.

But because they were not so much opposites as corollaries, this swing back to a continental strategy did not weaken the new emphasis on the defence of the empire. In fact, the revival of the imperial commitment became stronger in 1939, certainly stronger than at any time since 1919. Even when Chamberlain and his advisers recognized that there was no going back to the days of the Elder Pitt and that a field force would have to go to Europe, they pressed ahead with forming heavier garrisons outside Europe. By 1938 the government was clear that a field force had to be built up in Egypt. By 1939 these plans had broadened into larger schemes for military action in the Mediterranean, Egypt, Palestine Malta, Gibraltar and Cyprus, as well as in the Red Sea and in East Africa. These operations were intended to attack the Italian empire in Africa and the Italian presence in the Mediterranean, in a word, as the Chiefs of Staff explained with relish in April 1939, 'to knock out the weaker partner in the Axis as soon as possible'. By July they came to recognize that Mussolini could not be shoved down the trap-door quickly and that the possibility of war with Japan was likelier and troops would be urgently needed in Burma and Malaya. Once more, Laocoon was writhing between the serpents.

Reinforcing all these garrisons was not easy politically. In Egypt, few of the Pashas welcomed the prospect of Mussolini entering Cairo on his white horse, but they were nervous about the political repercussions of more British troops being tucked around the Suez Canal. Iraq was difficult too. So, too, was Persia; so obviously was Palestine. But much more serious was the question: where were all these troops to come from? Of course, they would have to come from India. In spite of the constitutional folderols of the nineteen-twenties, the imperial crisis of the late nineteen-thirties was so terrible that the British had to cut the constitutional corners. By 1938, in the event of a war with Italy, India was to be billed for two brigade groups and four air squadrons to go to Egypt, one brigade group and two squadrons to Singapore, a brigade to Persia, a battalion to Aden, and a force of indefinite size to Iraq. These were promissory notes. Next year, in 1939, they came up for payment. By now, everything was going wrong. There was fear of imminent war in Libya and in East Africa. The Egyptian garrison needed to be strengthened by moving a brigade from Palestine. But Palestine was in the middle of a rebellion. All these maddeningly intractable questions fitted into each other like Chinese boxes.

By 1939 the Chiefs of Staff wanted to give up these off-the-peg arrangements and to 'pursue a policy of self-sufficiency for our forces and defence in the Middle East'; they had in mind an Imperial Strategic Reserve. (Incidentally, this was discussed on 24 February, before Hitler's spring upon Prague.) The plan demanded that troops should somehow or other be disengaged from Palestine, and that more troops should be sent to Egypt from India. Chamberlain agreed with a bad grace. Simon agreed with Chamberlain, as he nearly always did until September 1939. Lord Zetland was anxious about India, but then he was always anxious. Consider, then, the military commitments of India by 1939. The promissory notes issued by 1938 have already been listed. Now to them must be added: Force 'Heron' to go to Egypt; Force 'Wren' scheduled to go to Burma; Force 'Emu' on call for Singapore; and Indian artillery for Kenya. Surely, then, the wheel had come full circle? Had we not been at this point before—in Curzon's time? Once more the Indian army was to be moved around the world in British interests. But in 1939 we are not in Curzon's time. Indeed the wheel had spun past full circle. Assuredly India could still be persuaded into providing troops, but they would not be supplied on the old terms.

Let us look, then, more closely at the Indian army, which would have to strive for Britain since so many beautiful people in Hampstead and Oxford itself were too valuable to be risked in war. What interests us are the political implications of Britain's use of the Indian army in 1938–39, and indeed until the end of the Second World War in 1945. In 1938, the establishment of the Indian army was 55,000 British troops, 20,000 Gurkhas and 120,000 Indians (of whom some 51,000 were Muslims, 46,000 Hindus and 23,000 Sikhs). Between the wars, this army had lagged behind the times. The poverty of government and the require-ments of those Indian politicians who were working the constitution of the Raj had both called for parsimony in military affairs. Step by step the army became obsolescent. Now *bandobast* and bluff were all very well for punishing Afghans on the frontier or for rough-housing Indian rioters. But if the army was to take on Germans, Italians and Japanese (and in the end it took on all three of them), then it had to be purged and it had to be re-equipped in a modern form. Nodding plumes and gleaming lances were no longer enough; automatic weapons would have to be brought in.

Once the world-wide scale of British commitments in the face of international pressure had become plain, then it would have to be the

Indian army which provided much of the imperial mobile reserve. That meant that this army had to be dragged out of the Old Curiosity Shop and modernized. Now we come to the political implications. The better the Indian army, the higher the cost. Who was going to pay it? Even the obsolescent army was costing more than half the budget of the Government of India. Now the Generals wanted more, at first Rs 21 crores (say £16 million). There was small chance of raising this from the Indians. Since 1937, Indian politicians had been working the new constitution in most of the provinces. The stability of their ministries depended on their keeping most of the taxes they raised and giving the central government as little as possible. If the Viceroy tried to raise the sums needed for rearmament, the Congress ministries in the provinces would not stand for it. Sir James Grigg, Finance Member in India (later Secretary for War in London), set out the alternatives: in the first place there was the political argument: 'I cannot tax for these extra demands . . . if I raid the Sinking Fund not to give the provinces more revenue but to provide more money for less troops there will be a storm . . . such that the Congress Governments would seize the excuse for walking out. . . . India should be relieved of this new burden.' If the relief was not forthcoming, the new constitution in India would fail. But there was a strategic argument as well. As Grigg put it: 'We [India] are at the end of our resources . . . India's lot in the scheme of Empire Defence should be re-determined on the basis . . . of the U.K. bearing everything that can reasonably be accounted imperial.' So this is what it came to. In the interests of Imperial defensive security, the Indian army was to cost more. But in the interests of Indian political security, most of the additional cost was to fall on Britain.

There was to be a motorized division in India. Britain would pay for it. The rest of the Indian army was to be thinned down and re-equipped. Should the British taxpayer pick up the bill for this too? The British Treasury hoped not and said so, but the burden was inescapable. During 1939 an expert committee, the Chatfield Committee, was suggesting that Britain should pay over £34 million of Indian military costs. Of course, there was to be no stopping there. By an agreement between London and Delhi in 1940, the division of Indian defence expenditure was settled. India was to pay only the cost of specifically Indian defence. Let us look at the figures. In 1940 to 1941 Britain's contribution to Indian defence was £40 million and India's contribution to Indian defence was £49 million; by 1941 to 1942 Britain's contribution to Indian defence was £150 million and India's contribution £71 million. By 1942 to 1943 the estimate of Britain's contribution to Indian defence had risen to £270 million. By 1942 India was spending less than three per cent of what Britain was spending on the war effort and about one-third that of Canada. Certainly in 1942, with the Japanese pressing against the frontiers of Bengal and threatening Calcutta, this was defence at bargain prices.

The relationship between Britain and India can usually be more deeply analysed in financial than in constitutional terms. The position we are probing is a good example of that. Gandhi and Nehru made much of Britain's having declared war on India's behalf, without having consulted India, in September 1939. So she did. The outcome in military terms was that India during the war exploited Britain. But how could this have come about? Are not colonies supposed to have been exploited by their imperialist masters? In India this was no longer happening because of political developments there. Britain had made the 1935 constitution, as the Viceroy wrote in 1939, 'because we thought that way the best way of maintaining British influence in India'. So it had been necessary to conciliate the politicians before the war. In 1940, with the threat of civil disobedience, and indeed the threat of Indian links with Japan itself, it became imperative to conciliate the notables and the rich. So there was to be no heavy taxation on them. Bombay millowners and north Indian landed magnates could not be pushed too far; few rupees could be screwed out of them, but all these thin contributions had to be gratefully received. As Sir John Simon sarcastically said, 'India was fortunate indeed in having us behind her.' Under the threat of war, the empire was revived at last. But for the first time since the eighteenth century, it was the British taxpayer that was going to pay for it. Here, then, would be a way of testing his will for empire.

Our interest in the Second World War is limited to its effects on empire, both short-term and long-term. In the main we are not much concerned with the period of European civil war to 1941, but rather with the spread of fighting later to a world-wide scale. In the short term, the impact of war considerably strengthened the empire, so much so that the period between 1941 and 1945 has striking resemblances to the period between 1916 and 1922.

In the first place, the world-wide threat of disaster puts into power men who would never have won it by the electors' choice in peacetime—Lord Lloyd, Bracken, Beaverbrook and, of course, the Prime Minister, Churchill himself. Churchill's imperialism was not as thoughtful as Milner's or Curzon's, but it was no less ardent. Already in 1939, as First Lord of the Admiralty, he was denouncing the policy of what he called 'running after Gandhi and the Congress which is steadily wearing down the pillar of British authority'. As Prime Minister he did far more to harass his colleagues when they tried to keep Indian leaders on the British side. Amery, the frustrated Secretary of State for India, complained to Smuts in 1942 that:

the idea that it might be possible to reconcile India to the Commonwealth by conceding Indian aspirations under a workable constitution, just means nothing to him [Churchill]. We either govern India or are kicked out. I don't think that he has the slightest idea of the extent to which we have been kicked out already, or how impossible it is to hold our present position indefinitely except on terms which mean that we certainly shall be kicked out in the end.

There are deeper similarities between the two periods, not merely of temperament, but of strategy. Once again, there was to be a German attack through south Russia, just as the Germans and Turks had attacked in 1918. The *Seekriegsleitung* (the German naval command), who scanned wider maps than the German army, suggested following up the Balkan campaigns by putting German pressure on the Middle East. But there was dissension inside the German high command and it was decided to postpone any German attack on the Arab oil-producing land until after the success of Barbarossa. Nevertheless, the British feared German thrusts into the region that was now priceless to them; hence the British occupation of Syria, of Iraq and of Iran; hence, too, the discussion, at Russian invitation, of a possible British move into south Russia. This was Curzon all over again. Moreover, Churchill was not a Lloyd George, pressing for withdrawal from these exposed positions. By 1945, with both British and Russian troops in Iran, Eden hoped to arrange a joint evacuation. But the Prime Minister enjoyed holding the position. 'We had much better stay. It is easy to go and hard to return'.

At the same time India had been massively re-garrisoned. The forces based there were so strong that the rising of 1942, the Quit India Movement, much more dangerous, potentially, than the rising of 1857, was crushed in a twelfth of the time, in other words, in one month. As a field of operations India was unimportant. No one seriously planned to invade her. Germany and Japan could not synchronize their propaganda about India for the Indians; the issue was not interesting to the German army, stuck in Russia, or to the Japanese army, stuck in China. But Indian troops were as vital to British purposes as they had been during the First World War, defending the oilfields and the Middle East. In the campaigns east of Calcutta, for Singapore, Malaya, and Burma, the British seemed to be the Italians of the war in Asia, the soft underbelly of the front against Japan. But here, too, the Indian army eventually proved its worth in the counter-attacks against Japan in 1944–45. Another sign of India's importance lies in war supply. By 1943 India was producing more goods for the war than Australia, New Zealand and South Africa combined. Consider again the scale of operations designed for the defeat of Japan. By October 1945 the planners meant to assemble in India more than twenty-seven divisions (apart from those on internal security duties), 2,100 landing craft and up to 156 squadrons of the RAF (not to mention the vast number of American planes).

The old rule remained true. India remained one of the twin centres of British power in the world. An acute observer noted this after 1918: 'If anyone imagines that England would let India go without staking her last drop of blood, this is a sign of absolute failure to learn from the world war.' This was Hitler writing in *Mein Kampf*. This was echoed by Churchill, reporting his conversations in Cairo with Roosevelt and Chiang Kai-Shek. He had made it clear, he said, that 'while the British empire did not seek any territorial aggrandizement, neither were we prepared to make any territorial sacrifices'. This held good of the disaster areas of British imperialism as well. The humiliations in South-east Asia had not persuaded the British that they must pack up and go, although they had gone a long way towards weakening Australia's trust in Britain. In 1945, Mountbatten's command was estimating that, after the Japanese occupation, what Burma needed was years of 'resolute military occupation'. In Malaya and Singapore again, the British entered in 1945 like a bridegroom coming into his chamber. And yet Burma went in 1946, India in 1947 and the colonial empire in Africa had been dismantled by 1964.

Why was this? We shall waste our time if we look for the answer in the electoral choices of Demos in 1945. Attlee and Bevin were no less imperialist in 1945 than the Churchill Government had been before 1945; it was merely that they worked by new techniques. People do not become imperialists as a matter of ideology; they do so as a matter of necessity. With these suggestions in mind, we shall move to the sombre theme of the end of empire.

VI

Between the wars British statesmen had been fearful for their empire. It had seemed so fragile that another great war might well knock it to pieces. That did not happen. Whatever caused the end of empire, it was not the Second World War, although this conclusion will not please those who think that the world came to an end in 1945, or those who think that the world's great age began anew in 1945. During the war, as we have seen, the British reoccupied most of the Middle East territories, Curzon's fantasy empire from which British rule had been withdrawn or relaxed during the nineteen-twenties and nineteen-thirties; they dealt with Indian rebels more ferociously than at any time since 1857; where they had been expelled, they had returned; by 1945 they were in Indonesia, for the first time since 1816.

But war-time occupations are responses to war-time pressures. We cannot safely infer from them any longer-term design. What, then, were the long-term designs for empire? Did the British feel that war had shown that the colonial game was up? That the time had come to take to the troopships and sail away? Their views emerged quite clearly in 1942, after the fall of Singapore in February. The State Department had long believed that colonies were an anachronism. In March, Roosevelt suggested to London that India should be handed over to an Indian government. He was snubbed. In May 1942 the State Department suggested a joint declaration on the future of colonies, proposing that they should all advance quickly to independence on agreed time-tables under the supervision of some international body. This suggestion that the colonies were an archaic survival which affronted the spirit of the age was badly received in Whitehall. But the country was heavily dependent upon American good-will and large tracts of its empire were almost abjectly dependent upon American support. Something had to be done, as the Foreign Office insisted, to humour the patron. It was essential to cajole the United States into entering 'some general defence scheme that would include the defence of the colonial areas . . . without impairing our unquestioned right to administer our own colonies including those which we have temporarily lost to the Japanese'. It was agreed to set up 'purely consultative commissions' for the West Indies, the Pacific, South-east Asia and Africa. All the powers with defence interests in any of these regions would sit on its commission, which would coordinate regional defence and economic development but which would not intervene in government. That would bring the British empire the help of American guns and dollars without the hindrance of American constitutional time-tables. The real British policy for British colonies was well defined by a Cabinet Committee in May 1943:

Many parts of the Colonial Empire are still so little removed from their primitive state that it must be a matter of *many generations* before they are ready for anything like full self-government. There are other parts inhabited by people of two or more different races, and it is impossible to say how long it will take to weld together these so-called plural communities into an entity capable of exercising self-government.

The Cabinet Committee which adopted this view was made up of Lord Cranborne (later Lord Salisbury), the Lord Privy Seal, Oliver Stanley, the Colonial Secretary, Anthony Eden, the Foreign Secretary, and the Deputy Prime Minister, Attlee. But in any case American pressure was soon lifted. The Defence Department overruled the State Department, insisting that after the war America could control territories not all that dissimilar from colonies in the Pacific and in Asia. Hence Washington dropped the slogans about political independence. Now the approach was to be about Freedom from Want and Freedom from Fear, rather more accommodating concepts. After the founding of the United Nations, there was to be a similar cycle—demands for a right of intervention in colonies, British resistance, and a compromise in which the British gave nothing away. Even during its greatest adversities during the war, then, the British Government was not minded to jettison its colonies. So we shall be wise to look elsewhere for the end of empire.

Perhaps we should seek it in the electors' choice in 1945 which brought Labour to power? It is characteristic of the political issues presented to Demos during this century that Labour's election manifesto in 1945 did not mention the tropical colonies at all. There was now some criticism of empire, but it is characteristic also of the continuities between post-war policies after 1918 and after 1945 that Attlee's Government had to grapple with Little Englanders just as Lloyd George's Government had done. The country was poor. Overseas commitments were costly. Development ought to begin at home. Mr Mikardo and Mr Crossman called for retrenchment in the Middle East—just as Labour MPs had done in 1920. Dalton prophesied that policing the world would bankrupt the country, just as Bonar Law had done in 1922. Dalton wrote (privately) of the 'pullulating, poverty-stricken, diseased nigger communities, for whom one can do nothing in the short run and who, the more one tries to help them, are querulous and ungrateful'. On the other hand, the Government, like that after 1918, contained men who were determined to defend the positions of British expansion and influence in the world. They included Attlee himself, A. V. Alexander and Bevin. During the war Bevin had believed that 'we may well become the leading influence in western Europe' and that 'the British empire should endeavour to become one Defence Unit'. In 1947 Bevin was to be found arguing (much as he had done in 1930) that Britain's solution to the dollar problem lay in an empire customs union. Indeed, a good argument for the Attlee Government's persistence with the old objectives is that it brought about no radical departures from the defence policy of the Churchill Government— except that it no longer had the Indian army at its disposal. So Britain's decision to quit India was not intended to mark the end of empire. Quitting India has to be seen in the light of the simultaneous decision to push British penetration deeper into tropical Africa and the Middle East.

Perhaps that is the real question. Whatever else it did or did not do, the Attlee Government presided over the independence of India. Surely here at last is a sign of grace? Something was done to quell the Old Adam of Colonialism. We cannot sink into the intricacies of the Indian problem between 1945 and 1947. In any case enough has been said about India already. But the vital point to grasp is the distinction between independence and partition. Independence for India meant only a new technique for keeping the British connection with India. Partition, which was unintended, meant the end or at least the weakening of British strategic interests as they were based in India. But, as we shall see, this was another question.

Already before the war there had been strong arguments, in terms of British interests, for shifting the basis of the connection between Britain and India. India's tariff autonomy was already cutting Lancashire's exports to pieces, while she was extorting wider and wider preferences in the British market. By 1938 the Cabinet had been driven to consider the possibility of a tariff war between the metropolis and her overbearing dependency. The war froze any chance of altering the relationship. But it made the relationship still more anomalous. We have noted the British indebtedness to India which was the result of incurring most of India's defence costs. By 1945 the sterling balances in India's favour amounted to some £1,300 to £1,500 million. Another result of war was to commit Delhi to a policy of rapid industrialization, and by 1945 a Cabinet Committee on India was staggered to learn that the Government of India (still a British Government, remember) wanted the power to nationalize some of the British firms in India and to discriminate against others in the issue of licences. As Simon commented, 'we risk throwing up everything without getting out of our responsibilities to India'. Already there was planning to get rid of these responsibilities. In March 1945, Attlee, Anderson and R. A. Butler were all agreeing that if the Indians would not settle on a constitution, then Britain should after the war devise one and enforce it upon her. So there would be no denial of independence, not from the British side anyway. But there were considerable difficulties in contriving it. In May 1946 the Cabinet Mission to India announced its plan for a three-tiered constitution crowned by a Union of India dealing with foreign affairs and defence. What they had in mind was a kind of United States of South Asia which would stress states' rights. The failure of this scheme pushed Wavell into devising his breakdown plan, for the Viceroy was convinced that power was draining out of the Raj. This brought Attlee's decision on 18 December 1946 to dismiss Wavell, as the Prime Minister was fearful of the effect upon parliament of announcing in advance a terminal date for the Raj. All these were desperate problems but they were problems in technique. Not until 1947, in Mountbatten's time, did London think about the unthinkable, namely a splitting of India which would leave no vestige at all of a unitary structure.

But partition was a much more serious blow to British interests. There was much to be said for a renewed type of linkage between India and Britain. But there was much to be said against splitting this into British links with Hindustan and British links with Pakistan. The first and the greatest casualty of partition would be the Indian army. That was one of the reasons why the Attlee Government was so reluctant to sanction partition and the reason why it so appalled the generals, such as Auchinleck and Allanbrooke. As the latter recalled, 'with the loss of India . . . the keystone of the arch of our Commonwealth defence was lost and our imperial defence crashed'. But this, the most momentous effect for Britain of the loss of India, was conceded by the Attlee Government as a cruel necessity. It was, however, far from an end of empire. The Government was intent upon replacing the lost eastern empire with another.

Not until the nineteen-forties was there a serious version of imperialism in tropical Africa. Until then, both the prospectuses of Joseph Chamberlain and the prognostications of Lenin on imperialism had turned out to be empty, leaving their words reading like Old Moore's Almanack. For there had been slight economic development, little capital investment, small markets and few business ventures in tropical Africa. Wars are usually the bearers of glad tidings to under-developed regions unless they become battlefields, and it was the Second World War which shook Africa out of its economic stagnation. The shortage of vegetable oils, copper and cotton combined with the British desire to control the sales of cocoa, tea and sisal to bring the government fully into the work of stimulating and regulating production in tropical Africa. This was not entirely new. What was new was the weight of intervention by the colonial régimes working at the behest of the embattled government in London. Hence the rise of the Commodity Marketing Boards, those colonial versions of Morton's Fork, which compelled African producers to sell cheap in the cause of cushioning them from price swings. More important was the extraordinary power over the open sectors of these African economies which was successfully claimed by the colonial governments, or their successors. For example, the records of the Anglo-American Economic Commission for French Africa show how even the most trivial items of import for the north African territories were controlled and husbanded by committees sitting in London, staffed in part by the dons from Oxford women's colleges, which may explain their severity.

This deepening intervention in the African economies was carried on by the Attlee Government. Again, the world shortage of vital commodities such as fats kept the wartime policy in being; but it was afforced by Britain's dollar problems which drove her to seek dollar savers. Again, no one really knew what geological jackpots Africa contained, because general neglect had skimped the necessary surveys. Here might lie God's Plenty which would rescue the pilgrim British economy from the Slough of Despond. In October 1948 Bevin, the imperial Micawber, told Dalton about the pie in the African sky: 'if we only pushed on and developed Africa, we could have the United States dependent on us, and eating out of our hand, in four or five years. . . . The United States is very barren of essential minerals, and in Africa we have them all.' But there were other, less palpable, reasons why a venture into African development was agreeable to the Labour Government after 1945. Some years before, another Labour politician, himself Secretary of State for India, had noticed: 'The negro has many more political friends in this country than the Indian. . . . Idealists of our Party care much more about the African.' That politician was the father of Mr Anthony Wedgwood Benn. Part of this affection sprang from the belief that the African was easier to influence and that he was more amenable to Christianity. Once again, God was working through his Englishmen, always a hall-mark of left-wing imperialism in England. So the same Labour Government which had liquidated most of British Asia went on to animate part of British Africa. Africa would be a surrogate for India, more docile, more malleable, more pious.

But if Africa was to come to the rescue of the British economy, then this result would have to be planned for. As Chancellor of the Exchequer, after Dalton had been hurled back into the Smoking Room, Stafford Cripps referred the whole question of colonial development to the planning section of the Cabinet Secretariat; and he proposed to integrate domestic and colonial investment programmes. Not much came of this. Nor did much come of the pressures to nationalize the United Africa Company or the copper firms in Northern Rhodesia. More was done by the device of public corporations. In 1946 the government accepted a scheme put up by the United Africa Company for producing ground-nuts on three and one-quarter million acres of Tanganyika, Kenya and Northern Rhodesia. This was to be directed by the United Africa Company as managing agents. By 1948, only 7,500 acres were under crop and the Overseas Food Corporation took over from the United Africa Company. It received advances from the Government of £21 million, but the entire scheme finally had to be jettisoned. So much for ground-nuts. As Andrew Carnegie once said, 'pioneering does not pay'. The Colonial Development Corporation of 1948 had a less turbulent and more useful life in backing agricultural and mineral projects in Britain's African territories.

But it is the political implications of the new course which bear closest on our argument. In 1941 Lord Hailey had reported that African politics were well in hand; there was little discontent anywhere except here and there in the Gold Coast and in southern Nigeria. 'Political elements' were a small proportion of the population; policy, he advised, should be to 'go cautiously at the centre and concentrate on local institutions'. But there were two weaknesses about this strategy. The new policy of crashing into development meant, of course, greater imperial intervention in the affairs of the African subjects. Well, by now, we are very familiar with the consequences of this sort of thing. We have seen its effects in North America, in Latin America and in India. We can predict, better than Lord Hailey, what the results would probably be. The other weakness of Hailey's assumptions was his hope that to 'concentrate on local institutions' would divert attention from the centre. But the famous Local Self-Government Circular Despatch of 1947 did not have that effect at all. Instead it allowed the feared African politician to turn his locality into his bailiwick, and then to bond together one bailiwick with another in wider arenas of political action.

To some extent these possibilities were glimpsed in London. It seemed likely to some of the men in the Colonial Office that African politics were now moving more swiftly than Hailey had predicted in the early nineteen-forties. 'We must assume', argued a Colonial Office committee in 1947, 'that perhaps within a generation many of the principal territories of the Colonial Empire will have attained or be within sight of the goal of full responsibility for local affairs.' The Gold Coast would make the swiftest constitutional advance, probably winning internal self-government in a generation. But elsewhere in tropical Africa progress would be slow. The British were to be surprised by the extraordinary scale of popular support which the nationalists were able to command. In West Africa, and very shortly in East Africa, territories which had been political deserts now seemed to pullulate with political parties that were the darlings of the masses, the tribunes of the people and the voice of the future. Where had these new mass parties come from? Who was the Frankenstein who had called them into being? The government itself. In Africa, as in India, much of the impetus behind the mass parties came from the policies of the government itself. It was the government which pushed ahead with economic development; consequently it had to intervene more continuously, more forcefully, inside African society than it had done before.

These interventions did not emanate from the local District Commissioner, but from the seat of government in Accra or Lagos. It was from there that orders came for pushing ahead with cash crops, for fixing their prices, for denying their producers the imported goods they desired. But the government also furnished the structure for mass parties. It produced the grievances; it also provided the way in which these grievances could find a vehicle for their expression. As it busied itself more in the affairs of its subjects, so it had to seek support (or at least acquiescence) from larger numbers of them. Perforce it had dragged them out of the politics of localities and districts into wider arenas, into the politics of provinces and finally of the nation. For this the constitution-makers had already supplied the framework, in the chain of representative councils from the district up to the province and from there to the nation. As the nationalist politicians clambered from one arena to another, they carried with them the mass support gathered at the lower levels over purely local issues and pointed to it as support for national issues. In West Africa, just as in India before it, mass parties were the sum of a series of local political situations converted by government machinery into the apparent expression of nationalist demands. In a word, government needed economic growth in West Africa. It suspected that this would have to be paid for by political concession. And so it turned out. But the scale of colonial political development grew much more quickly than official calculations had allowed for.

But where in all this are the freedom-fighters? Not in West Africa, that is clear, for there was nothing to fight over except a time-table. But the places to look for them are in East and Central Africa. And there they were the white settlers. In West Africa the question of independence hardly arose before the nineteen-forties. In East and in Central Africa it had been stormily discussed since 1919. There the powers of the white colonists had cancelled out the orthodox doctrines about the paramountcy of African interests, and all the schemes for African political advance had been dropped. The impact of war mainly confirmed this. Economic development in East and Central Africa depended upon the good-will of the white population. Moreover, London feared that the whites would fall more and more under the influence of South Africa. These fears were compounded by the coming to power in South Africa of the Nationalist party in 1948. This momentous event spurred the British Government into pressing for a Central African Federation of the two Rhodesias and Nyasaland, which was set up in 1953 and was dissolved ten years later. But there was to be no federation in East Africa. Here the Mau-Mau rising between 1952 and 1960 led to the overthrow of the white settlers. Once the British brigades had been committed to this war, local power no longer lay with the white population. By 1955, when it was costing the Government £10,000 to kill each rebel, there was little chance that London would allow Kenya to revert to *status quo ante Mau-Mau* which might provoke another expensive rebellion. There had to be reform; and this was bound to break the paramountcy of white interests. With that assured, East African politics could go the way of West African politics—independence for Tanganyika in 1961, for Uganda in 1962 and for Kenya in 1963. So political developments in the African colonies had evolved in a variety of different ways. But in all of them local politics had been able to build enough pressure to persuade the British Government to accept the facts and concede their demands for independence, a conclusion which is as true of Rhodesia as of any of the other territories.

It would be parochial to discuss the fate of the British world system simply in terms of constitutional concessions flipped like coins to African negotiators at Lancaster House. After the war, the British had set out to build a substitute for India in Africa. But Britain's world system was much larger than that. The country had emerged from the Second World War as much the strongest of the middle powers of the world. Her production by 1950 was two and one-half times that of France and fifty per cent more than that of West Germany. In 1952 she was still contributing more than forty per cent to the defence spending of the European members of NATO. Britain was still the rich man in his palace, not yet the poor man at the gate.

After 1945 the official mind of the British armed services continued to believe that influence in the Mediterranean and the Middle East was vital to the security of the British world position. This had been the British thesis since first Cromwell and then William III had placed a naval presence in the Mediterranean, and it had become standard policy since the Younger Pitt and Palmerston had worked upon the crumbling Muslim powers of the eastern Mediterranean. Even in the later nineteen-forties with the Indian Raj gone, command over the Mediterranean and influence over the Middle East seemed essential for linking Britain with her interests in South-east Asia. The strains of holding Greece, Lloyd George's old satellite, were unbearable by 1947; and the strategic orthodoxies about the Mediterranean were challenged by a heresy that the British line ought to fall back from the Inland Sea to a defensive frontier stretching from Nigeria to Kenya. Attlee was attracted by this view. The loss of India made nonsense of the old obsession with the Suez Canal. 'We should be prepared to work round the Cape to Australia and New Zealand', and Britain could pull troops out of Egypt and the Middle East. With the help of Bevin, the service chiefs stopped this. Their arguments revived a good deal of the case Curzon had made after 1918. Informal influence was all very well, but it was no substitute for a military presence. Palestine was unreliable. All the more reason for garrisoning Cyprus and Malta and for ensuring an RAF presence in Jordan and Iraq. But the doctrine went beyond Curzon's arguments after the First World War. Now, after the Second World War, it was argued that British oil interests could be secured only by continuous presence (which the history of Middle East oil refuted) and that the whole ambitious strategy could be assured if the United States could be dragged into sustaining the Mediterranean position. Here are the marks of a *folie de grandeur*, the passion for maintaining a world system by trying to look as tall as the two super-powers, defending oil interests against one of them and relying for help on the other. But this was a mad world with mad kings. One should not put one's trust in super-powers.

The ark of the covenant lay in the Suez base. Five hundred million pounds had been spent on it. It contained two hundred square miles of installations and 600,000 tons of stores. It employed 75,000 Egyptians and it could handle half a million tons a month. Magnificent, but all these amenities turned on keeping Egyptian domestic politics coopera-tive. After 1946 Egyptian politicians found new possibilities of leverage in agitating over the base. The agitation was manageable so long as Pharaoh ruled in Cairo. But after 1952 Pharaoh took to his travels. There were riots in Egypt. There was tension in the base. The labour force melted away. The Egyptians insisted on a total evacuation of Suez.

Gradually the spectre took shape, the loss of the base, the end of the special position that Britain had enjoyed in Egypt since 1882. Once more the Israelis volunteered to become Gurkhas serving Britain. Britain could use Haifa. Or Gaza. Nothing came of this. What, then, was to be done about Suez? To secure the base the British were now maintaining three divisions there, and locking up 75,000 troops in Egypt made it impossible to form a strategic reserve in Britain. Again the base could not function without a local labour force, but the labourers were vanishing. A running battle with the Egyptians over Suez was bound to foul British relations with the Arab states. Moreover, the role of the base in wartime could be stultified by the threat of thermonuclear weapons.

Here we have a striking proof of the obsolescence of the old colonial methods for keeping influence in the outside world. All systems of influence which called for holding territory depended upon political quiescence among the colonial populations and on controlling political development in the colony. By the nineteen-twenties this had already been dubious. By the nineteen-fifties it was impossible. The result was a base choked with British troops and starved of labour. Hence the case, strenuously resisted, reluctantly accepted and gloomily implemented, for coming to terms with Egypt. The treaty of October 1954 stated that all British troops should leave the base by 1956 but they might reoccupy it in the event of any power attacking an Arab state or Turkey. This treaty showed more vividly than any other transaction of the nineteen-fifties that Britain was nearing the end of an age. Ever since Gladstone's time, all British governments had accepted that the security of Suez was a major British interest, and that it could be assured only by a British presence around the Canal. Nevertheless they went, mainly because the development of Middle East politics was making it increasingly hard to stay. The Suez Expedition of 1956 completed the ruin of this position, and brought on the fall of the British position in Iraq and Jordan. Now the bastions of the British world system shifted to Singapore, Kenya, Aden and Cyprus. One by one, these bases, too, were to be denied to British troops. We seem to be nearing a finish. But we should not look on this as a sort of imperial end game with the British King harried and driven off one square after another on the chess board of the world. This is how the process would have appeared to Joseph Chamberlain, or to Milner or to Curzon, all of them imbued with the late nineteenth-century passion to control territory. The process would have seemed less tragic to the Younger Pitt, to Canning or Palmerston, all of whom were less concerned with rule and more concerned with influence. Now the British were growing more intent on using transport planes to ferry their strategic reserve from home to vexed areas, and to develop tiny sites, inconspicuously placed and immune from politics, as air bases. Now for the first time Gan and the Cocos Islands make their bow on the world stage. But beside these new searches of the maps appeared a new consideration: was it really worth the country's while to maintain a world system at all? What was this world system for? If there was not to be a British presence east of Suez, then there was precious little point in holding bastions and staging-posts, whether in the Mediterranean and the Middle East or in the Indian Ocean. If there was no necessity for imperialism then there was no reason for holding the vestiges of empire. This is not so much an end game as a refusal to play the game any longer.

The historian of imperialism is a person whose business has been much plagued by amateurs, by those who have found the subject difficult or morally repulsive, and have used it to patter out their credos of right and wrong, and by those who have sought to squeeze the facts into simple explanations accounting for the growth of imperialism in terms of some single, simple cause ranging from capital export to Joanna Southcott's box. Now that the study of how empires ended is being opened up, it is our duty to stop these forms of cant and folly from becoming embedded in it. First, we do know what decolonization is not. It was not a continuous process of decline, for the old cause of expansion frequently rallied, especially in wartime. Decolonization was not usually a victory won by freedom-fighters. Men did fight for freedom—in Algeria for instance—but it was seldom those who fought for it who won it. Decolonization was not the result of some single cause, such as domestic constraints or international pressures. From time to time, these causes had important parts to play, but not continuously. Decolonization was not the outcome of some noble rage for justice by enthusiasts and moralists. These people have never been in short supply in England, but their enthusiasm could never be attracted for long. Whatever happened to the sentimental pro-Africanists of the nineteen-sixties? Where is Bohun? Where is Mowbray? Where is Plantagenet? Where indeed is Kingsley Martin?

Secondly, we know in general terms what decolonization was. Every colonial power sustained itself by shifting the basis of its rule from time to time, dropping one set of colonial collaborators and taking up another. In principle, this process could have continued endlessly. The imperial croupier never found any shortage of colonial subjects ready to place bets with him at the table, although they usually staggered up from the table in some disarray. Certainly in India in 1947, and in Africa in the late nineteen-fifties, there were still plenty of groups ready to try a flutter. But this holds good only in principle. In practice, political developments in the colonies tended to take the game out of the croupier's hands. These colonial political developments are the one constant factor in decolonization. We have seen how from 1919 they were knocking imperial calculations askew, depriving Britain of the Indian army, making the longed-for Egyptian treaty into a kind of Holy Grail eluding the grasp of the Parsifals in the Foreign Office. And once the political bases on which the colony was held came under strain, so that more and more had to be conceded to the moderates, then the system might come under international pressures as well.

Therefore there was an increasingly good case for capitulating to the views of the age that imperialism was an obsolete method of projecting influence in the outside world. Again, in principle, this might have meant reverting to the techniques of the early nineteenth century, falling back on informal pre-eminence based upon influence and trade, not upon territory and rule. But this, the neo-colonialism excogitated by the European resident philosophers waiting at the court of Kwami Nkrumah in the nineteen-fifties, was not practicable. There was no going back to the nineteenth-century techniques of expansion. That had depended upon the existence of a British world system. But in the strenuous conditions of the nineteen-fifties and the nineteen-sixties, Britain lacked the economic power, the military fire-power, the expansive thrust for maintaining a world system against the competition of other world powers. In any case domestic and international considerations would have stopped her from attempting to rebuild such a system.

There was nothing spectacular about the end of the affair. The last Emperor of East Rome died fighting on the walls of Byzantium. The last King-Emperor, George VI, died in his sleep after reading a thriller in bed. Some writers have seen the empire as a triumph for the one over the many. Others have seen in it the hand of providence or the work of human wickedness. We have tried to depict it less dramatically, as a triumph, in the end of the many over the one, as a system which in its time played a great part in the world, and finally perhaps as a great ship carrying some hopes and some fears: the ship rides the waves; *fluctuat nec mergitur*; then it ships water; then it rights itself; then it gradually fills, and at last, without convulsion, without tremor and without agony, the great ship goes down.

Congress in Decline: Bengal, 1930 to 1939

JOHN GALLAGHER

I

DURING the twenty years after the First World War, Indian politics were moulded by two main forces, each of which drew strength from the other. Important constitutional changes devolved a range of powers to Indians. But the British did not plan these reforms of 1919 and 1935 as stages by which they would quit India, bag and baggage, but rather as adjustments in the methods of keeping their Indian connection while retaining intact most of its fundamental advantages. At the centre of government in India, the powers of the Raj were increased; in the provinces more and more authority was entrusted to Indians. This system canalized much of Indian political action into the provinces. Moreover, by placing the new provincial administrations upon greatly widened electorates, it gave the Raj a further range of collaborators, selected now for their mastery of vote-gathering. The reforms of 1919 provoked another seminal development. By widening the functions of local government bodies in municipalities and the rural areas, which were to be chosen by the same voters who elected the new provincial councils, they linked the politics of the localities more closely to the politics of the province.

The second main development arose out of these changes, since constitutional initiatives by the British prompted political responses by the Indians, cooperators or non-cooperators alike. Whether they chose to work the reforms or preferred to press for further concessions, the politicians in nearly all provinces of India had to take account of the new electoral system. Those interested in forming ministries had to secure their bases in local constituencies; those attracted by the greater patronage and influence which local bodies now possessed, were anxious to sink their teeth into them. Those who were active in building movements capable of challenging their rivals and of putting pressure on the Raj, also needed local bastions from which to extend their influence.[1]

Castigated and emended by Dr Anil Seal, to whom I am most grateful

[1] Thus Gandhi's programme in 1920 for non-cooperation allowed his followers to continue cooperating on local bodies.

Government impulse had linked much more closely the local and the provincial arenas of politics; and the general trend among Indian politicians, constitutionalist or not, was to react to this initiative by copying it.

In so doing, they altered the working of Indian politics. Politics, electoral and agitational alike, were now built upon organizations with broader constituencies, whether these were defined by the reforms or laid down by Gandhi. Provincial issues were less easily settled by a caucus; parties were harder to control by bosses in city chambers. Central leadership had to be more responsive to local needs; and there were more people to voice them. That is not to say that Indian politics had been tidied up into parties with programmes, tailored to fit the needs of coherent social groups. The main elements were still the links between patrons and clients, the connections in localities and the shifting alliances between factions; these continued to cut across the spurious unities which now seemed to have emerged. Nevertheless, there had been an important change: more localities had to be bonded together, and they had to be related to the politics of larger arenas. The lessons of these electoral systems followed the logic of administrative change. This had already begun to link province and district so that neither could ignore the other. For administrative and electoral reasons alike, leaders in the province had now to cultivate connections in the locality, and local interests needed a say in larger arenas.

Bengal fitted awkwardly into this pattern, and it was to remain out of joint until the province was finally repartitioned. Since the days of the Nawab, the administration of Bengal had been strikingly decentralized, particularly in its eastern districts. The Permanent Settlement in 1793 had ratified this state of affairs. It was a system of transferring many of the functions of government to those men in rural society who were ready to assume the tasks of collecting the land revenue and shouldering much of the administration of their neighbourhoods. To some extent the British had leased out franchises of this sort in many other parts of India, but elsewhere they had avoided the error of giving away as much as they had in Bengal. By the later nineteenth century government was coming to intervene with more determination in the affairs of the localities. But this bureaucratic counter-attack was bound to be less successful in Bengal than in other provinces. Consequently, the districts of Bengal, and especially those in the east, went on enjoying a good deal of immunity from the interference which was becoming normal elsewhere. Even when they were equipped with elective institutions of local self-government, some of this immunity survived, and so, district politicians lacked the incentive to link locality with province. Conversely, politicians at the centre of Bengali affairs could afford to leave the districts pretty much on their own. It looked as though the new trends did not apply to Bengal as much as to other parts of India. The politicians' base was Calcutta; by comparison with the power of the metropolis, the mofussil seemed to matter little. Moreover, in the eastern hinterland, combinations between one district and another were almost out of the question. The lay of the land and the water was enough to make this so.

This helps to explain why Bengali politicians concentrated upon their city and ignored the districts. During the nineteen-twenties, when they could still feel insulated from hinterland opinion, they enjoyed the luxury of quarrelling among themselves over the spoils of the city. But even if they had wanted stronger links with the localities, there were other reasons why these would have been hard to forge. The reversal of partition in 1911 had been the one resounding success of political Bengal. But in that success lay desperate complications for the future. Undivided Bengal kept together regions and peoples whose interests were hard to reconcile. In the east, Muslims were a majority, in the west, Hindus. In both regions, the socially dominant, Hindu in the main, had lines into the political leadership of Calcutta. But in both regions their local dominance was being challenged by other interests which did not possess links of that sort. Congress in Bengal was thus based on the great city. It was also the spokesman of interests which were now on the defensive. Therefore vigorous agitation in the districts was the last thing it wanted, since this might spill over into a demand for social levelling. In other provinces, Congress might become a champion of underlying forces and a coordinator of agitation. It would find it much harder to be so in Bengal. As the defender of interests vulnerable to social change and a wider franchise, the Bengal Congress needed to make a quick bargain with the British. But this neither the British nor the Congress outside Bengal was ready to permit.

The difficulties which the Bengali politicians faced in the nineteen-twenties are more apparent to the historian than they were to Chitta-ranjan Das and his successors. Since Bengal had been less affected by the reforms of 1919 than most other provinces, its politicians still enjoyed many of the luxuries and freedoms of the past. But by 1929 further constitutional reform was on its way. It was to turn these free-doms into servitudes. Government had no intention of picking and choosing between regions; the new reforms would have to operate throughout the Indian empire in a uniform way. In their search for new collaborators the British chose to leap in the dark by extending the franchise to thirty-five million voters, of whom eight millions were to be in Bengal. A self-governing Bengal shaped by these voters might well lead to the ruin of the Bengal Congress. The Communal Award of 1932 turned these fears into near certainties. Consequently, the Bengal Congressmen needed the support of the all-India Congress as never before. For all their scorn of Gandhism and for the simplicities of Hindustan, they were now beggars and could not be choosers.

But there lay further dilemmas. The all-India purposes of the Congress centre did not match the interests of the Bengal Congress. Preoccupied with the struggle against the British, with the desire to hold Muslim support, with the need to satisfy other provinces where the party worked with securer social bases and better electoral prospects than it had in Bengal, the centre took decision after decision which further weakened the Congress in Bengal. Gandhi forced civil disobedience upon the province and reactivated its districts. The high command prevented the Bengal Congress from campaigning against the Communal Award and made matters even worse by forcing it to accept the Poona Pact. One by one, these external directives stripped away the prestige and sapped the strength of the Bengal Congress. It had need of outside support, either from the British or from the Congress centre; but as matters turned out, neither of these had need of the Bengal Congress. It is with such melancholy themes that this essay is concerned.

II

These new trends were in the end to prove deadly for the political leaders in Bengal and for the unity of the province itself. In retrospect it might seem that the nineteen-twenties were their decade of lost opportunities; but it is hard to see how they could have staved off the troubles to come. For the time being, the skills of Das seemed to have steered the Bengal Congress through the reforms. At the height of its influence, non-cooperation had apparently galvanized the politics of Bengal. Once Das and his supporters had expelled Surendranath Banerjea, they set out to exploit, and at the same time to control, the new wave of discontents which followed the war. The hartals in Calcutta, the agitations among the railway-workers and tea-coolies, the peasant demands in east Bengal, the campaigns against union boards in Midnapore, were a series of local discontents combined into what looked like a unified political aim. At the same time, the movement was strengthened by the growth of agitation among the Muslims; indeed, in

Bengal as elsewhere in India, the Khilafat issue acted as supercharger to the whole non-cooperation campaign.

But what Das wanted was to bring the British to terms in a tidy, a precise, an un-Gandhian way. The opportunists of the Presidency did not share the same aims as the zealots of the centre, for Das and his lieutenants worked a system of non-cooperation with limited liability.[2] He was striving not to achieve Ramraj in India, but to squeeze the British into making constitutional concessions in Bengal without un-leashing a levelling movement inside his own province. When non-cooperation failed, Das and his faction judged that the best way of bringing the British to terms was by entering the Legislative Council. From their conservative point of view, these were sensible tactics. The reforms had enfranchised about 1,330,000 voters in Bengal, many of them Muslims and the richer Hindu peasants of east and west. When the logic of these changes came to work its way into electoral results, it would harm the interests of the Hindu leadership which viewed itself as the political nation of Bengal. Its best course lay in exploiting what was left of its electoral advantage while the going was good. The Bengal Congress was still a powerful body. While the policy of organizing the Congress into linguistic provinces had divided Madras and Bombay into three and five Provincial Congresses respectively, the Bengal Congress had retained all thirty-two of its districts.[3] Moreover, it still enjoyed great intellectual prestige. Bengalis delighted to remind the rest of India that their province had provided the most sophisticated spokesmen for the nationalist cause. This passion for advanced thinking was to become all the more ardent as their options for political practice grew narrower.

At first Das's tactics seemed correct for Bengal. In 1923 his Swarajists did so well in the elections that they could dominate the Legislative Council. Das also won the first election to the new Calcutta Corporation, with its greatly extended powers. Once he became mayor, he had gained for the party what was to become the poisoned crown of controlling the metropolis. But Das's success in swinging the party towards electoral politics, and his growing preoccupation with the affairs of Calcutta, drained the militant spirit out of the districts. When the issue was no longer how to challenge the state, but how to enter its councils, few of

[2] For Das's attitude towards the decision to boycott the councils, taken by the Calcutta Congress in September 1920 and ratified at Nagpur in December, see R. A. Gordon, 'Non-Cooperation and Council Entry, 1919–29', *Modern Asian Studies*, VII, 3(1973), pp. 443–73.

[3] The Bengal Provincial Congress Committee [PCC] controlled District Congress Committees [DCCs] in each of the twenty-six districts of the Presidency. In addition, Calcutta was divided into four DCCs, and the two Bengali-speaking districts of Cachar and Sylhet in Assam had committees under the jurisdiction of the PCC.

the party workers in the districts thought this cause was worth a broken head. For those veterans in the wars of non-violence, it was a matter of once non-cooperative, twice shy. The price of bidding for collaboration was local torpor.

Except for electoral purposes, the leadership now neglected the districts in east and in west Bengal alike. During non-cooperation, local enthusiasm had set up some 170 National Schools throughout Bengal, as a way of evading British control over education. By 1924 there were only seventy of them, and they were scraping along with meagre support.[4] But it was the fate of Das's Village Reconstruction Fund which showed where his priorities lay. The Fund was to bring tidings of great joy to the peasants, announcing to Muslims and Hindus alike that the Swarajya Party was their friend. Nearly two and a half lakhs of rupees were collected. But one and a half lakhs of the Fund were spent in buying the *Indian Daily News* and turning it into the *Forward*, a Calcutta daily, committed to the policies of Das. As the Government of Bengal reported with mordant pleasure, no more than Rs. 2,000 of the Fund seem to have been used on work in the villages.[5]

Already by 1923 Congress organization in the districts was plainly running down.[6] More and more the political activists became obsessed with winning control over the provincial machine in Calcutta, and they reduced the local organizations into mere vote-gatherers for electing their own supporters to the PCC.[7] Das's very success in guiding the

[4] Bengal fortnightly report [FR Bengal] for the second half of April 1924 [henceforth the first and second halves of the month will be indicated by (1) and (2)]; Home Poll file 112 of 1924, National Archives of India, New Delhi [NAI].

[5] FR Bengal September (2) 1924, *ibid.*

[6] The decline of the Dacca DCC illustrates this. Dacca, the second city of the province, was the strongest outpost of the Hindu bhadralok enisled amid the Muslim masses of east Bengal. Das and several of his lieutenants had strong connections with the district. It had been active in non-cooperation, and it was one of Das's chief bases during his struggle to recapture the Bengal Congress in 1923. Das was president of the DCC. Like the president, its two secretaries lived in Calcutta, one of them being Kiren Shankar Roy, an aide of Das's. By October 1923 the organization in Dacca was moribund, its only signs of life being 'a nice building with a sign board over the door and a few so-called volunteers residing therein', and its only function being to help the supporters and hinder the opponents of its masters in Calcutta. *Amrita Bazar Patrika*, 1 July, 6 October, 17 October 1923.

[7] During this period and until 1934 the Bengal PCC was composed as follows:

elected by DCCs on proportion of population	268
co-opted by these elected members,	
one for each DCC	32
Muslims	14
Women	10
Total	324

Bengal Congress into a policy of potential collaboration made it hard to reconcile the interests of the party as a legislative group with its interests as spokesman for the districts. In order to dominate the Legislative Council, the party had to attract some Muslim support; but its local members in the east Bengal districts detested any concession to Muslim pressures, especially over tenancy legislation. In order to placate its supporters in the districts, the party in council had to oppose tenancy legislation; and this endangered its Muslim alliance. Thus there was always the risk that the legislative wing of the party in Calcutta would fly apart from its membership in the mofussil. As a way of preventing this, Das himself held the offices of president of the PCC and Swarajist leader in the Legislative Council, roles which even he found hard to combine. On 16 June 1925, the death of Das removed the most brilliant opportunist in Indian politics, virtuoso of agitation, broker between irreconcilables, gambler for glittering stakes. Das was the last chance of the old system.

The end of his political adventure left his successor, J. M. Sen Gupta, with an impossible inheritance. Sen Gupta had talent and charm; he had the support of Gandhi; he controlled the PCC.[8] But he simply could not bend Das's bow, and in 1927 he was dislodged by the group led by Subhas Bose, who had been another of Das's would-be Dauphins. From then, until the outbreak of civil disobedience, the Bengal Congress was distracted by the efforts of rival bands of Calcutta politicians to dish each other. From time to time, the disgruntled leaders of the mofussil would have their little hour upon a larger stage. But local politics were still dominated by Calcutta, and back-biting in the mofussil was seasoned by vendettas imported from the metropolis. In 1925 the Atma Sakti group had denounced Das; in 1926–27 Sen Gupta was harshly attacked by the Karmi Sangha. Both these groups claimed to speak for the party workers in the districts. In each case the complaints were the same: Calcutta was corrupting the leaders. They were neglecting the countryside. They were pandering to the Muslims. At face value, these protests came from the sons of the soil, unpolluted by urban trickery; in fact they were encouraged by those camarillas which were out of power in Calcutta. The Atma Sakti demands were orchestrated by Calcutta politicians hostile to Das; the Karmi Sangha found backers in the Big Five, Calcutta politicians and businessmen hostile to Sen Gupta.

The political importance which the districts had won during the

[8] There is an account of Sen Gupta which stresses the charm, if not the talent, in M. Collis, *Trials in Burma* (London, 1945, second edition), pp. 84–137.

agitation of 1919–22 had itself been encouraged by the city politicians for their own ends. Now that they were preoccupied with electoral politics and the patronage of Calcutta, they had little time to waste on the affairs of the districts. In their thinking, they had no need to do so. The Bengal Congress was Hindu nationalism. Therefore Hindus of east and west Bengal would vote for it. The purpose of district branches was to bring out the votes which would give it control of the Provincial Council. There the city politicians could settle the future of the province before a widening of the franchise brought millions of fractious Muslims within the pale of the constitution. Local politicians then, might sigh, but they had to obey.

Nearly all these plans, as we shall see, were to be ruined. But during the nineteen-twenties they were still credible. Local politics had become enervated, but this was true in most provinces, where the downfall of non-cooperation had led to a slump in membership and an enfeebling of the party machine. In Bengal, it still seemed rational to run politics from the metropolis. No other Indian city dominated its hinterland as completely as Calcutta dominated Bengal. More than one million and a quarter persons lived in Calcutta during the nineteen-twenties; outside it, only 4 per cent of the population of Bengal were urban-dwellers, and indeed twelve and a half million Bengalis lived in hamlets with fewer than 500 inhabitants apiece.[9] The metropolis was the centre of almost all the higher education in Bengal; and so its cultural style was stamped upon the professional classes in all the districts. Equally, the city's economic predominance was manifest. Nearly 80 per cent of Bengal's income tax in 1918–19 was paid by Calcutta.[10] The city was a stronghold of the bhadralok; in 1921, half the Bengali Hindus in the city were Brahmins, Kayasths or Baidyas. Calcutta was pre-eminently their city. Just as they dominated its social life, so too they dominated its politics, and they had no intention of making Calcutta politics a career open to the talents of rustics without the right connections. When B. N. Sasmal became secretary of the PCC in 1927, the combined efforts of the four Calcutta DCCs quickly pushed him out of office;[11] not only was he an

[9] *Report of the Indian Statutory Commission* (London, 1930), I, 61–62.

[10] *Statistical Returns of the Income Tax Department, Bengal* (Calcutta, 1919), p. ii. Peasants in even the remotest hinterland felt the powerful influence of Calcutta. Jute, Bengal's most important cash crop, was grown in twenty-four districts; prices of jute in up-country markets were settled by Calcutta, and often artificially depressed by gambling in jute futures at Calcutta's Bhitar Bazar. *Royal Commission on Agriculture in India,* Volume IV, *Evidence Taken in the Bengal Presidency* (Calcutta, 1927), qq. 21498, 21599–606, 21644–47, 21716–18.

[11] *Forward,* 12 February 1927. Another reason for their hostility was their desire to keep Sasmal from gaining any of the patronage of Calcutta Corporation.

up-country man from Midnapore, he was also a Mahisya. The true heirs of Das were more presentable men, such as Subhas Bose, J. M. Sen Gupta, K. S. Roy (all three educated at Oxford or Cambridge), Anil Baran Ray and P. C. Guha Roy.

But the most revealing of the party's links in Calcutta was with men of great possessions. Das's newspaper, *Forward*, was backed by the group who later became celebrated in Bengal as the Big Five, and as supporters of Subhas Bose. Tulsi Charan Goswami was a great zemindar with rich interests in jute; Sarat Chandra Bose, brother of Subhas, was a leader of the Calcutta Bar; Nirmal Chandra Chunder was a wealthy solicitor who had become one of the leaders of Kayasth society in the city; Bidhan Chandra Roy was one of its most successful physicians and a man with industrial connections; while Nalini Ranjan Sarkar was first and foremost a businessman who had made his pile in insurance.

The most notorious result of the party's preoccupation with Calcutta was its shady role in the affairs of the Corporation. Once the Calcutta Municipal Act had been passed by Surendranath Banerjea in 1923, most of the workings of the city government came under the control of eighty-five councillors, five aldermen and the mayor they elected. When Congress candidates won the first election in 1924, they took command of an institution with an annual revenue of two crores of rupees and with large patronage to spread among businessmen, contractors, shopkeepers, municipal employees and ratepayers. With the severity of youth, Subhas Bose could jeer at old Surendranath as 'Tammany Banerjea';[12] but his own group soon picked up the same way of making friends. As the first mayor of Calcutta under the new system, Das made it plain that the spoils belonged to the victors, an understanding which held good throughout the nineteen-twenties (and long after) when Congressmen usually controlled the Corporation.[13]

Municipal patronage was too agreeable a perquisite to be shared with country cousins. When the PCC as a whole put up candidates for the Corporation in 1927, all five Calcutta DCCs protested, saying that the right of nomination was theirs. But even they could not bear to share it among themselves: in 1930 three of them were denouncing the other two as the puppets of the Big Five who were grinding down the faces of

[12] Subhas Bose to Sarat Bose, 17 July 1925, in *Subhas Chandra Bose: Correspondence, 1924–1932* (Calcutta, 1967), p. 59.

[13] The tone of municipal corruption was clearly set as early as 1924. Calcutta gossip was soon alleging that the party had made Rs. 50,000 by placing a waterworks contract with an understanding firm; and the shopkeepers in the Municipal Market were soon being squeezed into contributing to party funds. FR Bengal July (1) 1924 and December (1) 1924, Home Poll file 25 of 1924, NAI.

the poor.[14] But whichever of the Calcutta factions came to power, it did not usher the rule of the saints into the government of the city. One era of corruption succeeded another, and the victory of one faction merely spurred the other into making a new bid for control of these fruits of office. So obsessed were the politicians of Calcutta with their intrigues over the Corporation that in March 1930 they seemed oblivious of the larger events which were unfolding in India. On the eve of Gandhi's campaign, Jawaharlal Nehru was writing:

When everyone is thinking and talking of civil disobedience, in Calcutta people quarrel over the Municipal election.[15]

Here was a poor outlook for civil disobedience in Bengal. It was all the worse because of the party's decay as a link between the leadership and opinion in the districts. The districts of Bengal contained 150 sub-divisions; by 1928 only sixty of these sub-divisions possessed any Congress committees. At most, the total membership of the party in the province was about 25,000, a figure compiled from DCC returns which the PCC, perhaps prudently, did not try to check.[16] Moreover, the organization had lost its precarious footing in the villages: '... as far as I know', the secretary of the PCC had to report, 'there are very few Village Congress Committees: mostly the members are in the towns'.[17]

But the province was slowly coming under the influence of forces that were to change politics beyond the calculations of the Bengal Congress. In west and east Bengal alike, rural tranquillity had long depended on a smooth relationship between landlords and rich peasants or *jotedars*. In west Bengal many of these rich peasants were Mahisyas, a low caste which had been actively organizing since the late nineteenth century into caste sabhas, whose leaders deeply distrusted Calcutta.[18] In east Bengal the most conspicuous of the rich peasants were Namasudras, Hindu tenants who had more and more moved into opposition against their Hindu landlords,[19] and who were to use the new political rules

[14] *Liberty*, 19 February, 26 February and 1 March 1930; *Amrita Bazar Patrika*, 25 February, 1 March and 5 March 1930. For the purposes of this campaign the Twenty-Four Parganas DCC claimed itself as one of the Calcutta DCCs, in addition to North, South, Central Calcutta and Burra Bazar DCCs.

[15] J. Nehru to Secretary, Bengal PCC, 7 March 1930, file G120/186 of 1930 of the records of the All-India Congress Committee [AICC], Nehru Memorial Museum and Library, New Delhi.

[16] J. Nehru, 'Notes of Inspection, Bengal PCC', 14 March 1929, file P 28(i)/151, AICC.

[17] Kiran Shankar Roy to Secretary, AICC, 14 February 1929, file P24/148 of 1929, AICC.

[18] Their political role during the nineteen-thirties will be discussed below.

[19] For the earlier history of Mahisyas and Namasudras see B. B. Chaudhuri, 'Agrarian Economy and Agrarian Relations in Bengal, 1859–1885' (Oxford University,

after 1920 to make common cause with their Muslim fellow tenants. These new forces, more portentous for the future of Bengal than the log-rolling of the PCC, arose from the social changes which were slowly transforming the province. By the beginning of the twentieth century many of the districts of west and central Bengal were in agricultural decay, growing markedly less jute and fine grain than the districts of the east.[20] There the vitality of agriculture helped to raise the aspirations of the more substantial peasants, who pressed for firmer tenurial rights. By the Bengal Tenancy Amendment Act of 1928 these 'occupancy raiyats' were given full rights of transferring land; while many of the under-raiyats who in some districts were already exercising many of the rights of occupancy raiyats,[21] now formally obtained all the rights of their superiors except the right to transfer land.

The 1928 Act is a striking illustration of the constraints under which the Bengal Congress was labouring by this time. In the eastern districts its supporters were the class of rent-receivers. To them tenant-right was landlord-wrong, and the party was therefore bound to oppose the legislation; but in doing so it furnished unanswerable proof to the have-nots that it was the party of the haves. The grievances of the upper tenants ensured that there was no dearth of discontent in east Bengal. In 1923 tenants were restive in Tippera, in 1924 in Mymensingh and Dacca, in 1926 in Tippera, Mymensingh, Pabna and Jessore.[22] But both the Muslims and the less well-to-do Hindus had other grievances as well. Educational spending in Bengal was notoriously concentrated on the higher levels—only Assam had a smaller proportion of its boys proceeding upwards from Class IV; only the Punjab spent a smaller proportion of its educational expenditure on primary education; of the scandalously small sums spent on primary education in Bengal, more than one-third came from fees.[23] The politics of education in Bengal had a very seamy side. If the cost of higher education was out of all propor-tion to that of primary education, this was because of the selfishness of upper-class opinion and the ineffectiveness of the new voters enfran-

D.Phil. thesis, 1968); R. K. Ray, 'Social Conflict and Political Unrest in Bengal, 1875–1908' (Cambridge University, Ph.D. thesis, 1973).

[20] *Report of the Land Revenue Commission, Bengal* (Alipore, 1940), III, evidence of the British Indian Association, 279–96.

[21] *Ibid.*, I, final report of the Commission, 29.

[22] FR Bengal September (2) 1923, Home Poll file 25 of 1923; FR Bengal January (2) 1924, Home Poll file 25 of 1924; FR Bengal January (2) 1926, March (2) 1926, Home Poll file 112 of 1926, NAI.

[23] *Indian Statutory Commission. Interim Report. (Review of growth of Education in British India by the Auxiliary Committee appointed by the Commission) September 1929* (London, 1929), pp. 46, 258, 260.

chised by the Reforms. Government raised the bulk of its revenue from the agriculturists but spent only one-third upon them. Part of the reason for this lay in 'a certain fear among the upper classes in this country of the lower classes being educated'.[24]

There was nothing new about these grievances. But the progress of the eastern districts during the twentieth century gradually turned old complaints into political counters. The Montagu-Chelmsford reforms gave the aggrieved the chance to defend themselves. Before 1919 there had been five Muslims among the twenty-eight elected members of the Legislative Council, and they had been chosen by 6,346 Muslim voters.[25] The Act of 1919 gave the Muslims thirty-nine out of eighty-five territorial constituencies; thirty-three of these Muslim seats were for rural areas, mainly in the Dacca, Chittagong and Rajshahi divisions of east Bengal. Of the million and a quarter new voters in the province, more than four hundred thousand were in the Muslim rural constituencies.[26] With their 45 per cent of the territorial constituencies in the Legislative Council, the Muslims had the means to defend the community's interests in the districts. But they failed to make the most of this opportunity. Clumsy, naive and self-seeking, the Muslim members of the Council were easily split by Das and Sen Gupta. Faction was as rife among them as it was among Congressmen, and the passing of the Tenancy Act of 1928 owed more to the British than to the members whose constituents it was intended to protect.

In the Council the aggrieved got little protection. But they got rather more at lower levels where the union boards, local boards and district boards formed an ascending hierarchy of local government. The Bengal Village Self-Government Act of 1919 had confirmed union boards as village authorities and allowed them an elected chairman. By 1926, 2,419 of these boards had been set up, and they were elected by 881,773 voters.[27] Above these boards were the local boards, concerned with the affairs of a sub-division, and elected by the same franchise. In 1926 there were eighty-two of them, elected by 1,691,333 voters. At the

[24] *Royal Commission on Agriculture*, IV, evidence of Director of Public Instruction, Bengal, qq. 23509–10, 23549, 23555.

[25] *East India (Constitutional Reforms . . .) vol. I, Report of the Committee . . . to enquire into questions connected with the Franchise. . . . Cmd.* 141 (London, 1919), p. 38.

[26] *Ibid.*, p. 44. The Franchise Committee estimated that the total number of voters would be 1,228,000, and that the Muslim rural voters would amount to 422,000. At the first election held under the new constitution, 1,021,418 persons voted, of whom 449,382 voted in Muslim rural constituencies. *PP*, 1921, XXVI [*Cmd.* 1261], 10–13.

[27] The vote was given to persons paying Rs 1 as a cess or a chaukidari tax. The figure is for those who actually voted in 1926, and not the larger number who were entitled to vote.

top of the system were the district boards, most of whose members were elected by the local boards. By 1926, twenty six district boards had been set up.

The powers of district boards were quite extensive. They appointed almost all the petty officials of their districts, controlled road-building and water-supply and had some powers in the administration of vernacular education. District boards had the power to levy a cess in their districts, and together with their subordinate bodies they were responsible for substantial sums of money: in 1925–26 they spent Rs 10,237,988.[28] This position they intended to expand. Their powers over education in the districts were less than those in some other provinces, but by the later nineteen-twenties they were working to establish district education boards.

This was a situation full of hopeful possibilities for the enemies of privilege in the eastern districts, Hindu and Muslim alike. The number of voters for these bodies of rural self-government was much the same as the number who could vote in the rural constituencies for the Legislative Council. But there was a vital difference between the two systems of representation. Voting for the Council was done by separate electorates, but the members of the rural boards were chosen by joint electorates. By taking to organization in the eastern districts, and by winning the support of lower-caste Hindu voters there, the Muslims now had the opportunity of winning control of the local boards, and so of most of the district boards. Here at last was their chance to wrest the control of local patronage and perhaps of local education from the zemindars and their clients. Their progress towards these goals is traced in Tables 1 and 2.

[28] *Government of India: Memorandum on the Development and Working of Representative Institutions in the Sphere of Local Self-Government, February 1928*, pp. 31–64, 74–5, 83. This may seem a substantial sum, but it should be compared with expenditure in other provinces.

Expenditure of district boards and municipalities, 1920–21 and 1929–30, in lakhs of Rs

	1920–21		1929–30	
	district boards	municipalities	district boards	municipalities
Bengal	113.32	62.37	140.51	92.45
Bombay	129.81	165.97	198.91	235.90
Madras	221.44	100.29	410.18	167.00
UP	152.13	125.24	199.71	175.47

Source: Gyan Chand, *Local Finance in India* (Allahabad, 1947), pp. 312, 314 317, 319.

These comparisons help to explain why politicians in some other provinces took a livelier interest in the institutions of local self-government.

TABLE 1*

Muslim membership of Local Boards

	Total population	Muslim population	Percentage Exceeds 50%	Percentage Less than 50%	1920–21	1921–22	1922–23
BENGAL	47,592,462	25,486,124	53.55		37.13	37.3	38.1
Burdwan Division	8,050,642	1,082,122		13.44	14.6		12.6
Burdwan	1,438,926	266,281		18.51	19.0		19.05
Birbhum	847,570	212,460		25.07	25.0		25.0
Bankura	1,019,941	46,601		4.57	18.18		13.3
Midnapore	2,666,660	180,672		6.78	7.69		5.9
Hooghly	1,080,142	173,633		16.08	18.0		15.38
Howrah	997,403	202,475		20.30	12.5		12.5
Presidency Division	9,461,395	4,476,741		47.32	33.3		36.5
24-Parganas	2,628,205	909,786		34.62	27.7		33.8
Calcutta	907,851	209,066		23.03			
Nadia	1,487,572	895,190	60.18		31.3		28.79
Murshidabad	1,262,514	676,257	53.56		39.6		49.2
Jessore	1,722,219	1,063,555	61.75		33.3		33.3
Khulna	1,453,034	722,887		49.75	35.8		37.9
Rajshahi Division	10,345,664	6,349,689	61.38		49.29		44.7
Rajshahi	1,489,675	1,140,256	76.54		65.0		66.6
Dinajpur	1,705,353	836,803		49.07	35.1		40.0
Jalpaiguri	936,269	231,683		24.75	Nil		11.1
Rangpur	2,507,854	1,706,177	68.03		54.54		53.7
Bogra	1,048,606	864,998	82.49				59.25
Pabna	1,389,494	1,053,571	75.82		50.0		47.2
Malda	985,665	507,685	51.51				
Darjeeling	282,748	8,516		3.01			5.26
Dacca Division	12,837,311	8,946,043	69.69		49.5		50.0
Dacca	3,125,967	2,043,246	65.36		29.7		29.8
Mymensingh	4,837,730	3,623,719	74.91		62.0		61.0
Faridpur	2,249,858	1,427,839	63.46		42.2		45.4
Bakarganj	2,623,756	1,851,239	70.56		54.7		56.4
Chittagong Division	6,000,524	4,356,207	72.60		60.32		64.22
Tippera	2,743,073	2,033,242	74.12		52.77		65.96
Noakhali	1,472,786	1,142,468	77.57		70.37		68.75
Chittagong	1,611,422	1,173,205	72.81				56.66

Source: calculated from *1921 Census, Bengal*, V, part II, 464–99 and *Government of Working of the District Boards in Bengal* [after 1930, *District and Local Boards*, on title-
* I am indebted to the SSRC Modern Indian History project and Mr. C. Emery

in all Bengal districts, 1920-35

1923-24	1924-25	1925-26	1926-27	1927-28	1928-29	1929-30	1930-31	1931-32	1932-33	1933-34	1934-35
36.2	38.3	40.9	40.45	46.0	43.3	43.7	45.4	45.6	46.51	47.14	47.0
11.8	12.16	12.5	13.6	14.53	14.65	14.32	15.1	15.4	17.3	16.85	17.2
19.05	19.05	19.4	19.75	20.98	20.98	19.75	20.98	22.22	22.22	22.22	23.45
25.0	25.0	25.0	25.0	30.0	29.16	29.16	33.3	33.3	33.3	33.33	33.3
13.3	13.3	6.6	6.6	6.6	6.6	3.3	3.3	3.3	10.0	10.0	10.0
5.1	5.1	5.98	8.5	8.5	8.5	8.5	8.5	8.5	12.3	11.1	11.1
13.8	13.8	13.8	13.8	15.2	15.2	15.2	16.6	16.6	16.6	17.0	17.1
12.5	16.6	16.66	16.66	16.66	16.66	17.9	17.9	17.9	17.9	17.9	18.4
38.83	38.46	42.3	41.1	44.82	43.9	44.2	44.8	45.4	47.7	48.02	48.02
33.8	32.4	32.3	30.8	29.41	29.4	27.9	27.9	27.9	35.2	35.3	35.3
28.79	30.15	46.9	43.9	40.99	40.9	45.45	45.4	45.45	45.45	46.9	46.9
49.2	49.2	49.2	50.79	50.79	50.79	50.57	50.7	50.79	50.0	50.0	50.0
43.83	42.46	43.8	43.83	64.38	60.27	58.9	61.6	61.64	65.75	65.7	65.7
37.93	37.93	39.6	36.2	36.2	36.2	36.2	36.1	39.65	39.65	39.6	39.6
44.7	44.6	48.6	47.47	50.2	53.3	54.0	55.2	54.9	51.7	53.8	52.8
68.7	68.7	68.7	68.7	70.8	75.0	75.0	75.0	75.0	62.5	66.6	64.5
37.8	51.1	51.1	51.1	60.0	62.2	62.2	62.2	57.7	57.7	57.7	57.7
11.1	13.3	22.2	22.1	22.22	11.1	11.1	38.8	33.3	22.2	22.2	22.2
53.7	53.7	51.85	51.85	51.85	53.7	57.4	57.4	59.2	59.26	66.66	64.8
59.25	59.25	59.25	59.25	59.25	59.2	59.2	74.0	74.07	74.07	74.0	74.0
47.2	47.2	58.3	50.0	55.5	66.6	66.6	66.6	66.6	66.6	66.6	63.8
							44.4	50.0	50.0	50.0	50.0
5.26	5.3	5.2	5.3	5.3	7.8	7.8	7.8	7.8	5.2	5.2	5.2
51.5	51.2	50.5	53.2	58.4	58.1	58.4	59.5	63.5	63.9	66.5	66.5
31.5	29.8	28.07	24.5	44.8	44.8	44.8	44.8	44.8	50.0	58.6	60.3
65.5	65.5	64.5	67.7	65.5	65.5	66.6	66.6	73.4	71.3	73.4	72.3
43.4	43.4	43.4	52.2	52.2	52.2	52.2	57.9	60.8	60.8	62.3	62.3
56.4	56.4	56.4	57.7	65.4	64.2	64.1	62.9	67.9	67.9	67.9	67.9
63.3	70.0	70.64	71.55	68.8	68.8	74.3	74.3	73.39	75.22	74.52	73.59
63.8	63.83	68.09	70.21	64.0	65.96	70.21	70.2	68.08	70.21	69.56	67.36
68.8		68.75	68.75	70.0	70.0	81.25	81.25	81.25	81.25	83.33	83.33
56.6	76.66	76.66	76.66	76.6	73.33	73.33	73.3	73.33	76.66	73.33	73.33

Bengal. Local Self-Government Department. [Annual] *Resolution reviewing the Reports on the*
page] *during the year 1920-1 to 1934-35* (Calcutta, 1922-37), Appendix G.
for help with this and subsequent tables.

TABLE 2
Muslim Membership of District Boards

	Total population	Muslim population	Percentage		1920–21	1921–22	1922–23
			Exceeds 50%	Less than 50%			
BENGAL	47,592,462	25,486,124	*53.55*		31.78	34.4	32.1
Burdwan							
Division	8,050,642	1,082,122		13.44	13.56		11.11
Burdwan	1,438,926	266,281		18.51	11.11		11.11
Birbhum	847,570	212,460		25.07	18.75		18.7
Bankura	1,019,941	46,601		4.57	18.75		8.3
Midnapore	2,666,660	180,672		6.78	12.5		8.3
Hooghly	1,080,142	173,633		16.08	15.3		15.3
Howrah	997,403	202,475		20.30	5.55		5.55
Presidency							
Division	9,461,395	4,476,741		47.32	22.01		25.19
24-Parganas	2,628,205	909,786		34.62	20.8		23.3
Calcutta	907,851	209,066		23.03			
Nadia	1,487,572	895,190	*60.18*		20.8		20.0
Marshidabad	1,262,514	676,257	*53.56*		33.3		44.4
Jessore	1,722,219	1,063,555	*61.75*		16.6		16.6
Khulna	1,453,034	722,887		49.75	18.7		18.7
Rajshahi							
Division	10,345,664	6,349,689	*61.38*		41.73		35.6
Rajshahi	1,489,675	1,140,256	*76.54*		*63.6*		*54.5*
Dinajpur	1,705,353	836,803		49.07	31.8		33.3
Jalpaiguri	936,269	231,683		24.75	11.7		14.3
Rangpur	2,507,854	1,706,177	*68.03*		45.09		44.44
Bogra	1,048,606	864,998	*82.49*		43.7		*50.0*
Pabna	1,389,494	1,053,571	*75.82*		46.65		41.6
Malda	985,665	507,685	*51.51*		46.6		33.3
Darjeeling	282,748	8,516		3.01			10.0
Dacca							
Division	12,837,311	8,946,043	*69.69*		43.0		40.0
Dacca	3,125,967	2,043,246	*65.36*		32.1		27.2
Mymensingh	4,837,730	3,623,719	*74.91*		*50.0*		45.8
Faridpur	2,249,858	1,427,839	*63.46*		45.8		41.6
Bakarganj	2,623,756	1,851,239	*70.56*		45.8		*50.0*
Chittagong							
Division	6,000,524	4,356,207	*72.60*		46.42		*57.14*
Tippera	2,743,073	2,033,242	*74.12*		44.44		*53.33*
Noakhali	1,472,786	1,142,468	*77.57*		57.9		*70.83*
Chittagong	1,611,422	1,173,205	*72.81*		36.84		*50.0*

Source: as in Table 1.

in all Bengal Districts, 1920-35

1923-24	1924-25	1925-26	1926-27	1927-28	1928-29	1929-30	1930-31	1931-32	1932-33	1933-34	1934-35
33.8	35.5	35.5	36.89	38.0	40.8	42.4	42.3	42.4	41.73	41.87	41.8
10.07	10.2	10.8	11.1	13.07	13.07	13.07	14.9	14.9	14.28	14.28	14.84
11.11	11.11	11.11	16.66	16.66	16.66	16.66	16.66	16.66	16.66	16.66	20.9
18.7	16.66	16.6	16.66	20.8	20.8	20.8	25.0	25.0	25.0	20.9	20.9
8.3	8.3	4.2	4.2	4.2	4.2	4.16	4.16	4.16	4.16	4.16	4.0
6.06	6.06	6.06	6.06	6.06	6.06	6.06	8.82	8.82	8.82	11.76	11.76
13.3	13.3	13.3	13.3	16.6	16.6	16.6	16.6	16.6	13.3	13.3	13.3
5.55	5.55	16.66	16.66	16.66	16.66	16.66	22.22	22.22	22.22	22.22	22.22
27.4	28.57	27.6	29.07	28.3	38.29	41.8	41.1	40.81	37.41	37.41	37.4
23.3	23.3	23.3	23.3	23.3	23.3	30.0	26.6	26.66	30.0	26.6	26.6
29.33	20.69	20.0	23.3	23.3	23.3	33.33	33.33	33.33	33.33	33.3	33.3
44.44	44.44	44.4	40.74	40.74	40.74	40.74	44.44	44.44	33.33	33.3	33.3
20.83	30.0	26.66	33.33	30.0	70.0	70.0	66.6	66.66	56.6	60.0	60.0
25.0	25.0	25.0	25.0	25.0	33.3	33.33	33.3	33.33	33.3	33.3	33.3
37.4	40.22	43.2	45.81	46.36	45.8	46.3	46.3	44.5	43.2	42.7	43.2
66.6	66.6	66.6	70.3	66.6	51.8	48.1	48.1	48.1	44.4	44.4	44.4
37.03	44.4	51.9	51.9	51.85	55.5	55.5	55.5	48.1	48.1	48.1	48.1
14.3	14.3	14.3	19.05	19.05	19.0	14.2	14.2	14.29	12.5	12.5	12.5
40.74	48.15	48.15	48.15	48.15	51.8	51.8	51.8	44.44	44.44	48.15	55.5
44.44	44.44	44.44	66.66	66.66	66.6	61.11	61.1	61.11	61.11	61.11	61.11
41.6	41.6	54.2	54.2	54.2	54.2	75.0	75.0	75.0	75.0	62.5	62.5
33.3	40.0	40.0	33.3	46.6	46.6	46.6	46.6	50.0	50.0	50.0	50.0
10.0	10.0	10.0	10.0	10.0	15.0	10.0	10.0	10.0	10.0	15.0	10.0
46.8	48.4	45.6	47.6	53.1	57.1	57.1	56.3	55.5	58.4	59.5	58.7
27.2	27.2	24.2	24.2	18.2	33.3	33.3	33.3	33.3	34.3	45.4	45.4
63.6	66.6	66.6	66.6	75.7	75.7	75.7	72.7	66.6	66.6	66.6	63.63
46.6	46.6	41.3	53.3	56.6	56.6	63.3	66.6	66.6	66.6	60.0	60.0
50.0	53.3	50.0	46.6	63.3	63.3	56.6	53.3	56.6	66.6	66.6	66.6
55.95	61.90	60.71	60.71	58.3	60.7	66.6	65.43	71.42	71.42	72.28	71.08
53.33	56.66	56.66	56.66	53.3	53.33	56.66	53.57	66.66	63.33	63.3	63.33
66.66	62.5	58.33	58.33	54.16	58.33	75.0	75.0	75.0	75.0	78.25	78.25
50.0	66.66	66.66	66.66	66.66	70.0	70.0	68.96	73.33	76.66	76.66	73.33

TABLE 3

Elections to Local Boards in all

	Total population	Muslim population	Percentage Exceeds 50%	Less than 50%	1920–21	1921–22	1922–23
DACCA	3,125,967	2,043,246	*65.36*			29.7	29.8
Sadar Subdivision	1,079,723	662,201	*61.33*			25.0	22.2
Narayanganj Subdivision	869,961	675,977	*77.70*			40.0	41.6
Munshiganj Subdivision	683,876	374,390	*54.75*			37.5	33.3
Manikganj Subdivision	492,407	330,678	*67.16*			11.1	22.2

Source: as in Table 1.

The course of elections to the local bodies, with their active electorate of more than one and a half millions, reveals the history of the voters' choice. In twelve of the fifteen districts of Rajshahi, Dacca and Chittagong divisions, the Muslims were a majority of the population. In 1920–21 they controlled more than half the local boards in six of these districts. By 1934–35, they controlled that many in twelve of these districts. Apart from Jessore district in the Presidency division, the electoral swing was greatest in Dacca district, where the Muslim share of local boards increased from 29.7 per cent to 60.3 per cent. This result is all the more striking because of the concentration of bhadralok in Dacca and the importance of their connections with education and politics in Calcutta. Nevertheless the trend is quite clear throughout the district, as Table 3 shows. The course of the district board elections shown in Table 2 says less about the popular choice, since not all members of district boards were elected. The Hindus' local influence and the importance of their interests worked in their favour. It is noticeable that throughout the period they kept control of the Dacca district board. Nevertheless, the Muslim upsurge was remarkable. In 1920–21 Muslims controlled two of the district boards in the Rajshahi, Dacca and Chittagong divisions; by 1934–35 they controlled nine.

In the short run, these changes had little immediate effect. Just as the incompetence and faction of Muslim members let their case go by default in the Legislative Council, so too the Muslim members of rural boards were often at sixes and sevens. After the local elections in Mymensingh in 1927, the District Magistrate reported:

Subdivisions of Dacca District, 1920–35

1923–24	1924–25	1925–26	1926–27	1927–28	1928–29	1929–30	1930–31	1931–32	1932–33	1933–34	1934–35
31.5	29.8	2807	24.5	44.8	44.8	44.8	44.8	44.8	50.0	58.6	60.3
22.2	22.2	22.2	16.6	44.4	44.4	44.4	44.4	44.4	61.1	61.1	61.1
50.0	50.0	50.0	41.6	50.0	50.0	50.0	50.0	50.0	50.0	66.6	66.6
33.3	27.7	22.2	22.2	44.4	44.4	44.4	44.4	44.4	44.4	44.4	50.0
22.2	22.2	22.2	22.2	40.0	40.0	40.0	40.0	40.0	40.0	70.0	70.0

Not a Hindu has been elected. Yet . . . never was intrigue and faction more alive in the District and Local Boards than at present.[29]

But experience together with communal rancour soon put this right, and by the nineteen-thirties the Hindu politicians of east Bengal faced the cheerless prospect of losing control of the districts they had dominated for so long.

The longer-term implications of these changes were more important. Since elections to local boards were by joint electorates, their results allowed both Hindus and Muslims to measure the likely consequences of abandoning the separate electorates which had been in force in conciliar elections since 1909. It was now clear that in east Bengal the Muslims had nothing to fear from joint electorates; in west Bengal on the other hand, where they were generally in small minorities, separate electorates would be their only hope of winning any representation at all. For the Hindus, it was the other way round. In west Bengal they would gain from joint electorates, but in the east they would lose badly and might find their social dominance in ruins. Consequently, any demand for joint electorates would accurately divide the interests of Hindus and Muslims in the eastern and western districts alike.

III

Thus did the Bengal Congress, obsessed with Calcutta, neglectful of the

[29] FR Bengal March (2) 1927, Home Poll file 32 of 1927, NAI.

localities, weakening in the eastern districts, devoid of mass support, enter the nineteen-thirties. At the start of that decade the civil disobedience movement was to drag into the open the internal constraints which were to cripple the Congress in Bengal. Later the initiatives of the British Government, and the responses of the Congress centre to those initiatives, were to reveal the external constraints upon the politics of the province.

Civil disobedience was forced upon Gandhi (who had his own constraints) by a rising militancy in some of the provinces and by his failure to bring Irwin to terms in 1929. The strategy to which he had to turn in 1930 was meant to exert an increasing pressure on the British by unifying a series of regional resistances against them. To the Bengal politicians (and some others) this was a distasteful prospect, only too likely to upset their provincial applecarts. When Gandhi opened the campaign on 12 March 1930 they had to fall in line; but with one of their finer touches they did so by forming two rival civil disobedience councils. In the event, none of the Calcutta factions had much influence on the course of the movement. The Bengal PCC, controlled by Subhas Bose, claimed to have organized eleven centres of civil disobedience; but ten of them were in the district of Twenty-Four Parganas, only next door to Calcutta.[30]

In the districts it soon turned out that civil disobedience could succeed only where there were local grievances which the agitators could exploit. Its disasters in east Bengal showed how impotent the movement was when local grievances were of the wrong sort. There the Gandhians had been working among the people for a decade. Now the time had come to collect the political dividend. Members of the Nawabganj ashram tried to ignite Dacca district; the Khalispur ashram preached civil disobedience in Khulna; khadi workers in Faridpur and members of the national school in Dinajpur called for resistance, while satyagrahis from the Vidyasram in Sylhet agitated in that district and in Noakhali.[31] But instead of attracting mass support, the campaign provoked wide opposition. In Dacca, Faridpur, Bakarganj and Mymensingh, the Muslims asserted themselves against civil disobedience; while the vast majority of the Namasudras either remained aloof from the movement or, as they did in Faridpur and Bakarganj, actively worked in

[30] Six DCCs controlled by Bose's faction also set up such centres. But those in Khulna, Noakhali, Tippera, Bakarganj and Howrah were ineffective, and the success of the sixth (Mahisbathar, in Twenty-Four Parganas) owed more to the Gandhians. The claims of the Bengal PCC are set out in *Liberty*, 17 April 1930.

[31] Bengal Council of Civil Disobedience to AICC, 6 November 1930, file G 86/186 F, 177 N of 1930, AICC.

Government's favour.[32] The contrast with the non-cooperation movement is striking: from the end of 1921 until March 1922, many eastern districts, conspicuously Tippera, Rangpur and Noakhali, had refused to pay taxes.[33] But those days had gone, and now the Government of Bengal could report with relief that:

The movement is generally confined to volunteers of the bhadralok class, and generally speaking, few of the villagers have so far taken part in it.[34]

Some of the western districts showed what could be done by exploiting local grievances. The Mahisbathar sub-division of Twenty-Four Parganas was successfully aroused—but less by the Congress volunteers than by the lucky chance that a local zemindar was at odds with Government; the Arambagh sub-division of Hooghly also responded well—but once again because of local circumstances. Arambagh had large numbers of discontented Mahisya *jotedars*; in any case it was contiguous to Midnapore. There the movement was so effective that when he contemplated civil disobedience over the whole of India, the Secretary of the Home Department in Simla concluded:

... I would put Midnapore as the district where the prestige of Government has fallen more than in any other.[35]

Gandhi's negotiations with Irwin ended the first phase of civil disobedience in March 1931. The campaign had much increased the prestige of the Congress centre. Gandhi had decided when the movement was to begin. Twelve months later it was Gandhi who brought it to an end. Admittedly, while the campaign was being fought, with the Working Committee in gaol and the provincial movements harried by the police, there was no chance of day-to-day control from the centre. Nevertheless the trend was there. Not even the Bengal PCC could stand aloof from civil disobedience, however much they disliked its leadership and tactics. Moreover, in regaining the initiative he had possessed in 1921, Gandhi now enjoyed once more the great political advantage which it brought. Civil disobedience had mobilized Indians into politics on a scale which had been unknown for nearly a decade. It was to the centre, to the Mahatma, that they looked, not to their local leadership. This gave the all-India centre the chance to settle accounts with the Bengal Congress.

[32] FR Bengal June (2) 1930, Home Poll file 18/7 of 1930, NAI.
[33] Note on Movements for the Non-Payment of Revenue, Taxes or Rent, n.d., Home Poll file 168 of 1929, NAI.
[34] FR Bengal April (1) 1930, Home Poll file 18/5 of 1930, NAI.
[35] Minute by H. W. Emerson, 20 June, 1931, on Government of Bengal to Home Department, Government of India, 11 June, 1931, Home Poll file 14/8 of 1931, NAI.

Within a month of Gandhi's pact with Irwin, the leaders of the PCC were embarrassed by the charge that they were out of line with his policy.[36] By stages the Mahatma moved into the role of the supreme authority, whose rulings came to Bengal Congressmen over the heads of their own leaders, and whose attitude towards these leaders could make or break them.[37] Seeing which way the wind was blowing, B. C. Roy, who was now mayor of Calcutta, began to move away from Subhas taking on the role of the centre's candid correspondent from Bengal. Soon there was fresh trouble over Calcutta Corporation, with Sen Gupta calling for purifications. 'I know', B. C. Roy told Vallabhbhai Patel, 'what purity there was during the four years that Mr Sen Gupta was the Mayor. . . .'[38] Evidently the soul of Tammany Banerjea went marching on.

This new outburst of intrigue gave the centre its chance. In August Vallabhbhai Patel directed M. R. Aney of Berar to enquire rigorously into Bengal affairs. Earlier enquirers from the centre had restricted themselves to tossing olive branches to both factions and then jumping thankfully into the train at Howrah. Aney's intervention was far more decisive and far more partisan. As usual, the Corporation was blamed for much of the mischief, but Aney came down heavily against the Subhas group, removing them from office and installing the Sen Gupta faction as the rulers of the PCC.[39] Nirmal Chandra Chunder, one of the Big Five, previously the patron of Subhas, agreed to become its acting president—another mark of the latter's decline.

A further result of civil disobedience was that political life was reviving in the districts. The campaign had shown that the leaders were lagging behind their followers. As the Bengal Council of Civil Disobedience had found: 'The people as also the workers . . . wanted a more forward programme.'[40] In Bengal that meant that they had to construct it for themselves. During the campaign, unhampered by

[36] On 14 April 1931, *Liberty,* Subhas's paper, deplored and denied attacks of this sort which were appearing in Sen Gupta's *Advance* 'and its supporters in the Calcutta gutter press'.

[37] The episode of the Bengal floods in 1931 illustrates this change. Naturally, both factions formed relief committees. To combat the general belief that Gandhi was supporting Sen Gupta's committee against his own, Subhas found it worth his while to send a telegram to the Mahatma (by then on his way to London) asking for impartial support for both relief funds. *Advance,* 19 August 1931; *Liberty,* 8 September 1931.

[38] B. C. Roy to Vallabhbhai Patel, 7 September 1931, file P 15/379 of 1931, AICC.

[39] Report by M. R. Aney on Bengal Congress Disputes, 25 September 1931, file G 25/506 of 1934–35, AICC.

[40] 'The Bengal Council of Civil Disobedience, a Brief Account of its Work', n.d. (*circa* 30 September 1930), file G 86/186 E of 1930, AICC.

leadership from Calcutta, they were bound to go their own ways; and this unusual experience of freedom left them very touchy about metropolitan control once the campaign was over. By June 1931, Sen Gupta and his municipal purifiers had been able to persuade twenty-two of the thirty-two DCCs to rebel against the dominant faction on the PCC; by July, twenty-six had come out in opposition.[41]

Once the Congress centre had restored the Sen Gupta faction to power, Subhas could now play tit-for-tat by poking the fires in the districts. This proved easy to do. After Gandhi had failed at the Second Round Table negotiations, a Bengal Political Conference was held at Berhampore in December 1931. Its members resolved 'that Government has practically ended the Gandhi-Irwin Pact', and 'that the time has arrived for resumption of the Satyagraha campaign for attainment of independence'. Until it was resumed, not only British goods, but also those banks, insurance companies, steamships and newspapers controlled by the British, should be boycotted.[42] This sounded so much like fighting talk that Nirmal Chandra Chunder resigned as president of the PCC.[43]

Admittedly, tempers at Berhampore had been inflamed by fresh Government ordinances against terrorism, but the violence of district representatives at the conference is plain. When Bankim Mukherjee (later to become a Communist leader in Bengal) called for a 'country-wide no-rent and no-tax campaign', his motion was narrowly beaten by 189 votes against 143.[44] But the best evidence about district opinion is that even the PCC, now dominated by the centre's men, did not risk rebutting it. They held back as long as they dared, hoping that 'Bengal will not precipitate matters until she has heard what Mahatmaji has to say'.[45] But Mahatmaji was still at sea, too far away to save them from the pressure of local opinion; and on 19 December they surrendered to it by accepting the boycott resolution.[46] Bengal's slide into militancy, together with a similar development in the UP, were among the chief reasons why the Government of India suddenly struck at the Congress in the first week of January 1932 and thus precipitated the second campaign of civil disobedience.

In its second phase, civil disobedience worked under much greater difficulties than in the first. This time authority was well prepared, and the Bengal Government immediately locked up the entire Congress leadership in the province. At once the connection between the Congress

[41] *Liberty*, 4 June 1931; *Advance*, 17 July 1931.   [42] *Liberty*, 7 December 1931.
[43] *Ibid.*, 13 and 14 December 1931.   [44] *Advance*, 8 December 1931.
[45] *Advance*, 15 December 1931.   [46] *Liberty*, 18, 20 and 25 December 1931.

and the districts was snapped; while the districts themselves, bereft of the local men who had led them in the first campaign, had now to depend on their ability to generate mass movements. Nearly everywhere, that was an impossibility, for it took more than dire threats against British banks and insurance to bring the peasants out of the fields. Once again everything depended upon the presence or absence of local grievances for which the British could be blamed. The slump in crop prices might have seemed a promising issue.[47] But this did no good in east Bengal. Here the economic crisis caused agitation in the districts, but it was against the Congress, since the troubles of the tenants were blamed on the landlords and their party. In these districts the cry could now be heard that the peasants would never prosper until '. . . the control over the Government was transferred to the people',[48] when moneylenders and landlords (often the same persons) would get their deserts. But it was not only among the Muslims that the Hindu gentry was running out of credit. At its meeting on 20 December 1931, the Bengal Backward Classes Association, voicing the opposition of the Namasudras, noted a '. . . want of faith in Congress professions of sympathy for the Backward classes and . . . signs of revolt against the Congress. . . .'[49] Consequently, civil disobedience in the eastern districts was easily

[47] *Jute Prices in Calcutta, Rs per 400 lb. bale.*

1929	71–4
1930	50–4
1931	37–5
1932	31–12

Source: *Statistical Abstract for British India, Cmd.* 4835 of 1935, p. 760.

Common Rice Prices, Rs per maund.

	Calcutta	Dacca	Midnapore
1929	8–8	6–9	5–4
1930	7–7	6–4	4–9
1931	5–5	4–5	3–0
1932	4–2	3–2	2–7

Source: *ibid.*, p. 765.

[48] *Liberty*, 2 November 1931. This affair is a good example of the way in which the Muslim political ferment had reached the village level, where it was organized with the help of the district towns. At meetings of tenants in villages of Madhupur, Mymensingh district, '. . . the discussions practically centred round the question of payment of rent and of the dues of the Mahajans [moneylenders]'. The meetings were addressed by three Muslim members of the district bar.

[49] *Liberty*, 27 December 1931.

snuffed out; deprived of mass support, the young bhadralok had to console themselves with terrorism, the second to last throw of a privileged class near the end of its tether.[50]

The efficient repression of 1932 also crimped the movement in most of the districts of western Bengal. There, militancy was not absent, and there were games of tip-and-run in Calcutta, where the young sparks organized a Congress Postal Service and, more durably, their underground newspaper, *The Challenge*.[51] In some areas of west Bengal a mass resistance was successfully organized. In April 1932 Government identified Bishnapur in Bankura, Arambagh in Hooghly, and the entire Midnapore district as the most recalcitrant areas of Bengal;[52] and Arambagh and Midnapore were to persist in civil disobedience almost until the end of 1933, long after it had petered out in the rest of the province.[53]

Once more, local grievance gave the leverage. In November 1931 a new revenue settlement had been imposed upon Arambagh 'to the utter dismay and surprise of the distressed peasantry',[54] but to the advantage of the agitators.[55] In Midnapore the resumption of civil disobedience was the signal for reviving the agitation against the chaukidari tax which had been active in the district in 1930. Both these issues were especially important to the richer peasantry who dominated Arambagh and Midnapore alike. It was their domination which gave the resistance the flavour of a mass movement in those areas, so that Imperial Chemical Industries (India) glumly reported about Midnapore: 'There appears to be a network of volunteers, and passive assistance to the movement is given by the villages and merchants.'[56] And that was why during the second civil disobedience movement sixty-four of the seventy-six union boards in Contai sub-division took part in the agitation against chaukidari taxes. Between January and the end

[50] The last was to be Marxism.

[51] Postmaster-General, Bengal, to Director-General, Posts and Telegraphs, 13 February 1932, Home Poll file 21/7 of 1932, NAI. *The Challenge* was a pert and rather charming cyclostyled paper. There are a few copies in the AICC files.

[52] FR Bengal April (1) 1932, Home Poll file 18/7 of 1932, NAI.

[53] Until October 1933, numerous telegrams from Bengal to Delhi continued to report resistance in Arambagh and Midnapore. Home Poll file 3/1 of 1933, NAI.

[54] *Liberty*, 12 November 1931, letter from Profulla Chandra Sen (a future Chief Minister of west Bengal).

[55] 'Arambagh War Council: Report from January to June 1932', file 4/406 of 1932, AICC.

[56] Imperial Chemical Industries (India) to Bengal Chamber of Commerce, 5 September 1932, enclosed in Bengal Chamber of Commerce to Commerce Department, Government of India, 27 September 1932, Home Poll file 195 of 1932, NAI.

of June 1932, 5,900 persons were arrested in Tamluk, 4,343 in Contai.[57]

In Arambagh and Midnapore alike, the power of the rich peasants, Kaibarttas transmuted into Mahisyas, could turn civil disobedience into a mass movement. In Tamluk, where almost the entire population consisted of Kaibarttas, the threat of boycott by the caste saw to it that no one came to the rescue of the persecuted chaukidars.[58] As he grappled with Midnapore, the Commissioner of the Burdwan division recognized that the root of his difficulties lay in '. . . the solidarity of the opposition due to the fact that most of the inhabitants are Mahisyas'.[59] The result was that political activity went deeper than elsewhere, affecting many unlettered men. Many of those imprisoned in Midnapore for civil disobedience were of lower social standing than in the other districts of Bengal.[60] That is why the movement was so strong.

Midnapore was the only counterpart in Bengal to such districts as Kaira and Surat in Gujarat, or Guntur and Nellore in Andhra: where local leaderships took up issues popular with the richer peasants, confidently relying on their solidarity. But what was good for other provinces was not good for the Bengal Congress. The old firm did not welcome a lower class of customer. As the ardent editors of *The Challenge* had to note with regret:

Of the 32 Congress districts, the fringe of the mass has been touched in only a few of them, but in the majority of the districts, the so-called middle-class gentry and educated young men have been drawn into the movement.[61]

The only district of Bengal which did exploit local grievance took care to keep out of the control of its PCC:

Midnapur [*sic*] D.C.C. has been trying to work with as little outside control as possible . . . the whole of Midnapore have all along being trying to keep themselves aloof . . . from the quagmire of Bengal party politics.[62]

[57] 'Tamluk Sub-Divisional War Council: Report on Civil Disobedience Movement in Tamluk from January to June 1932', n.d. (*circa* August 1932), 'Statistical Report of the Civil Disobedience at Contai, Midnapore, from January to July 1932', 24 August 1932, file 4/406 of 1932, AICC.

[58] Narendra Nath Das, *History of Midnapur, Part-Two* (Calcutta, 1962), p. 164.

[59] FR Bengal July (2) 1930, Home Poll file 18/8, NAI.

[60] By the end of 1932, Hijli gaol had housed some 2,957 prisoners convicted during the second civil disobedience movement. Nearly all of them came from Midnapore and Bankura. They were described as 'corner boys' or 'village youths' whose level of literacy was much lower than that of the other civil disobedience prisoners in Bengal, who were predominantly bhadralok. Report on Types of Civil Disobedience Prisoners in Bengal, n.d., enclosed in Government of Bengal to Home Department, Government of India, no. 5394, PJ, 26 November 1932, Home Poll file 23/66 of 1932, NAI.

[61] *The Challenge*, 11 July 1932.

[62] 'Civil Disobedience in Tamluk', a report by G. Singh, Director of Tamluk

All that was left under the control of the Bengal Congress were the sectors of stagnation; all that was dynamic in the eastern and western districts was slipping out of its control. Civil disobedience had exposed the underlying trend of politics:[63] in the east, local power was dribbling through the fingers of the landed supporters of the Congress; in the west, the rich peasants resisted the British and Calcutta alike. Both in the eastern districts, where its allies were being knocked off their perches, and in the western districts, where its nominal supporters kept it at bay, the internal constraints upon the Calcutta clique were growing apace. Sapped by these weaknesses, it had now to face a tightening of external constraints from British political initiatives and the responses to these initiatives from the all-India centre of nationalist politics.

IV

The Communal Award, announced by the British Government in August 1932, was a new sign of its determination to warp the Indian question towards electoral politics. During the late nineteen-twenties there had been many discussions about revising the Montagu-Chelmsford Act so as to put provincial government into Indian hands. All of them had smashed against the question how the communities were to be represented in the new provincial legislatures. Should they be represented by separate electorates as Muslims had been since 1909? In what proportions? And by what franchise? When he went to London for the second session of the Round Table Conference in 1931 Gandhi had hoped to cut through these controversies by insisting that Indian control of the central government must precede communal settlements in the provinces.[64] At the conference, the Minorities Committee would not hear of this. A self-governing India would mean a central government dominated by Hindus. But once the issue of provincial self-government was compounded by a demand for *purna*

Civil Disobedience Council, no date [early 1931], file G 86/186 E, 177N, of 1930, AICC.

[63] During the first half of 1932, some 16,383 persons were arrested in the province, most of them for picketting. The total compares poorly with the 11,025 arrests in Gujarat, a region with only one-sixth of Bengal's population, *The Challenge*, 25 July 1932.

[64] When challenged to be more precise, all he would suggest were joint electorates and a reservation of seats for both Hindus and Muslims on the basis of their populations in those provinces where either community was less than 25 per cent of the population. *Indian Round Table Conference (Second Session), Proceedings of the Minorities Committee*, Appendix I.

swaraj, everyone wanted to see where he stood. Before coming to that point, minorities meant to entrench their own positions. This brought about a deadlock, and towards the end of the conference, MacDonald, the British Prime Minister, announced that since there could be no constitutional progress without settling the issue of communal representation, he would decide between the competing claims.

It was in Bengal and the Punjab that the most vexing problems lay. In most of the provinces of British India the Hindus stood in unchallengeable majorities, and there the only task was to get the best possible terms for the minorities. The North-West Frontier Province was a special case: while possessing a Muslim majority of more than 90 per cent, it was still without a council. Sind was not yet a province. But Bengal and the Punjab were provinces of the first importance, and in both of them the Muslims were a majority, in Bengal of nearly 55 per cent, in the Punjab of nearly 57 per cent. Unless the new constitution ensured their hold on these provinces, the Muslim politicians could not afford to accept it. On the other hand, a British acceptance of their claims would bring bitter protests from the most vociferous Hindu politicians of Bengal and the Punjab, not to mention Sikhs who were 13 per cent of the population of the latter.

In so thorny a question the British were not quick to move.[65] What set them to work on their decision were all-India considerations, in the form of a warning from Willingdon, the Viceroy, 'that the Muslim position is extremely shaky . . . their leaders cannot control them. . . .'[66] Hoare, the Secretary of State for India, reported to the Cabinet that 'unless an undertaking to issue a decision was made before the Mohammadan Conference at Lahore on March 21st, the Mohammadan communities would probably not co-operate further in the work of the Round Table Conference Committees. . . .'[67]

When Hoare first set his mind to drafting the terms of the Award, he was clear that British interests would be served by bettering the existing Muslim position in Bengal and the Punjab; but he believed that in each province, Hindus and Muslims ought to get seats in proportion to their shares of the population. In principle, the Governors of the two pro-

[65] There were, however, good technical reasons for delay. The question was bound up with whatever extensions might be made to the franchise; the Indian Franchise Committee did not report until May 1932. Moreover, the Cabinet was still uncertain whether to put its plans for provincial self-government and for federating India into one and the same Bill; indeed it was not yet committed to producing any Bill at all.
[66] Willingdon to Hoare, private, 21 March 1932, Templewood Papers, vol. 5, Mss Eur E 240, India Office Library, London [IOL].
[67] Cabinet Minute, 23 March 1932, file 49 of Private Office Papers [L/PO], IOL.

vinces agreed with this view.[68] From Calcutta, Anderson advised that out of a Council of 250 for Bengal, the Muslims should have 111 seats or 44.4 per cent of the whole, and the Hindus 107 or 42.8 per cent; the rest were to go to special interests, especially those of the Europeans. But the Government of India felt scant concern for holding a communal balance in Bengal; they proposed to give 121 seats to the Muslims, or 48.4 per cent of the total, and to the Hindus ninety-six, or 39.2 per cent of the total.[69]

Hoare thought that New Delhi was being unfair to the Bengal Hindus. But when he pressed the Government of India to reconsider, the Viceroy came out with his political reasons for turning down Anderson's plan:

Governor naturally has approached problem solely in its provincial aspect in the light exclusively of Bengal conditions. Our own responsibilities compel us to take a wider view. We cannot afford to ignore reactions outside Bengal. ... Governor's proposals ... will alienate from us Moslem support not merely in Bengal but throughout India. ... No words that I can use ... can overstate the importance which I and my colleagues ... attach to a decision by His Majesty's Government accepting our proposals in preference to Governor's. ...[70]

With some reluctance, Hoare accepted the Viceroy's case, and the Cabinet settled the matter on 4 August. Previously, the Hindus had forty-six seats to the Muslims' thirty-nine in the Bengal Council; the Award gave them eighty General seats to the Muslims' 119.[71] This was a stunning blow to the Hindu politicians and their patrons. But when they struck it, the British did so for reasons that in the main were not connected with the province at all, but with averting 'reactions outside Bengal', or in other words to satisfy the Muslim politicians of the UP and the Punjab.

Having been smitten by the British, the Bengal Hindus were now

[68] Hoare to Willingdon, telegram, secret, 22 March 1932; de Montmorency to Willingdon, private, 29 April 1932; Anderson to Willingdon, private, 5 May 1932, *ibid.*

[69] Anderson to Hoare, secret, 7 June 1932; Willingdon to Hoare, telegram 438-S, 14 June 1932, *ibid.* At the same time the Viceroy and his Council thought that the seats to be allotted to the Depressed Classes—then estimated at about ten—should come from the Hindus' ninety-six.

[70] Willingdon to Hoare, telegram 493-S, 9 July 1932, *ibid.* One member of the Viceroy's Council dissented. This was the Law Member, Sir B. L. Mitter. He was a Bengali.

[71] Annexure to *East India (Constitutional Reforms)*: *Communal Decision, Cmd.* 4147 of 1932, in fact, Hoare was harder on the caste Hindus than Willingdon had been, since some of the General seats were meant for the Depressed. Of course, caste Hindus could expect to pick up a few more from the special constituencies.

squeezed by the Congress. The Award had prolonged the system of separate electorates for Hindus, Muslims and Sikhs, and it had extended the system to those whom the draftsmen ambiguously described as the Depressed Classes. At the same time the fourth paragraph of the Award stated that the British Government would not take part in any negotiation to amend the decision, but that it might agree to any 'practicable alternative' which the Indian communities might settle for between themselves. This easement left still darker the prospects of the Bengal Congress. When Gandhi's fast led to the Poona Pact, this meant that the Congress centre bought up the separate electorates awarded to the Depressed Classes; the price it had to pay was to reserve for them a share of the Hindu seats in every province. Generosity on this scale was all very well for the Congress leaders in provinces where, on any assumptions, there would be a copper-bottomed Hindu majority. But in Bengal the caste Hindus had nothing to spare. Matters were all the worse for them because of the obscurity of the term 'Depressed Classes' in the province. In the event it was defined so widely that almost all the non-bhadralok castes were able to get themselves included in the category. At first, Government had intended that the Depressed Classes in Bengal should obtain ten seats. The intervention by the Congress centre raised this number to thirty, and these came from the seventy-eight in the Hindu quota, shrinking it still further.[72]

V

But at first Hindus and Muslims in Bengal were able to work out their attitudes to the Award without much prompting from their all-India patrons. The Congress centre had become a victim of the Ordinance Raj and was closed down; the Muslim League and the Muslim Conference were neither of them credible spokesmen for the all-India interests of the community. The first reaction among politically minded Hindus was one of united commination. Over this issue, at least, there was no disagreement between the factions of the PCC. *Liberty*, which was still writing in the Subhas interest, denounced the terms of the Award as:

... insulting and positively mischievous. ... The Hindus are rendered politically impotent, and the reactions of this process on the cultural, economic and political life of the province will be disastrous.[73]

[72] The Bengal Congress could reasonably hope to win some of these thirty seats.
[73] *Liberty*, 17 August 1932.

Advance, which spoke for Sen Gupta, repeated these indictments:

... the award has sacrificed the province to the Moslem and European communities and has left no real autonomy to the children of the soil.[74]

When Government ruled that eighty-seven Bengal castes were to be included in the Depressed Classes, both newspapers protested again. *Liberty* wrote that this was tantamount to saying that '... the Bhadra-logs of Bengal are the only undepressed class', whereas they had merely acted for the good of all the rest:

The political interests of socially inferior classes never suffered for reasons of their social inferiority.[75]

Advance took the same line, blaming the Namasudras and Rajbansis for allowing themselves to be classed as Depressed. In any case:

... there does not exist in Bengal any caste or castes which may perpetually come under the definition of 'depressed'.[76]

Whatever their dissension over other issues, when the Bengal factions did agree, their unanimity was wonderful. It is easy to see behind this concord their anxiety for the safety of the Permanent Settlement, if the Award were to give the Muslims control of a self-governing Bengal. Further tenancy legislation would really hurt 'the children of the soil'. Since both groups were candidly devoted to the landholder interest,[77] this initial unity was natural. But it was not to last. Towards the end of the year a Unity Conference at Allahabad considered the communal question in India as a whole. For Bengal they proposed that the Muslims should be given an absolute majority of seats (127) in the Legislative Council. In return for this assurance of control, the Muslims were to agree that representation of the Hindus should be increased to 112. More important, the Muslims were to agree to joint electorates. Now there were many Indian politicians who specialized in Unity

[74] *Advance*, 18 August 1932.

[75] *Liberty*, 22 January 1933. Although the Poona Pact was made on 25 September 1932, it was not until the following January that the Government of Bengal ruled which castes in Bengal were to be included under its arrangements for the Depressed Classes. By defining some substantial peasants as Depressed, the Government showed once more how British administrative categories rode rough-shod over Indian social facts.

[76] *Advance*, 22 January 1933.

[77] During the civil disobedience movement, *Advance* took the opportunity of describing a Muslim motion in Council for further amendment of the Tenancy Amendment Act of 1928 as 'grotesque'. *Advance*, 23 November 1932. Its rival wrote that 'The better type of landholder[s] in Bengal ... have inspired the best of our cultural movements and financed every public endeavour that has had for its object the accomplishment of something great and good.' *Liberty*, 1 March 1933.

Conferences, where they turned real conflicts into bland unrealities. So we need not take the Allahabad proposals very seriously. But what is interesting about them is their reception in Bengal. Some Congressmen were firmly against them, but others wobbled. None of them liked the notion of an absolute Muslim majority, but they were divided over the notion of joint electorates. In the western districts, with their Hindu majorities, Congressmen had nothing to fear from joint electorates. But in the eastern districts, the trend of the district board elections had shown how much they had to lose. In the event, the scheme came to nothing, but the divisions it opened were a portent of greater trouble to come.[78]

Even in the short run the Award was managing to divide the Bengal Muslims as well. When news of its terms first reached Calcutta, the Bengal Government telegraphed its impression that 'Muslims are satisfied but are determined to continue demand for statutory majority, more as offset to Hindu demands than as demand in itself sustainable.'[79] All the Muslim political groups complained that their 48 per cent of representation in the council would leave any Muslim ministry dependent on the good will of others. Their demand for the elusive 51 per cent was voiced by Fazl-Huq, the Bengal Muslim League and the Bengal section of the Muslim Conference; but it was also expressed by the few Muslims who belonged to the Congress. With the whole community jubilant at the prospect of becoming the masters, no Muslim party could flout that mood by not pressing for an absolute majority. But in every other respect, the Award divided these parties. Predictably, the Congress Muslims, following the party's line, attacked separate electorates. So too did the Bengal wing of the Muslim League, whose members were close enough to the populist roots of east Bengal to realize that they had nothing to fear from joint electorates. On the other hand, the old-fashioned Central National Muhammadan Association, which derived its strength from Calcutta and the western districts, where the community was weaker, held strongly to separate electorates.

[78] For brevity, this account neglects the role of the Hindu Mahasabha. During the 1920s Bengal had rejected the Mahasabha. After the failure of Das's Pact, the temper of the Bengal Congress was sufficiently anti-Muslim for it to perform the Mahasabha's work without acknowledgement. But the Award gave the Mahasabha a fresh chance in Bengal. It was active in protest (e.g. *Advance*, 21 August 1932; *Liberty*, 5 September 1932). It strongly opposed the Allahabad scheme, making impossible stipulations and finally inducing Congressmen to make them as well. For the negotiations over the proposals see *Advance*, 29 November 1932, and *Liberty*, 12, 26, 28 and 29 December 1932.

[79] Government of Bengal to Secretary of State, telegram, 22 August 1932, Home Poll file 41/4 of 1932, NAI.

This was also the view of the Bengal section of the Muslim Conference which was dominated by wealthy men such as Sir A. K. Ghaznavi and Nazimuddin, who had no wish to see Muslim radicalism encouraged by campaigns fought in joint electorates.[80] All these preliminary divisions among Hindus and Muslims in Bengal were to be widened once the issue of the Award came to be examined on the stage of all-India politics.

In devising their attitudes to the Award, the spokesmen of all-India interests, Muslim and Hindu alike, were aware of its enormous implications for electoral politics. From their all-India standpoints, the root problem was that the Award affected both communities in different ways in different provinces. In Bombay, Madras, the Central Provinces, Bihar and the United Provinces, it was not contentious, since there the Hindus were bound to win in any case. In Sind, if Sind were to become a separate province, Muslims of some sort were bound to win, and so they were in the North-West Frontier Province, although here the winners were likely to be unsympathetic to the Muslim centre. The rub came in Bengal and the Punjab, where the composition of the new legislature was likely to strip the Hindus of much of their previous political importance. Here was an apple of discord for the Congress. Its claim to be spokesman for the entire Indian nation rested on its carrying a Muslim wing of its own. For these Congress Muslims there was no choice but to accept the Award in Bengal and the Punjab. Opposing it would have meant their political extinction. This would also have extinguished the credibility of Congress claims to represent Indians of all communities. On the other hand, for the Congress to acquiesce in the Award would enrage its Hindu members in Bengal and the Punjab.

At first, civil disobedience postponed the dilemma for the Congress centre. Gandhi and the other leaders were in gaol; the police broke up the annual sessions; and anyway, with nothing precisely known about the new constitution, there was nothing immediately to decide. From his prison, Gandhi advised his followers to keep mum;[81] and for seven months after his release in August 1933, he was able to bottle up discussion of the awkward issue. But it was bound to spill out. Early in 1933 a White Paper outlined the British Government's suggestions about the shape of the reforms.[82] Here was a powerful stimulus to electoral poli-

---

[80] Ghaznavi and Nazimuddin told the Governor of Bengal that the Muslims should be given an absolute majority of seats for otherwise 'the strong section which has always favoured joint electorates without reservation of seats would again assert itself. . . .', enclosed in Anderson to Hoare, 22 July 1932, file 49 of L/PO, IOL.

[81] Gandhi to Birla, 21 January 1933, G. D. Birla, *In the Shadow of the Mahatma* (new edition, Bombay, 1968), p. 87.

[82] *Proposals for Indian Constitutional Reform, Cmd.* 4268 of 1933.

tics, for now it was reasonably plain that under the new constitution the provinces would practically govern themselves. For many Congressmen this was a much more glowing prospect than sticking in the dead end of civil disobedience; moreover, the approach of the interim elections to the Delhi Assembly provided an excuse for reviving the Swarajist Party. Here, as usual, calculations of provincial interest were everything. In provinces with a majority of Hindus, the chances of Congress-Swarajist candidates for the Assembly would be bright; but brighter by far would be the chances of these candidates for provincial elections under the new constitution, when there would be everything to play for, and when there would be Hindu majorities guaranteed by the Award. Men of that sort, ready to rush for nomination, did not share Gandhi's anxiety about snapping the unity of the movement. There was no gainsaying them; and at a meeting of the All-India Congress Committee at Patna, between 18 and 20 May 1934, the bargain was struck. On his side, Gandi agreed to abandon civil disobedience and to sanction a programme of fighting the elections to the Assembly. For their part, the new Swarajists swallowed the argument that since Congress was totally opposed to the reforms which were taking shape in London, the question of its attitude to the Award simply did not arise. Therefore, Congress, it was announced, neither accepted nor rejected the Award.[83] So sybilline a statement warded off trouble, but the trouble was bound to return. To fight the elections meant setting up a Parliamentary Board to supervise nominations and expound the party's views, including its views on the most vexed issue in Indian politics—the Award.

What were these views? Gandhi still hoped he would not have to say. But when the Working Committee met members of the Parliamentary Board in June, the clash of interests showed that the cat could not be kept in the bag. Malaviya and Aney, with their Mahasabha connections, thought it scandalous that Congress should not candidly denounce the Award, and they threatened to resign unless it was rejected. On their side, the Congress Muslims, Khaliquzzaman, Asaf Ali and Dr Syed Mahmud, protested that such a rejection would finish their influence with their own supporters. If the Award was denounced, they too threatened to resign, and their leader, Dr Ansari, would go with them. Harassed by both sides, Gandhi improvised a new resolution.

[83] For new evidence about the evolution of this decision, see K. M. Munshi, *Indian Constitutional Documents*, vol. I (Bombay, 1967), pp. 357–82. There is an illuminating account in 'The Communal Award', a memorandum prepared by Chandrashankar Shukla, Vallabhbhai Patel Papers. Shukla had acted as one of Gandhi's secretaries in 1934. There is further information in Rajendra Prasad, *Autobiography* (Bombay, 1957), pp. 378–9.

Congress rejected the White Paper. Only a constituent assembly could settle the communal problem. 'The White Paper lapsing', he continued in a daring *petitio principii*, 'the Communal Award lapses automatically'. Nevertheless,

Since, however, the different communities in the country are sharply divided on the question of the Communal Award, it is necessary to define the Congress attitude on it. The Congress claims to represent equally all the communities composing the Indian nation and therefore, in view of the division of opinion, can neither accept nor reject the Communal Award as long as the division of opinion lasts. . . . Judged by the national standard the Communal Award is wholly unsatisfactory, besides being open to serious objections on other grounds.[84]

So it had come to this. On one of the most crucial of issues before the country, the divisions inside Indian society forced Congress to move from one tongue-tied position to another. First, the self-styled spokesmen for India could not speak. Then, when they were driven into speaking, they had nothing to say. This was good enough for the Congress Muslims, who were too beggared of support to be choosers; but for the Mahasabha wing of the Congress, who were not short of other options, it was merely a word game. Gandhi did his best:

The more I think about it, the clearer I become that the Working Committee . . . resolution is faultless. . . . Non-committal is the only position the Congress can take up. We must not tease the communal boil. The more we tease it, the worse it becomes. In my opinion it is a fatal blunder to turn our opinion from the White Paper. If the reforms are not killed, the Award will stand in spite of agitation. The reforms can be killed by sustained effort.[85]

By July 1934, this was a sanguine statement. It did not convince Malaviya and Aney. They quit the Parliamentary Board and went on to organize a new Congress Nationalist Party, designed to cripple the Swarajists at the elections by dilating on the wrongs of Bengali and Punjabi Hindus. When they began marshalling their forces at the All-India Communal Award Conference held on 25 October, most of the old faces from the Mahasabha breakaway of 1926 were to be seen. Their conference was attended by Kelkar, Moonjee and Aney, veterans from the Tilak school of politics, by Bhai Parmanand and

84 The text of the resolution, as it was approved by the Working Committee, is printed in *The Indian National Congress, Resolutions 1934-6* (Allahabad, n.d.), pp. 19-20. Gandhi's draft, which differs in unimportant ways, is in Appendix 2 to the memorandum by Chandrashankar Shukla, *loc. cit.* The account of these discussions in June by Chaudhry Khaliquzzaman, *Pathway to Pakistan* (Lahore, 1961), pp. 123-26, differs in some details, and also in some dates.

85 Gandhi to Aney, 12 July 1934, quoted in Shukla, 'The Command Award', Vallabhbhai Patel Papers.

Radha Kumud Mukerji, also of the Mahasabha persuasion, and by
Raja Narendranath and Master Tara Singh, a couple brought into
startling and short-lived agreement by the grievances of Hindus and
Sikhs in the Punjab. The conference castigated the Congress attitude to
the Award as 'a virtual acquiescence in the decision'.[86] Of course it was.
The point was taken in Bengal as well. Objurgations and appeals from
the province poured into the AICC, most of them from east Bengal,
conspicuously from Dinajpur, Barisal, Chittagong, Khulna, Dacca,
Pabna, Jessore, Mymensingh and Brahmanbaria.[87]

These complex events were now enlivened by another round of
quarrelling inside the Bengal PCC. By now the old paladins were no
longer there, for Subhas had gone to Europe and Sen Gupta had died,
and their factions had passed into the hands of B. C. Roy and J. C.
Gupta respectively. The latter group had been alarmed that the new
Swarajist machine for fighting elections in Bengal would fall under the
control of their rivals;[88] after this quarrel had been patched up,
there was another struggle for control of the Corporation, and for a
while Calcutta was graced by the presence of two rival mayors. It was
not that the factions differed in their attitude to the Award; all that
separated them over this issue was that B. C. Roy, now leader of the
majority in the PCC, had tacked so close to Gandhi that he had to
accept the Working Party's ambiguous statements about the Award;
J. C. Gupta, on the other hand, with the freedom of leading the outs,
kept on demanding that the Congress centre should permit open
agitation in Bengal against it.[89] But these were no more than tactical

[86] Resolution of the first session of the All-Indian Communal Award Conference,
enclosed in Ramanand Chatterjee to Rajendra Prasad, 27 October 1934, file G/24 of
1934–36, AICC.

[87] Here are some of the messages of protest from east Bengal all addressed to
Vallabhbhai Patel, President of the Congress: Joginchandra Chakravarty [Dinajpur],
telegram, 7 September 1934; Saratchaira Guha, telegram, 7 September 1934;
Mohin Das, 7 September 1934; Mymensingh conference, 7 September 1934; Khulna
Congress Committee, telegram, 6 September 1934; Pabna Congress Committee,
8 August 1934; Jhenida Congress Committee [Jessore], 12 August 1934; statement by
President, Dacca DCC, enclosed in Secretary, Congress Nationalist Party, Bengal,
to AICC, 6 August 1934. There were also protests from Hooghly, Burdwan, Calcutta
and Birbhum in west Bengal, file G 24 of 1934–36, AICC.

[88] For the development and the temporary settlement of this devious affair see
K. M. Munshi to Gandhi, n.d. [circa 8 April 1934], in Munshi, Indian Constitutional
Documents, I, 369; Bhulabhai Desai to unnamed correspondent, 10 May 1934, in
M. C. Setalvad, Bhulabhai Desai (New Delhi, 1968), pp. 120–1; J. C. Gupta, Amarendranath Chatterjee, D. C. Chakravarti and others to AICC, 11 May 1934, file G
25/506 of 1934–35, AICC; Munshi to Gandhi, 23 May 1934, in Munshi, Indian Constitutional Documents, I, 374.

[89] J. C. Gupta to Gandhi, 16 August 1934, Vallabhbhai Patel Papers.

differences; their inwardness was expressed by the Gandhian workers of Bengal, who were without any hope of power in the PCC, and so could afford to play the role of impartial observers:

'Amrita Bazar Patrika' is communal. The vernacular 'Basumati' is frankly sanatanist. 'Ananda Bazar Patrika' . . . is a vehement supporter of the Hindu Sabha. . . . 'Advance' is a close ally of the 'Ananda Bazar Patrika'. These two papers seized the opportunity of the resignations of Panditji [Malaviya] and Sj. Aney . . . to make their party strong by damning the Parliamentary Board and the Working Committee as having played into their hands. . . . 'Forward'[90] has no love for the Working Committee or for you either. But it supports because it has to.[91]

The communalism of Bengal Hindus, which seemed so deplorable to the Congress centre, seemed indispensable to the PCC in Calcutta, if they were to make headway against the Nationalists in the forthcoming elections. B. C. Roy pleaded with Gandhi to permit the Bengal Congress to come out against the Award. Would he allow them to announce that their candidates for the Assembly would vote against any move to support the Award there? Gandhi would not. Nor would he allow these candidates to be dispensed on conscientious grounds from obeying the Working Committee resolution: 'Those . . . who want dispensation have simply to belong to the Nationalist Party.'[92] At the same time, the all-India interests, for whose sake he was hobbling the Bengal Congress, were driving him to try for an electoral pact with the Nationalists. But Malaviya and Aney pitched their price too high.[93] Their party persisted with its campaign against the Congress, and when the Assembly elections took place in Bengal, they carried all seven seats in the General constituencies: Congress won none. The new policy of strictly subordinating Bengal to the centre had produced another ominous result.

[90] *Forward* was *Liberty* under a new name.
[91] Birendra Nath Gupta to Gandhi, 21 August 1934, Vallabhbhai Patel Papers. Like everyone else in Bengal, the Gandhians had their factions. B. N. Gupta belonged to the group led by Suresh Chandra Banerji.
[92] B. C. Roy to Gandhi, 22 August 1934; Gandhi to B. C. Roy, 25 August 1934; Gandhi to B. C. Roy, 30 August 1934; Vallabhbhai Patel Papers. In fact, Gandhi had offered a version of the conscience clause to Malaviya. He proposed to apply it in individual cases. Malaviya demanded that it must apply to all candidates.
[93] Malaviya and Aney demanded twenty seats. Gandhi and Vallabhbhai then proposed local arrangements in which the 'demonstrably weaker party' should retire. Forwarding this second scheme, Gandhi commented: 'I do not know what view the Parliamentary Board will take but Sardar [Patel] accepts it in substance.' Gandhi to Malaviya, 3 September 1934, Vallabhbhai Patel Papers. This is an interesting commentary on the powers of the Board.

VI

At this point Bengal was whirled into the vortex of the all-India problem, for reasons of which its politicians knew little, and by agencies of which they disapproved. Once again, the initiative came not from India but from Westminster. When the Joint Select Committee reported in October 1934, the lines of the imminent Government of India Act became clear. In the long term, India was to be federated, although the shape of the federation was still up in the air. In the short term, the provinces were to receive self-government, although the imperial safeguards were somewhat fussier than they had been in the White Paper. In its decadence, British imperialism was swinging between the concessions of 1933 and the safeguards of 1934. But the Congress leaders could now be sure that they were dealing with a power which knew it must give way in the provinces.

For the right-wing men who dominated the Congress leadership, men such as Vallabhbhai Patel, Rajendra Prasad and Rajagopalachari, this initiative in British policy underwrote their own choice in favour of electoral politics. During the nineteen-twenties they had argued for no-change against the Swarajists of those days. Das and Motilal Nehru, those frustrated collaborators, had entered the Councils. But they had never controlled the ministries. Now the survivors could do so. Provincial power was in sight for the Congress right wing. They had waited long for it. They meant to take it. Better still, the British were on the run; so the independence of all-India might be within grasp, especially if the Muslims could be brought into a nationalist coalition. How then were the Muslims to be paid? Obviously by tactical concessions in Bengal and the Punjab. In Wardha and Ahmedabad and Madras this seemed a fair price to pay.

But which Muslims were to be squared? The Award, it is true, dealt the community high cards to play against Congress, if the latter needed a joint opposition against the British. One obvious way of playing the hand would be by a long, slow game, cashing its immediate winnings from the Award, and ultimately settling for an independent India with a weak centre and strong provinces—a United States of India where the Muslims would be entrenched in their own majority regions. The argument for the waiting game was well expressed by the Aga Khan, one of the leaders of the Muslim Conference:

The Conf[erence], the League or any other body, if it is to meet & discuss, will open the door to the other elements to counter-attack the Com[munal]

Award, and by making, thanks to the Hindu press, all powerful, such a noise as to frighten the B[ritish] Gov[ernment] to go back & say 'as important Muslims are opposed to it, they are not prepared to push it through Parliament'. . . . By all means let us have . . . our Unity conferences . . . but *only after the Com[munal] award is law of the land & Act of Parliament a reality.*[94]

The community should stand pat. It should eschew negotiation. It should be wary of schemes of self-government at the centre. As for the Muslim League, it was in disarray until Jinnah returned to take the lead, but it was clear that Muslims must hold on to 'those rights which have already been conceded to them'.[95]

But this was the view from Delhi or the Ritz Hotel. In fact there was no more a general interest for all Muslims than there was for all Hindus. In their majority provinces, what preoccupied Muslim leaders were the interests of their followers in those provinces, and in different districts of those provinces. In the Punjab, Sind and Bengal, where the Award had rendered their majorities secure, some of them were ready to flirt with joint electorates.[96] Without an effective centre, with the Muslim Conference a network of notables and the Muslim League a cockpit of rivals, the position of the community was chaotic. Some Muslims wanted the Award and wanted the reforms as a way of buttressing it. Others wanted the Award but would not hear of the reforms. Some worked for joint electorates, others worked against them. Some glimpsed provincial power moving into their grasp; others saw it vanishing for ever.

But after March 1934, when Jinnah was back in power in the Muslim League, the position became a little simpler. His rivals, Fazl-i-Husain and the Aga Khan, had placed the Muslim Conference firmly behind the Award, but many Muslims from east Bengal were ready to bargain about it. This gave Jinnah an alternative way of playing the hand which the British had dealt: he could offer the Congress the League's co-operation over joint electorates if in return the Congress would accept

[94] Aga Khan to Fazl-i-Husain, Private, 21 January 1934, Fazl-i-Husain Papers [italics in original].

[95] Resolutions of the Muslim League on the Communal Award, 25-6 November 1933, *All-India Muslim League Resolutions, 1924-36* [n.d.], pp. 57-8.

[96] In 1933 the Muslim leaders of the Punjab calculated that by conceding joint electorates they could turn their representation of 49 per cent, guaranteed by the Award, into an absolute majority. But the plan cleft the Muslims of west Punjab, where the majority was large, and the Muslims of east Punjab, where the Hindus had the majority in the Ambala division. Moreover, the plan exposed the split of interests between the rural Muslims of the west, and the urban Muslims whose chance of representation in Lahore and Amritsar would be much reduced. Fazl-i-Husain to Zafrullah Khan, 8 May 1933; to Shafat Ahmad Khan, 19 June 1933, Fazl-i-Husain Papers. For Sind, see Fazl-i-Husain to Abdulla Haroun, 16 December 1932, *ibid.*

Muslim majorities in Bengal and the Punjab. Jinnah had sound reasons for seeking agreement with Congress. If he was to beat the Conference, then he had to broaden the basis of the League. An agreement with Congress would be helpful and might be possible, since he was as opposed to safeguards as they were, and his Bengal followers would accept joint electorates. This would mean trouble in the Punjab, where Muslim politics were controlled by Fazl-i-Husain, but he had little to lose there.[97]

Twelve months earlier, the Congress high command had been aware that they might buy Jinnah's support against the British, at the cost of selling out the Hindus in Bengal and the Punjab.[98] Now in January 1935, when the Joint Select Committee's report gave them a solid incentive to do so, Jinnah made his offer in plain terms:

I have nothing in common with the Aga Khan. He is a British agent. I am devoted to my old policy and programme. . . . If the Congress can support the Muslims on the question of the Communal Award, I would be able to get all the Muslim members except 7 or 8.

I . . . take the view that the J.P.C. [Joint Select Committee] Provincial constitution would be acceptable if the powers of the Governor and the legislative independence of the police department were removed. . . .

I am for the complete rejection of the proposals relating to Central Government. . . .

As things stand, the practical way would be for just a few leaders of political thought to combine for the purpose of preparing a formula which both the communities might accept. The Congress I admit would have to change its attitude in some respects, but looking to the great interests at stake Congress leaders should not flinch. I think that the future is with the Congress Party and not with me or the Aga Khan.[99]

[97] In any case, Jinnah still saw himself less as a party leader than as a go-between whose role lay in the central Assembly (to which he had been re-elected in October 1934). There the support of the Congress members would strengthen his claim to be a national leader.

[98] In January 1934 Jinnah had suggested a combined attack against the proposals of the White Paper, if Congressmen would accept the Communal Award; Munshi to Gandhi, 27 January 1934, in Munshi, *Indian Constitutional Documents*, I, 360, 361.

[99] 'Summary of conversation between Mr. Jinnah and myself', Vallabhbhai Patel Papers. This document is unsigned and undated. It is uncertain who made the summary, since copies of many documents circulating among the Congress high command found their way into Vallabhbhai's papers. But its date is fairly clear. The report had been published in December 1934. Jinnah returned to India in January 1935. The Aga Khan was also in India during that month. Jinnah's unknown interlocutor suggested that if there were to be conversations, they 'should take place before the Muslim League met'. The Council of the League met on 25-6 January. We may therefore conclude that the date of the conversation must have been very shortly before 23 January, when the talks between Jinnah and Rajendra Prasad did, in fact, begin.

On 23 January 1935, Rajendra Prasad, now president of the Congress, opened negotiations. He soon found that Jinnah was ready to bargain about the Award; for a price he would agree to joint electorates.[100] The Congress right wing had now to settle how much they were ready to pay. On the evening of 30 January, the Congress president, together with Vallabhbhai, Malaviya and Bhulabhai Desai agreed on the price: they would give the Muslims 51 per cent of the seats in Bengal and in the Punjab—more than the British had awarded them. [101] When this was put to Jinnah on the following day, he asked for more, observing 'that he was unable just yet to see any way to induce the Punjab although he felt that he had good grounds for recommending joint electorates to Bengal'; the Muslims would be more readily persuaded, if they were granted a differential franchise as well.[102]

At that point the talks were adjourned for twelve days, so that both sides might sound their followers. It says much for the anxiety of the Congress leadership to clinch the agreement that they made no immediate difficulties over Jinnah's higher terms; and still more, that they deliberately let the bulk of Bengal Congress opinion go by default, even when their province was coming up for auction. The only Bengal politician consulted by the Congress centre seems to have been B. C. Roy, who could speak convincingly for the rich men of Calcutta but not for the opinion of the districts.

On 13–14 February, Prasad and Jinnah finally nerved themselves to

[100] 'Substance of conversation . . . on the 23rd January 1935', Rajendra Prasad Papers [RPP] XI/35/1/2; 'Notes on conversation on 28 January 1935', RPP XI/35/1/6.

[101] 'Notes of conversation between . . . Malaviya . . . Patel . . . Desai . . . and . . . Prasad . . . on the 30th of January 1935', RPP XI/35/1/9. This meeting ratified the agreement reached earlier that day between Prasad and Jinnah, that in all provinces other than Bengal, the Punjab and Assam, the weightage given to minorities under the communal decision should stand; and that in Bengal both Hindus and Muslims should try to persuade the Europeans to surrender some of their seats. These were then to be divided between the two communities.

[102] 'Notes of conversation . . . on 31st January, 1935', RPP XI/35/1/10. If a given percentage of seats was to be reserved for either Hindus or Muslims under a system of separate electorates, this could be contrived by allotting to each community that percentage of constituencies which were bound to elect Hindu or Muslim members. In the Punjab the Sikhs possessed separate constituencies as well. This system had existed under the Montagu–Chelmsford constitution. But if separate electorates were to be replaced by joint electorates, then seats might still effectively be reserved by altering the terms of the franchise. Such schemes for a differential franchise implied altering British proposals by readjusting the franchise so that the electoral rolls reflected the proportion of population formed by Hindus and Muslims in Bengal and the proportion of Hindus, Muslims and Sikhs in the Punjab.

agree on a formula 'as a basis for further discussion'. Joint electorates were to replace separate electorates in the voting for the central and provincial legislatures. Bengal and the Punjab apart, in all the other provinces of British India the number of seats reserved to the Muslims under the Communal Award was to stand. In Bengal and the Punjab, the franchise was to be adjusted on a differential basis. In Bengal, 'the seats allotted to the Muslims under the award are to remain reserved for them', and if the Europeans surrendered any of their seats, these were to be divided between Hindus and Muslims in proportion to their population in the province—which would give the Muslims an absolute majority.[103]

The drafting of this 'basis for further discussion' was very cautious; its inwardness lay in generally accepting, although not in so many words, the Communal Award. Congress had bought out the Muslim asset of separate electorates at the cost of acquiescing in the certainty of Muslim control of the Punjab and the likelihood of Muslim control of Bengal. From his all-India point of view, Rajendra Prasad was satisfied with the bargain. The loss of Bengal and the Punjab was regrettable, but there was the compensation, as he reminded Vallabhbhai Patel, that:

Joint electorates are in themselves important as opening a way for joint action which has great possibilities for the future. Hindus have always attached great value to them and if they can be had they should be prepared to pay some price.[104]

From the summit of the Congress high command (as of the Government of India) it was easy to assume the existence of some solid mass defined as 'Hindus'; but that assumption slid over the awkward local facts. It was not the Hindus as a whole who would have to pay the price, but some Hindus in some districts of some provinces. In the Ambala division of Punjab, and the Presidency and Burdwan divisions of Bengal, the Hindu majorities had nothing to fear from joint electorates; just as on the other side of the hill, the Muslim majorities in west Punjab and east Bengal stood to gain from them. But where the shoe pinched was in areas where socially powerful minorities of Muslims and Hindus would be trapped in constituencies which they could never hope to capture. The Jinnah-Prasad proposals could expect no support from the urban Muslims of the Lahore division or from the

---

[103] 'Notes on conversations . . . on the 13th and 14th February, 1935', RPP XI/35/1/17. The Muslims were also to keep the one-third share of seats in the new central legislature which Hoare had allotted them.

[104] Rajendra Prasad to Vallabhbhai Patel, 14 February 1935, Vallabhbhai Patel Papers.

upper-caste Hindus of the Dacca, Rajshahi and Chittagong divisions. As for the Sikhs, they had already blocked an earlier scheme of differential franchise for the Punjab, and it was hard to see how any variant could secure them their 18 per cent of seats under the Award. These were not hopeful signs.

The combined efforts of Bhulabhai Desai, Patel and Prasad gradually won over the Hindus of the Punjab, but this was to be their only success. At first, the Congress president hoped to carry Hindu opinion in Bengal; apparently B. C. Roy and his coterie in Calcutta persuaded him that the formula 'may be accepted by other influential Bengalis also'.[105] But the time had gone when influential Bengalis could credibly speak for the Hindus of their province. So far as the Congress politicians in the districts were concerned, the issue cut too near the bone for them to leave their case in the hands of a few Congress notables. Other troubles were mounting as well. The Sikhs would not hear of the Punjab formula. The Hindu Mahasabha denounced the Bengal formula.[106] So did Malaviya, the voice of Hindu orthodoxy.[107] But Jinnah was now stipulating that Sikhs, Mahasabha and Malaviya must all agree before he would risk trying to push the scheme through the Muslim League.[108] Sceptics were coming to wonder whether the negotiations were more than a charade, a view expressed by Sir N. N. Sarcar, the Law Member of the Government of India: 'I feel . . . that the peace talk is pure moonshine. Jinnah is humbugging the Congress and the latter know that they are being humbugged'.[109]

Whatever Jinnah's motives may have been, his conditions gave the Bengal Congress a way out of its isolation. Now it could band together with the disgruntled from other provinces against the Congress centre. With Malaviya and the spokesmen for the Sikhs and the Mahasabha milling around him in Delhi, Prasad had enough difficulties. His troubles were compounded by the arrival of emissaries from the Bengal Congress, those pastmasters of faction. They brought their own splits

[105] Rajendra Prasad to Vallabhbhai Patel, 14 February 1935, Vallabhbhai Patel Papers.

[106] The Mahasabha were demanding that no seats should be reserved for either community in Bengal; Hindu Sabha to Prasad, telegram, 16 February 1935; Ramanand Chatterji, H. N. Dutt, J. N. Basu, Rajendra Dev, B. N. Majumdar and Indra Narayan Sen to Prasad, telegram, n.d. (?16 February 1935); Secretary, All-Bengal Hindu Conference to Prasad, 16 February 1935, RPP XI/35/1/21.

[107] Malaviya also opposed the scheme for giving the Muslims too much in the new central legislature.

[108] 'Daily Notes', 20 and 22 February 1935, RPP XI/35/30.

[109] Sarcar to R. M. Chatterji, 18 February 1935, N. N. Sarcar Papers, Nehru Memorial Museum and Library, New Delhi.

with them. The division between Hindu interests in east and in west Bengal had been dragged into the open by the Prasad-Jinnah plan. East Bengalis were prominent among the root and branch group who wanted to knock the Bengal formula to pieces by scrapping the differential franchise, limiting the reservation of seats to ten years, pulling down the Muslim share of seats from 119 to 110, and pushing up the Hindu share to about ninety. Pitted against them was a more moderate view, expressed by the west Bengal leaders, P. N. Bannerji and Amarendranath Chatterji, who supported the first two demands but who were prepared to leave the distribution of seats alone.[110]

When Prasad confronted the Bengalis and the all-India leaders of the Mahasabha on 25 February, he was both perplexed and irritated by the demands of the Bengal opposition. Expounded by Sarkendranath Roy, Indra Narayan Sen, Dinesh Chakravarty and Makhen Lall Sen, these had a pronounced flavour both of the Hindu Sabha and of east Bengal. The Congress president's own notes describe the clash:

I told the gentlemen present that so far as I could see there was no chance of these proposals being accepted by Mr. Jinnah and I took it that their instruction was that I should break off negotiations. . . . Some Bengal friends said that sooner the negotiations were broken off the better, but Dr. Bannerji [West Bengal] said that there was a sharp difference of opinion and I should not take that as the Bengal opinion. . . . Dr. Bannerji asked Malaviyajee to take the question in his hand, accept anything he considered fair and reasonable and they would all accept it. Mr Anney [Mahasabha] said that he would not give that authority to Malviyajee alone. Dr. Moonjey [Mahasabha] said that they should all assist Malaviyajee in finding a formula. Pandit Malaviyajee said that seeing that there was such sharp difference of opinion he would not take any such responsibility on himself. . . . I said . . . I would show their demands to Mr. Jinnah but I had no hopes of their being accepted. I pointed out that we were losing a great opportunity of getting Joint Electorates about which we had been speaking so much.[111]

Clearly there was no hope of meeting Jinnah's conditions. But so anxious were Prasad and Vallabhbhai Patel to save their bargain that when the Congress president met Jinnah on 27 February he suggested confining the agreement to the Congress and the League, leaving aside the more intransigent bodies. Jinnah refused. That was the end of the affair.[112] Another all-India leader of the Congress, a man eager for electoral victory in his own province, commiserated with Prasad: 'It is very tragic'.[113]

[110] 'Daily Notes', 25 February 1935, RPP XI/35/30.
[111] *Ibid*.
[112] 'Daily Notes', 27 February 1935, RPP XI/35/30.
[113] Rajagopalachari to Rajendra Prasad, 2 March 1935, RPP XI/35/40.

Perhaps the odds had always been against success; but the history of the negotiations is revealing. Prasad's account shows that in his view it was the Bengal Hindus who used Jinnah's conditions to upset the bargain. Ever since 1932, they had been alarmed by the new electoral arithmetic. From the British India Association to the University, from the zemindars to the literary men, from chairmen of district boards to members of the Legislative Council, they had shouted their hatred of the Communal Award from the housetops. It had been in the interest of Hindu politicians in all districts to do so.

But their general solidarity was dividing into regional interests of east and west. At one time they had rightly seen that from one end of Bengal to another, their advantage lay in pressing for joint electorates; even where they were outnumbered by Muslims, as in the districts of east Bengal, their local influence could win seats for them. But these calculations dated from the golden days of Hindu predominance. By the nineteen-thirties they had everything to lose in the eastern districts by joint electorates. In west Bengal, where joint electorates were in the interest of the political oligarchy, the Jinnah-Prasad formula would rescue something from the Award. But in east Bengal, where their last hope now lay in preserving separate electorates, the formula would ruin them completely. Rajendra Prasad had been misled by his Calcutta advisers, for as he ruefully admitted:

When we came to discuss the merits of the proposed formula it appeared that there was difference of opinion as regards the value of joint electorates some friends saying that separate electorates would suit Hindus in Eastern Bengal better.[114]

Birla put the point more bitingly when he reported to Gandhi that

Among the Bengal Hindus those who come from West Bengal are favourably disposed towards joint electorates. On the other hand, East Bengal is simply frightened of it.[115]

This glaring division of interests put a further strain upon the Bengal Congress. The all-India leadership had already brought it to heel. Every fresh act of control by the centre added to the difficulties under which the Bengal Congress had to work. The centre had unleashed civil disobedience and unsettled the preponderance of Calcutta. It had demolished the power of the majority faction. It had surrendered thirty seats to the lower castes. Now it had clearly shown that in the pursuit of its wider interests it meant to abandon Bengal to the Muslims.

[114] 'Daily Notes', 26 February 1935, RPP XI/35/30.
[115] Birla to Mahadev Desai, 28 February 1935, Birla, *In the Shadow of the Mahatma*, p. 150.

VII

By their strategy of concentrating on the greatest good of the greatest number of Hindus in other provinces, Prasad and Patel had shown how little value they placed on Bengal. When the Congress president visited Calcutta in March 1935, he found Congressmen still full of resentment about the negotiations with Jinnah and fearful of new encroachments from the centre. Central agencies such as the All-India Village Industrial Association which Gandhi had recently set up, were regarded with suspicion, in case the high command intended them to supplant the PCC.[116] But for all its rodomontades, the Bengal Congress could not evade the power of the centre. Even without Subhas and Sen Gupta, their followers still jockeyed for position, since the lure of controlling Calcutta Corporation was still strong. Now Sarat Bose and Suresh Majumdar were pitted against B. C. Roy and K. S. Roy, and when the former group won a majority, the opposition appealed again to the centre, alleging that many of the membership lists were bogus. One of Rajendra Prasad's tasks in Bengal was to enquire into this shady affair. Rather contemptuously, he confirmed the Bose-Majumdar group in power.

These internal quarrels meant more external intervention. But the high command now held a better surety for the good behaviour of the provincial Congress. The elections which were due in January 1937 would decide who were to be the masters of the province. Whoever they might be, they could hardly be the Bengal Congress, but it was important for the PCC to do as well as possible. After all, other parties in Bengal had their factions as well, and a sizeable bloc of votes in the new Assembly would be a useful bargaining factor. But under the new constitution many more Bengalis would have the vote. One and a third million of them had been enfranchised in 1920; now eight millions were to receive the vote. After its cold-shouldering of the districts, most of these persons were outside the influence of the PCC.

How unrepresentative was the Bengal Congress, how etiolated its condition becomes plain from its own returns to the Mass Contact Committee in 1936. At first sight its membership still seemed fairly high:

---

[116] 'Summary Report of informal talks held ... at Bengal P.C.C., 19-3-35'; 'At Dr. B. C. Roy's residence, 19-3-35'; 'Conference with Congress Workers ... outside the present Bengal Executive, 20-3-35', RPP IV/36/1.

TABLE 4

Strength of the Bengal Congress by Districts, 1936

District	No. of members	No. of Primary Committees
Twenty-Four Parganas	1765	31
Jessore	1529	22
South Calcutta	1018	3
Central Calcutta	1087	6
Rajshahi	1913	5
Jalpaiguri	1015	3
Howrah	4790	27
Burdwan	792	16
North Calcutta	1844	6
Bankura	1545	11
Midnapore	nil*	nil*
Murshidabad	819	16
Dinajpur	1932	8
Nadia	1350	55
Sylhet	2831	15
Dacca	798	17
Noakhali	1436	21
Khulna	1296	40
Burra Bazar	1565	1
Hooghly	797	18
Birbhum	606	2
Rangpur	1161	12
Malda	1014	5
Bogra	1154	15
Pabna	1314	10
Mymensingh	2737	18
Faridpur	726	7
Barisal	661	29
Chittagong	71	2
Tippera	8958	19
Cachar	516	3
Total	49040	443

* The Congress was still banned in Midnapore.

Source: DCC answers to question 1/1 of questionnaire, Report of Congress and Mass Contact Sub-Committee, Bengal PCC, enclosed in Bengal PCC to Congress Mass Contact Committee, 16 August 1936, RPP IX/36/31. An earlier version of this table is enclosed in Bengal PCC to AICC, 10 July 1936, file P6/707 of 1936, AICC. This is a more optimistic and a less reliable estimate: e.g. it credits Midnapore with eighty-six Congress Committees.

But even the Bengal PCC did not believe their own figures about the number of primary committees:

The committees cannot all be said to be actually functioning today.[117]

Their estimates of total membership deserve a similar scepticism.[118] But in any case, whatever the nominal strength of the Bengal Congress may have been, the effective influence of its workers was small. Even on their own estimates, the popular appeal of the DCCs did not spread far:

TABLE 5
Mass contacts established by the DCCs

	Constructive Programme
Twenty-Four Parganas	'unsatisfactory'
Jessore	'to a little extent'
South Calcutta	'practically nothing'
Central Calcutta	'little opportunity'
Rajshahi	'no real constructive work'
Jalpaiguri	'we could do nothing'
Howrah	'constructive work did not help towards the contact with masses'
Burdwan	'some extent'
North Calcutta	'not . . . sufficiently worked to elicit effect'
Bankura	'libraries, schools, dispensaries, village industries'
Midnapore	'National School, Khadi work, health and industrial exhibition and arbitration work'
Murshidabad	No answer
Dinajpur	'No attempt made'
Nadia	'educational works among depressed classes'
Sylhet	'during last thirteen years Khadi, untouchability and other constructive works failed to create any consciousness of enthusiasm'
Hooghly	'in Arambagh Sub-Division whole-time workers running primary schools, doing Khadi work, by medical work and other constructive activities have been able to develop contact with the masses effectively'
Pabna	'flood relief'
Dacca	'to a small extent'
Noakhali	'no serious attempt made except through Khadi work'
Faridpur	'no constructive work'

Source: DCC answers to question 1/5 of questionnaire, Report of Congress and Mass Contact Sub-Committee, Bengal PCC, enclosed in Bengal PCC to Congress Mass Contact Committee, 16 August 1936, RPP, IX/36/31.

Only twenty of the thirty-two Congress DCCs in the Bengal province bothered to report, but the general position is clear.

[117] Bengal PCC to AICC, 10 July 1936 file P6/707 of 1936, AICC.

[118] At first, the Bengal Congress claimed that its membership was 56,750; after checking the lists, the AICC reduced the figures to 42,385. Rajendra Prasad to Bengal PCC, 8 March 1936, RPP IV/36/21. The PCC accepted the correction; the higher figures given in Table 4 were alleged to have been the result of later recruitment.

The same picture emerges from the reports of the DCCs about the nature of their membership. When they estimated the number of 'peasants' and 'workers' among their members they tied themselves into knots, just as the British census commissioners did with their own unreal categories. Nevertheless, the returns are revealing, especially when they are read with the returns about the presence or absence of peasant organizations in the districts.

TABLE 6

Reported Percentages of 'Peasants' and 'Workers' in Bengal DCCs, and Peasant Organizations in those Districts

	Percentages of 'Peasants' or 'Workers'	Peasant Organizations
Twenty-Four Parganas	Peasants 5 Workers 5	'The particulars are not known'
Jessore	Peasants + Workers = 5	Nil
South Calcutta	Both 'negligible'	No answer
Central Calcutta	Peasants nil; Workers 'hardly any'	Nil
Rajshahi	No answer	No information
Jalpaiguri	'50% are peasants and landless labourers'	Nil
Howrah	Peasants 50 Workers 10	Nil
Burdwan	'75% cultivators, i.e. those who live upon land.'	District Kisan Samiti
	'Actual tillers and workers form a small fraction'	District Ryot Association
North Calcutta	Nil	Nil
Bankura	'actual tillers nil'	Nil
Midnapore	'Question does not arise'	Nil
Murshidabad	No answer	Nil
Dinajpur	Peasants + Workers = 16.5	District Praja Samiti
Nadia	Peasants 75 Workers 5	Nil
Sylhet	Peasants 6 Workers 'negligible'	Surma Valley Peasant Association
Dacca	'nothing worth mentioning'	District Praja Samiti
Noakhali	Peasants 1	District Krishak Samiti
Hooghly	Peasants 50 Workers 10	'We are not aware of any'
Faridpur	'Negligible'	Nil
Pabna	Peasants 'hardly any' Workers nil	Nil

Source: DCC answers to question 1/7 and 2/1 of questionnaire, Report of Congress and Mass Contact Sub-Committee, Bengal PCC, encl. in Bengal PCC to Congress Mass Contact Committee, 16 August 1936, RPP IX/36/31.

When Tables 4 and 5 are read together, there is a plain correspondence between the districts which had been militant during civil disobedience and those which in 1936 were reporting strong membership or useful mass contacts. The Mahisyas in Midnapore, in parts of Bankura and in the Arambagh sub-division of Hooghly remained active. In east Bengal, Mymensingh, Noakhali and Rajshahi still claimed large memberships,119 but here some of the traditional centres of Congress strength, such as Dacca, Chittagong and Barisal, were clearly in decline. But apart from these crude (and probably exaggerated) figures of membership, Tables 5 and 6 show how few were the districts where Congress possessed any influence whatever among the new electors. This isolation from the people was most marked in the east Bengal districts, where the new electors were mostly Muslims or lower-caste Hindus.

Consequently, for many of the new voters there would be little charm in the appeals of the Bengal Congress. But if they would not vote for a caucus in Calcutta, they might vote for a Mahatma in Wardha. The prestige of the Congress centre, the impact of its all-India agencies, its new financial strength, its apparent denial of caste distinctions, all worked to make the centre a greater electoral asset than the PCC. Here was the surety which bound the Bengal Congress to the high command. But in the meantime the Bengal Congress was hampered by the demands of its own constituents. After all, the new electors were birds in the bush; the old supporters were birds in the hand. On the one side, the Congress centre forbade them to denounce the Award; on the other, their old supporters insisted that they should do so. The final period before the elections left the Bengal Congress hopelessly caught in the nut-crackers.

When the Government of India Act reached the statute book in 1935, the Communal Award became law. By 1936, with the elections drawing near, the beleaguered Hindu notables of Bengal made one last effort to press London into amending it by Order in Council.120 To this end they drew up a memorial, signed by all Hindu members of the Legislative Council, by twenty-three chairmen of municipalities, by eight chairmen of district boards, and by thirty-six 'representative Hindu leaders'. Here is the roll-call of Hindu eminence in Bengal, for they included members of the Council of State, great zemindars, the

---

119 The huge membership figures returned from Tippera are an obvious overstatement. Nevertheless, membership may have been quite high, since Congress had benefited from the disputes between the Raja and his tenants.

120 They argued that the Act of 1935 empowered the British Government to amend its terms by Order in Council, subject to the approval of both Houses of Parliament.

mayor of Calcutta, the vice-chancellor of Calcutta University, Sarat Chandra Chatterji, the novelist, Sir P. C. Ray, the chemist, Ramanand Chatterji, editor of the *Modern Review*, Sir Nilratan Sircar, the eminent doctor, Rabindranath Tagore and Sir Brajendranath Seal.[121] Out of this memorial came a last campaign in which the thwarted collaborators of Bengal repeated their grievances in Calcutta, Dacca, Barisal, Howrah and elsewhere.[122] The Indian Association was active in the movement; so was the Hindu Sabha. By July, the political implications of the campaign were brought into the open by the Mahasabha who now threatened to contest the Bengal elections as Congress Nationalists;[123] the following month they gave Congress their terms for standing down. The terms were simple: unqualified rejection of the Communal Award.[124]

Majumdar and Sarat Bose did their best to make the Congress Working Committee relent. Once the Lucknow session of Congress had gone through the motions of rejecting the new constitution and had installed as president Jawaharlal Nehru, still regarded as the hammer of the Congress Right, they begged for a harder line against the Award, '... with a view ... to bring about the much needed United front in the Congress ranks in Bengal ... so far as this province is concerned, the only difference between the two groups centres round the issue of non-rejection by the Congress of the Award'.[125] But Nehru replied that: '... the question has to be tackled on an all-India basis',[126] it was an answer that might have been written by Prasad or Patel.

The next move from the PCC was one of its ritual gestures. K. S. Roy of the minority faction, hopefully cast bread on the waters by denouncing Majumdar and Bose to the centre as enemies of official Congress policy.[127] Nothing floated back from Allahabad. Both factions in the PCC had failed. But by now they understood their electoral dangers. At last the factions preferred unity to acrimony and agreed to share power in the Bengal PCC. Elections had joined together those whom the Corporation had put asunder.

Indeed, the need for unity between these oligarchs was urgent. In its

[121] Memorial enclosed in Maharaja of Burdwan to Zetland, 4 June 1936, *Bengal Anti-Communal Award Movement; a Report* (Calcutta, 1939), pp. 3–9.

[122] *Ibid.*, pp. 11–35.

[123] *Advance*, 8 July 1936.

[124] Statement by Indra Narayan Sen Gupta, General Secretary, Congress Nationalist Party, *Amrita Bazar Patrika*, 22 November 1936.

[125] Suresh Chandra Majumdar to Jawaharlal Nehru, 18 July 1936, file P6/707 of 1936, AICC; cf. Sarat Bose to Nehru, 11 August 1936, *ibid.*

[126] Jawaharlal Nehru to Suresh Chandra Majumdar, 6 August 1936, *ibid.*

[127] K. S. Roy to Jawaharlal Nehru, 6 August 1936, RPP IV/36/83.

election manifesto, the AICC rejected the new constitution but refused to sanction agitation against the Communal Award, on the gnostic ground that such an agitation would be one-sided. The Congress Nationalists of Bengal pounced on this statement,[128] and on 2 September they decided to run their own candidates. To level the bidding, on the same day Sarat Bose moved a resolution before the new Executive Council of the Bengal PCC:

That inasmuch as the Communal decision, apart from being an All-India problem, is one of the gravest and most vital problems affecting the province of Bengal . . . it is the duty of the provincial Congress organisation . . . to carry on agitation both in and outside the legislature for the rejection of the Communal decision. . . . [129]

Since these were now the days of unity, the resolution was carried unanimously. The PCC prudently failed to report it to the Working Committee, but there were other friends who did so. When Nehru protested, Sarat Bose was unrepentant:

You are well aware of the volume of popular feeling in our province against the communal decision. . . . The electorates . . . are not willing to tolerate any uncertain or equivocal attitude towards the communal decision. To ignore that fact would be to court defeat at the coming elections; and we shudder to think what the effect of such a defeat would be on the Congress organisation as a whole.[130]

Nehru found it best to confront this challenge in ideological terms, complaining that, as he had predicted, the Bengal Congress was losing its doctrinal purity:

It seemed to me that they were gradually converting themselves into the Nationalist Party. That fear seems to me even more justified now after the last decision of the B. [engal] P.C.C.[131]

That was true enough. But a problem which jeopardized the Congress in the all-India elections could not be solved by doctrinal definitions. At this time Nehru was acutely dependent on the support of the conservatives in the Working Committee. In July they had protested that his socialist turns of phrase would do the party electoral damage, and

[128] Statement by Akhil Chandra Dutta, President of the Bengal Congress Nationalist Party, *Amrita Bazar Patrika*, 27 August 1936.

[129] Resolution enclosed in Sarat Bose to Jawaharlal Nehru, 19 September 1936, file G 24/710 of 1936, AICC.

[130] Sarat Bose to Jawaharlal Nehru, 19 September 1936, *ibid.* He went on, maliciously, to quote Nehru's own judgement: 'The Congress attitude to the Communal Award was extraordinary. . . . It was the inevitable outcome of the past neutral and feeble policy'. J. Nehru, *An Autobiography* (London, 1936), p. 575.

[131] Jawaharlal Nehru to Sarat Bose, 4 October 1936, file G 24/710 of 1936, AICC.

their threat of resignation had curbed his experiments with truth. During the confrontation with Bengal in September and October it was they, and not the Congress president, who shaped the tactics of the centre. What moved Patel and Prasad were not ideological niceties but electoral needs, and these demanded a hard line against Bengal. They needed to cow the province. Now they had the ideal weapon at hand.

One of the first tasks of the newly united PCC had been to appoint a Provincial Parliamentary Committee, to scrutinize candidates nominated by the DCCs for the forthcoming elections. Once they had approved the list, the Bengal Committee wanted to publish it quickly, partly so that it might appear before 20 October, when the Puja holidays would bring politics to a standstill,[132] and partly, perhaps, because half the candidates they had approved were members of the Congress Nationalist Party.[133] But the list had also to be approved by the All-India Parliamentary Committee. With India standing on the brink of the elections, this body was one of the most powerful organizations in the entire Congress. Its president was Vallabhbhai Patel and its secretary was Rajendra Prasad.

Vallabhbhai had an old dislike of the Bengal Congress and of the Bose brothers. Now he seized the chance to use the full powers of the centre against provincial indiscipline:

The interpretation that has been put by the Bengal Executive Committee on the A.I.C.C. electoral statement about the Communal Decision is entirely wrong and unless the candidates whose recommendations are forwarded by you agree to accept the policy and programme of the [AICC] Manifesto, it would not be possible for the Central Parliamentary Committee to accept the recommendations, and there would be consequently considerable delay in getting a decision from authoritative sources afterwards.[134]

The leaders of the Bengal Congress might be united in detesting the Award; but they were no less united in desiring to contest the elections. So there was nothing for it except to surrender. On 8 November, the offending resolution was replaced by another which said nothing about destroying the Award; and this time the PCC punctiliously informed all members of the Working Committee that it had changed its mind.[135]

[132] B. C. Roy to Rajendra Prasad, 4 October 1936, *ibid.*

[133] Statement by Indra Narayan Sen Gupta, Secretary, Bengal Congress Nationalist Party, *Amrita Bazar Patrika*, 22 November 1936.

[134] Vallabhbhai Patel to B. C. Roy, 9 October 1936, file G 24/710 of 1936, AICC.

[135] Secretary, Bengal PCC to all members of the Working Committee, 13 November 1936, *ibid.*

The centre had disciplined a united Bengal. Bengal retaliated by embarrassing a divided centre. Sarat Bose appealed to Nehru as one advanced thinker to another:

... pro-ministry wallahs like Patel ... & others will sidetrack the main issue but Bengal will always stand by you in the fight for independence.[136]

But there was nothing to be gained by declaiming long-term slogans to a Congress president who was trapped in a Working Committee obsessed with a short-term aim. Nehru could not help. In any case Vallabhbhai had not finished with the Bengal PCC. On 8 November that body had transferred all the powers of its Parliamentary Committee to Sarat Bose and B. C. Roy. When Bose's list of candidates came before the All-India Parliamentary Committee, a number of them were rejected. He resigned from the task, leaving it to an apprehensive B. C. Roy,[137] who then received this encouragement from Nehru:

I do not know what you expect from me in the way of inspiration and guidance, but if I may venture to offer a suggestion—why not arrange for some of the Gilbert and Sullivan operas to be shown in Calcutta for the free entertainment and instruction of our over-worked and over-worried colleagues. Of course there is that other sovereign remedy of standing on one's head which the Bengal Parliamentary Board and the B.P.C.C. might indulge in with advantage. I can commend this method from personal experience. . . .[138]

Roy found no pleasure in this advice. Next the All-India Parliamentary Committee began to reject his nominees as well. It was now his turn to resign.[139] When the Bengal Congress fought the elections in January 1937, it was as the captive of the centre.

These low affairs have to be placed in a larger setting. All over India the provincial Congress parties were now squarely facing the demands of electoral politics; and most of them saw the need for integrating themselves into local centres of power. This they did, in the United Provinces, the Central Provinces and Bihar; after some difficulty they did so in Berar and Maharashtra;[140] and most conspicuously of all, they did so in Madras.[141] In that province Congress won 74 per cent of seats in the elections to the new provincial Assemblies under the new fran-

[136] Sarat Bose to Jawaharlal Nehru, 18 November 1936, *ibid.*
[137] B. C. Roy to G. B. Pant, 30 November 1936, file P 6/707 of 1936, AICC.
[138] Jawaharlal Nehru to B. C. Roy, 3 December 1936, *ibid.*
[139] B. C. Roy to G. B. Pant, 17 December 1936, *ibid.*
[140] Now that important powers were at stake, provincial politicians were compelled to woo the localities.
[141] C. J. Baker, 'Political Change in South India' (Cambridge University, Ph.D. thesis, 1972), Chapter IX.

chise; in Bihar it won 65 per cent, in the Central Provinces 62.5 per cent, in the United Provinces 59 per cent, and in Bombay 49 per cent. In the elections in Bengal, Congress won 21.6 per cent.[142]

This was a feeble result. The best that could be said of it was that no party did well in Bengal. Hence for a while, members of all the factions, such as J. C. Gupta, B. C. Roy, K. S. Roy, Sarat Bose and T. C. Goswami, could hope to take office in alliance with the Muslim-Namasudra party of Fazl-Huq.[143] But the Working Committee would not hear of it.[144] Reluctantly Bengal Congressmen had to watch portfolios floating away from them:

The Proja party members headed by Moulvi Fazul Huq begged of the Congress members to form a coalition with them. . . . Due to Congress decision we were unable to accede to their request. . . .[145]

As it turned out, there was never to be a Congress ministry in an undivided Bengal. But its disappointed Hindu politicians had one last fling. In provinces with Congress ministries there were other disappointed politicians. They might be recruited into a foray against those in possession. In 1937 Subhas Bose had returned to India, and he became president of the all-India Congress the following year. He was soon at odds with the right wing at the centre, because of his dislike of the Congress ministries and his outright opposition to federation. Stands of that sort were meat and drink to his supporters in Bengal, and they also won over the aggrieved factions in other provinces. This coalition forced through his re-election in January, 1939.[146] Not that it mattered. The opposition of the right wing, led by Gandhi himself,

[142] Congress candidates in Bengal won forty-three of the forty-eight General Seats, six of the seats reserved for the Depressed Classes and five of the seats reserved for Labour. Of the 250 seats in the new Assembly they won fifty-four.

[143] Nalinaksha Sanyal to Nehru, 20 February 1937; file E 5/840 of 1937, AICC.

[144] On 18 March the Working Committee agreed in principle that in provinces where Congress held a majority of Assembly seats, they might consider forming ministries. Of course, this did not apply to Bengal. On 29 April this permission was withdrawn. On 8 July, after a great deal of negotiating with Government, the Working Committee again granted permission for accepting office, but Nehru directed that in Bengal the Congress should not negotiate for membership of any coalition.

[145] J. C. Gupta to Jawaharlal Nehru, 14 August 1937, file P 5/868 of 1937, AICC.

[146] Bose won support from the Punjab and Bengal, provinces without Congress ministries. He also won support from the UP, where some sections of the provincial Congress were opposed to the tenancy legislation of the Pant ministry; from Madras, where the Rajagopalachari ministry had alienated a number of supporters; and from Karnatak, where there was dislike of the tenancy legislation of the Kher ministry in Bombay. For details of this coalition I am indebted to the work of Mr B. R. Tomlinson of Trinity College, Cambridge.

forced Subhas to resign in April, 1939.[147] He retaliated by founding the Forward Bloc and the Left-Consolidation Committee, efforts to give organized form to his inter-provincial alliance of the aggrieved. These picked up little support except from men who had been tossed and gored by Vallabhbhai. In August the Working Committee removed Subhas from all his positions in the Congress. The coalition vanished. Deserted by the M. N. Roy group, by the Trade Unionists, by the Congress Socialists and by the National Front,[148] Subhas was now a general without an army, reduced to demonstrating in front of British statues on the Calcutta maidan. In January 1941, he fled from India, disguised as a Muslim insurance agent.

It was the misfortune of Bengal that the history and social structure of the province made a jigsaw which no longer could be teased into a solution. Perhaps the best friend of the old politicians had been the pro-consul whose partition of Bengal would have cut away their troubles in the eastern districts. But they had rejected the surgery of George Nathaniel Curzon. By the nineteen-twenties their options inside undivided Bengal were closing. By the time of the Communal Award and the wider franchise, self-government for Bengal could only mean the rule of others. No one would permit Bengal to contract out of the empire on Burmese lines; and in any case the province lacked the internal solidarity to pull the Bengali peoples out of India. Inside the province the balance had tilted against the Hindu politicians, so radical in style, so conservative in practice. Inside India as a whole, it had tilted against Bengal. Only a new partition could salvage something from the wreck.

The modern history of Bengal has often been taken as the exemplar of Indian nationalism. In fact, Bengal more and more deviated from it. In the nineteenth century the province had done much to establish the trends in the national movement; by the nineteen-thirties it was struggling against them. By their failure to link province with locality, its politicians were bound to lose in the great game of the last days of the Raj. No province had done as much to develop theories and programmes for the national movement. Yet this narrative should have shown how irrelevant ideology turned out to be in this most ideologically minded of Indian provinces. It also demonstrates the need to reintegrate the study of Indian history. Bengal's fate had been largely determined by national and imperial considerations which were outside its control. Locality and

[147] For the moves and counter-moves between Subhas and Gandhi, see S. C. Bose, *Crossroads* (London, 1962), pp. 126–70.
[148] This was the Communist Party of India in sheep's clothing.

province cannot be studied in isolation from the nation and the empire to which they belonged.

There was a tragic sense to the struggles of the Bengal Congress as it tried to hold its own against the unsentimental calculations of the British and the Congress centre. Those Bengalis who once had gained so much by their enthusiastic acceptance of British rule and culture, were finally cast aside by the Raj. The province which had inspired Indian nationalism was sacrificed for its sake. Imperialism devours its own children. Nationalism destroys its own parents.